THE HYPHENATEDS

To Mom and Dad,
for teaching me the stories
(Deut. 6:7)

THE HYPHENATEDS

How Emergence Christianity Is Re-Traditioning Mainline Practices

Edited by Phil Snider

CHALICE
PRESS
ST. LOUIS, MISSOURI

Bible quotations, unless otherwise noted, are from the *New Revised Standard Version Bible,* copyright 1989, Division of Christian Education of the National Council of the Churches of Christ in the United States of America. Used by permission. All rights reserved.

"Give Me Your Hand," written by Aaron Strumpel. Recorded on *Enter the Worship Circle, Fourth Circle* © 2008. Used with permission.

Cover image: *Our Lady of the New Advent Icon* as created from Christmas advertising at House for All Sinners and Saints, Denver, Colorado. Photo copyright © 2011 by Amy Clifford. All rights reserved. Used by permission.

Cover and interior design: Scribe Inc.

Visit www.chalicepress.com

10 9 8 7 6 5 4 3 2 1   11 12 13 14 15 16

Paperback: 9780827214897 EPUB: 9780827214903
EPDF: 9780827214910

Library of Congress Cataloging–in–Publication Data

The hyphenateds : how emergence Christianity is re-traditioning mainline practices / edited by Phil Snider.
    p. cm.
Includes bibliographical references (p.   ).
ISBN 978-0-8272-1489-7
1. Emerging church movement. 2. Protestant churches. I. Snider, Phil, 1973- II. Title.
BV601.9.H97 2011
270.8'–dc23   2011031502

Printed in the United States of America

Contents

Acknowledgments

I am thankful to each of the contributors who made this book possible. Their collective wisdom has often influenced my vocational life, and it has been a privilege to personally collaborate with each of them. I am also grateful to Phyllis Tickle for supporting this project from the start. When I first told her about it, her encouragement and enthusiasm confirmed to me that it was indeed an important project to pursue.

I would also like to extend my thanks to Cyrus White and Chalice Press for their bold commitment to the future of the church. You have provided hospitality to many of us attempting to figure out what ministry in the twenty-first century might look like, and your example serves as an inspiration and challenge not only to the Christian Church (Disciples of Christ) but also to mainline communities across the board.

I remain grateful for the community of Brentwood Christian Church (Disciples of Christ), which has given me reason to be hopeful for the future of the mainline church. Thank you for encouraging me to pursue my ideas in writing and for believing that the story of our community is an important story to tell.

As always, I reserve my deepest thanks for my family: Amanda, Eli, Sam, and Lily Grace. We are learning the stories together, just as my mom and dad taught the stories to me when I was a child. It is to my parents that I dedicate this book.

–Phil Snider

About the Contributors

Phyllis Tickle (foreword), an Episcopalian, is one of the leading authorities on religion in North America and a much sought-after lecturer on the subject. She is the founding editor of the Religion Department of *Publishers Weekly*. In addition to lectures and numerous essays, articles, and interviews, Tickle is the author of over two dozen books on religion and spirituality, most recently *The Great Emergence: How Christianity Is Changing and Why*.

Doug Pagitt (afterword) is the founder of Solomon's Porch, a holistic missional Christian community in Minneapolis, Minnesota, and one of the founders of Emergent Village. In addition to being the author of several books (most recently *Church in the Inventive Age* and *A Christianity Worth Believing*) he is a speaker, radio host, and co-owner with Tony Jones of the event production company JoPa Productions.

Mike Baughman, an ordained elder in the United Methodist Church, is a pastor at Custer Road United Methodist Church in Plano, Texas. He previously served as lead pastor for an alternative worship gathering, *veritas . . .*, in Fort Worth, Texas. Mike has lectured on the emerging church at Perkins School of Theology and leads workshops on postmodern preaching and evangelism. He coauthored the book *Worship Feast: Lent*, contributed to several curriculums for Abingdon Press, Augsburg Fortress, and Barefoot Press, and has authored articles for the *Encyclopedia of Religious and Spiritual Development*.

Nadia Bolz-Weber, an ordained minister in the Evangelical Lutheran Church in America, is the organizing pastor of House for All Sinners and Saints, a Lutheran emerging church in Denver, Colorado. As one of the most sought-after workshop leaders and lecturers on the emerging church, she has been a featured speaker at numerous events, including Christianity 21 and the Greenbelt Festival (U.K.). In addition to being a featured blogger for *Sojourners*, she is the author of *Salvation on the Small Screen? 24 Hours of Christian Television* and a contributor to *Rising from the Ashes: Rethinking Church*. Nadia blogs at http://www.sarcasticlutheran.com.

Emily Bowen, an ordained minister in the Christian Church (Disciples of Christ), is a pastor at Brentwood Christian Church in Springfield, Missouri, where she lends leadership to the *Awakening*, an emerging worship gathering deeply rooted in progressive theology. She leads numerous workshops on emerging approaches to worship and is the coauthor of *Toward a Hopeful Future: Why the Emergent Church Is Good News for Mainline Congregations.*

Nate Frambach, an ordained minister in the Evangelical Lutheran Church in America, is Professor of Youth, Culture, and Mission at Wartburg Theological Seminary in Dubuque, Iowa, and is the author of *Emerging Ministry: Being Church Today.* He has published articles on ecclesiology and missiology in *Currents in Theology and Mission, Word and World,* and *The Journal of Youth and Theology* and has spoken on these themes in various venues including synod assemblies and theological conferences. He also serves on the Board of Directors of the ELCA Youth Ministry Network. You can visit his web home at http://www.nateframbach.com.

Matthew Gallion is a graduate student at Missouri State University where he is pursuing an M.A. in Religious Studies. Matt studies responses to American evangelicalism in postmodern contexts, particularly the emerging church and the emergent conversation, and the intersection of faith and culture, particularly in crossing the "digital divide." He is the author of "The Price of Freedom: Bribery, the Philippian Gift, and Paul's Choice in Philippians 1:19–26," which won the prize for best graduate paper at the annual meeting of the Central States Society of Biblical Literature. He received his B.A. from Southwest Baptist University and currently serves as Pastoral Resident at National Avenue Christian Church (Disciples of Christ) in Springfield, Missouri.

Brandon Gilvin, an ordained minister in the Christian Church (Disciples of Christ), currently serves as the Associate Director of Week of Compassion and is the author of *Solving the Da Vinci Code Mystery,* coauthor of *Wisdom from The Five People You Meet in Heaven,* and coeditor of Chalice Press's *WTF? (Where's the Faith?)* series.

Elaine A. Heath is the McCreless Associate Professor of Evangelism at Southern Methodist University, and the director of the Center for Missional Wisdom. She is ordained in the United Methodist Church. Her recent publications include *The Mystic Way of Evangelism: A Contemplative Vision for Christian Outreach; Naked Faith: The Mystical Theology of Phoebe Palmer,* and *Longing for Spring: A New Vision for Wesleyan Community,* coauthored with Scott T. Kisker.

Carol Howard Merritt, an ordained minister in the Presbyterian Church (U.S.A.), is a pastor at Western Presbyterian Church in Washington, D.C. She is the author of *Tribal Church: Ministering to the Missing Generation* and

Reframing Hope: Vital Ministry in a New Generation. She leads numerous workshops around the country as well as webinars sponsored by the Alban Institute. She is also the co-host of the podcast *God Complex Radio,* with Bruce Reyes-Chow and Landon Whitsitt.

Ross Lockhart, an ordained minister in the United Church of Canada, is the Lead Pastor at West Vancouver United Church in West Vancouver, British Columbia. In addition to being the author of *Gen X, Y Faith* and coeditor of *Three Ways of Grace,* Ross is a leader for the United Church of Canada's "Emerging Spirit" initiative.

Christopher D. Rodkey, an ordained minister in the United Church of Christ, is Pastor of Zion "Goshert's" United Church of Christ in Lebanon, Pennsylvania, and teaches at Lebanon Valley College. He holds doctorates from Drew University (Ph.D.) and Meadville Lombard Theological School (D.Min.). His work as pastor and scholar focuses upon a forced intersection between pastoral theology and philosophy, with particular interests in radical expressions of the Christian faith. His book, *The Synaptic Gospel,* engages phenomenology and neuroscience to offer a pastoral theology of pangenerational worship and religious education. He lectures often on the practice of youth ministry and is an occasional contributor to the blog, *An und für sich.*

Nanette Sawyer, an ordained minister in the Presbyterian Church (U.S.A.), is the founding pastor of Wicker Park Grace, an emerging faith community that gathers in an art gallery on the west side of Chicago. She has blogged for the *Christian Century* at http://www.theolog.org and at http://www.thehardestquestion.org. In addition to being a featured speaker at various events, including Christianity 21 and The Big Event of RevGal-BlogPals, she has taught as an adjunct instructor at McCormick Theological Seminary. She is a contributor to *An Emergent Manifesto of Hope* and the author of *Hospitality: The Sacred Art.*

Phil Snider is an ordained minister in the Christian Church (Disciples of Christ) and a pastor at Brentwood Christian Church in Springfield, Missouri. He is the coauthor of *Toward a Hopeful Future: Why the Emergent Church Is Good News for Mainline Congregations* and contributor to *Banned Questions about Jesus.* He blogs at http://www.philsnider.net.

Timothy Snyder is cofounder of The Netzer Co-Op, an emerging community in Austin, Texas. A graduate of Texas Lutheran University and Luther Seminary, he is the author of several articles on the emerging church, faith, and culture. He is currently the managing editor of GENERATE

Magazine and a lay minister at Hope Lutheran Church in St. Paul, Minnesota. He blogs regularly at http://www.curatingthejourney.org.

Stephanie Spellers, an ordained priest in the Episcopal Church, is the lead organizer of The Crossing, an emergent community rooted in St. Paul's Episcopal Cathedral in Boston, Massachusetts. In addition to serving as cochair of the Episcopal Church's Standing Commission on Mission and Evangelism, she is the U.S. editor and contributor to *Ancient Faith, Future Mission: Fresh Expressions in the Sacramental Tradition* and author of *Radical Welcome: Embracing God, the Other and the Spirit of Transformation.*

Foreword

Religion books, generally speaking, are not exciting. At least not in my experience. And never . . . absolutely never . . . are they exhilarating. I can say that with renewed confidence nowadays, because the exception that proves my rule is in your hands this very moment.

About every five hundred years or so, our latinized civilization goes through a period of upheaval and the reconfiguration of all its parts, including its forms and presentations of religion and much of its theology. We are in such a time now. Just as in the sixteenth century we named the upheaval as The Great Reformation, so now, five centuries later, we speak of our twenty-first–century tsunami as The Great Emergence.

The Great Reformation gave us humanism, the rise of the middle class, the birth of capitalism, the growth of the nation-state, and so on. It also gave us Protestantism as a new or fresh expression of the Christian faith. In a similar way, The Great Emergence is giving us globalization, the extended family, extreme urbanization, social networking, and so on; and along with all of these, Emergence Christianity as a new or fresh expression of Christian faith.

Protestantism, when used as an overarching term, simply names a set of sensibilities and values shared by a very multifaceted form of Christian belief and praxis. Were that not true, there would only be Protestants and not distinct denominations such as Lutherans, Presbyterians, Baptists, and so on, all flying under the banner of Protestantism. Thus it is with Emergence Christianity as well. That is to say that the words "Emergence Christianity" name a set of values and sensibilities shared by some half-dozen or so distinct groups functioning within and under the larger label. Gathered under Emergence Christianity, for instance, are Emerging Church, Emergents, Neo-monastics, Missional Church, and so on, and, most remarkable of all, I suspect, the Hyphenateds.

While one can easily draw many parallels between The Great Reformation and our own Great Emergence, there are also some significant differences; and from the point of view of religion, none of those differences is more absorbing to watch or more portentous than is the presence within Emergence Christianity of the Hyphenateds. They have no analog. They occupy new territory. They are the future for millions of Christians.

Hyphenateds, by definition, are Christians who are citizens of The Great Emergence and appreciators of its values, assets, and ways of being, as well as of the theological questions it is eliciting. At one and the same time, however, they are also reverent and proud inheritors of the traditions, praxis, and structure of their own inherited denominations and communions. They wish, in other words, to retain the best of the institutional Church and meld it seamlessly with the best of Emergence Church. They got their strange name as a direct result of that intention.

Originally, Christians who sought to "re-tradition"[1] the inherited or institutional Church were called Metho-mergents, Presby-mergents, Catho-mergents, Luther-mergents, Angli-mergents, and so on, and thus their name. In time and as their numbers grew somewhat exponentially, the hyphens became an annoyance and were dropped. The result was Methomergents, Presbymergents, Cathomergents, and so on. The form changed, in other words, but the name stuck.

And by any name, they need watching, for what they are about is a totally new thing.

What they are about is changing in some God-drenched ways the face of both the Faith and the Church. This book, then, is exhilarating, because it is, so far as I know, the first volume to collect some of America's Hyphenated leaders and thinkers into one set of covers for public viewing. Here a baker's dozen of the most influential Hyphenateds in this country talk boldly and unapologetically about what they are doing, how they are doing it, and why they are doing it.

Whether one is an Emergence Christian or a mainline Christian or a traditional Christian or even a disaffected Christian, one has the opportunity here to look at the future through the lens of an evolving present. What's written here is intimately told, without apology, and with no holds barred. The writers do not all agree with one another or with other theorists and observers like me; but what they do agree about is the passion of the call, its immediacy, and its holiness. Let us pray God may grant them traveling mercies all the way home.

—Phyllis Tickle

Note

[1] The term "re-traditioning" was first coined by the scholar Diana Butler Bass several years ago and has become the name of choice for what the Hyphenateds are about.

Introduction

Phil Snider

It would be a mistake to think that the critique of Christianity as a religion is primarily an attack that is launched by those outside the tradition; rather, it would be better to think of it as an integral part of Christianity itself.
—PETER ROLLINS[1]

Christians are bound by a tradition whose goal, if we allow it, is to set us free.
—DOUGLAS JOHN HALL[2]

In the heart of John Calvin's beloved Geneva, two contrasting images stand opposite one another. On one side of the main town square stands St. Peter's Cathedral, a striking architectural wonder that has dominated the center of the city ever since construction began on the original building in 1160. The hallowed ground of St. Peter's has long represented the power and allure of the institutional church, and it is best known as the cathedral that John Calvin commandeered as part of the Reformation, making it the hub of his preaching from 1536 to 1564.

Yet on the opposite side of the town square stands a statue of the prophet Jeremiah, which was carved by one of Rodin's students as an act of protest against the institutional church. Jeremiah's face is provocatively turned away from St. Peter's Cathedral in frustration and disgust, representing the righteous critique that always accompanies the prophet's witness.

When confronted with these contrasting images, one is tempted to determine which best represents the proper Christian perspective. Should one's loyalties be with the institutional church, which is the guardian and curator of sacred traditions held dear? Or should one join Jeremiah's prophetic protest, which always calls into question the practices of institutions, particularly institutions that claim to hold the power and authority on all things orthodox?

It is commonly assumed that the statue of Jeremiah represents Christians who have engaged the emerging church conversation over the better part of the last ten to fifteen years (a conversation that goes by many names, as we will discuss later). They are viewed as protestors who have turned away from the institutional church in disgust. Conversely, Christians who remain loyal to the institutional church (even those churches that were birthed as part of a protesting movement) are often viewed as representatives of St. Peter's Cathedral: those who consistently resist and domesticate the vision of Jeremiah, often because of an unspoken desire to maintain power and authority. This tension has become even more pronounced within the changing landscape of postmodern culture, when it seems as if so many established institutional churches and practices (read denominational churches and practices) are on the way out, and no one knows what kind of ecclesiastical communities will be forged in their wake.

Yet to understand the current ecclesiastical milieu in such a polarizing way not only misses the import of emergence Christianity, but also misreads the structure and purpose of Christian traditions in general, particularly those shaped by a reformed perspective. A more helpful understanding recognizes that both St. Peter's Cathedral and the statue of Jeremiah need each other, both are dependent upon each other, and both operate out of a deep commitment to the Christian tradition.

This can be compared to the theologian's calling to be both "bound and free."[3] On one hand, theologians are *bound* to the schools of thought they have inherited, that is, the traditions that have formatively shaped them. On the other hand, the responsibility of the theologian is to be set *free* from these schools in order to develop new frameworks for understanding that can move Christian theology forward. Moving into these new frameworks doesn't denigrate the traditions that have been handed over, but, quite to the contrary, is only possible because of them. For any kind of new theological work to be done, one must have served a kind of apprenticeship to the tradition, an apprenticeship that binds one to what has been handed over, precisely in order for one to be faithful to the given tradition by being set free from it. In other words, the test of our authentic appropriation of the tradition is ultimately about whether or not it leads to the birth pangs of theological freedom. From this perspective, the tradition can be viewed not just in terms of a static inheritance that we receive, but rather as a task that we do.[4]

In the same way, contrary to the popular distortion, mainline church leaders on the precipices of emergence Christianity are not abandoning the traditions that have shaped them; rather, they are attempting to faithfully appropriate their beloved traditions in new and innovative ways. They are part of what Diana Butler Bass has called a "re-traditioning,"[5] and they recognize that being responsible to the tradition demands that new life spring from it. As Peter Rollins observes,

> The Christian is one who is, in the moment of being a Christian (i.e., standing in a particular tradition), also the one who rejects it (remembering the prophets of old who warned us about how

any tradition could become idolatrous)–betraying it as an act of deep fidelity.[6]

This is why the church, in order to be faithful to its once and future task, always stands between the images of St. Peter's Cathedral and the statue of Jeremiah, embracing both the tradition and the prophet's critique of the tradition, manifesting elements of both priest and prophet, sometimes even undermining the tradition as a result of being apprenticed to the tradition.[7]

The essays in this book stand between these two images as well, thus offering space for Christian communities to consider how they might move forward in ways that are both faithful and prophetic. Indeed, this is the radical space that defines emergence Christianity.

In the following pages, several prominent leaders from mainline communities share their hopes, dreams, and visions for the future of the mainline church. Each of the contributors can be referred to as a "hyphenated Christian," which is to say a Christian who has roots in both emergence Christianity and the mainline church (Presbymergents, Anglimergents, Luthermergents, Methomergents, and so on). With a passion for mainline traditions and an understanding of emergence Christianity–coupled with the recognition that these are not separate entities–hyphenated Christians offer a vibrant and contagious vision of the ways in which mainline communities might faithfully and prophetically incarnate the love of Christ in the midst of an ever-changing postmodern world. Contributors to this volume offer wisdom from a variety of contexts: Some pastor churches that are typically referred to as emerging or missional, while others are engaged in ministry at more established congregations. Some are scholars or professors, while others are graduate students. Though the bulk of the emergent conversation has been dominated by the voices of Eurocentric males, this collection is much more diverse in scope.

As the essays in this book show, the mainline church has a very bright future. It just may not always look like what we expect.

Emergence Christianity: A Very Brief History

Over the last several years, theorists have tried to get a handle on the import of the emerging church conversation that dominated Christian circles throughout the first decade of the new millennium, and several theorists now use the phrase "emergence Christianity" (first coined by Phyllis Tickle) in order to capture the dynamics that have been at play throughout this time frame.[8]

In the early 2000s, the emerging church was all the rage, especially in evangelical contexts. Books were written from a variety of emerging perspectives, and conferences were organized in order to discuss the "emergent church." Even PBS joined the parade by putting together a documentary that explored whether or not the emerging church would represent the definitive way of embodying Christian community in the twenty-first century. Some proponents viewed the emerging conversation as the salvation of the church, while others decried it as the latest in a series of fashionable "postmodern" or "liberal" heresies. Most of the participants who gravitated toward emergent Christianity viewed it as a way to enter into conversation with others about what it means to be a Christian, all the while valuing the commitment to share in meaningful Christian community even while leaving room for disagreement on various doctrinal issues. For the most part, emergents held to the conviction that love, not doctrine, held them together.

Simultaneously, several new Christian communities were radically reconsidering cherished practices of the church. In the early days of emergent Christianity, these communities consisted largely of evangelical expatriates who had grown increasingly uncomfortable with what they viewed as trite and superficial forms of contemporary worship ("four songs in the key of perpetually happy," as Sally Morgenthaler memorably described it), and they longed to return to worship practices that drew upon ancient traditions and rich symbols of the faith.

These new "emergent churches" were enamored with theology. As a result, they started asking all kinds of questions about the theological meaning of every single practice of the church. They sought to inscribe all their communal activities with theological depth. So for instance, when couches in a circle replaced pews in a row, it wasn't because couches were more hip and trendy or neo-Beatnik than pews but rather because sitting in a circle conveyed a sense of participation and mutuality as opposed to observation and hierarchy, which, to them, was an important theological statement to make. Inscribing every ecclesiastical practice with theological meaning extended well beyond worship, and soon emergent communities were challenging Christians of all stripes to seriously evaluate why they do what they do. Though one of the early critiques of emergent Christianity was that it baptized the church in the name of the culture, a more thorough analysis revealed that it was actually coming much closer to doing the opposite. In the process—almost as a by-product—emergent communities challenged established churches to ask if their tried-and-true practices were more informed by theological convictions or cultural norms. The answers were sometimes disturbing.

Of course, several groups wanted to hitch themselves to the "emerging" bandwagon. It looked like the new way of being church, especially among younger generations. It was believed that, with a few cosmetic changes here and there, congregations could go through a metamorphosis of sorts and wondrously come out on the other side as an "emerging church," which would then put them in the coveted position of connecting with Millennials and Gen Xers in the same way that Willow Creek and Saddleback had connected with Baby Boomers a generation or two before.

This perspective led to the most substantial rift that took place in the emerging conversation, even among those who were incredibly instrumental in the earliest stages of emergent Christianity and initially shared many of the same goals. The main impasse had to do with theological doctrine. For many, the emerging church was supposed to be nothing more than a new way of doing church in a so-called postmodern culture,[9] an approach that could make church more relevant and interesting for younger people who otherwise had no interest. These folks argued that emerging expressions of Christianity pointed to a *style* that should be implemented in order to help evangelical congregations connect with the "unchurched." The idea was no different from any other gimmicky approach that tried to get people through the doors of the church so that the standard evangelical message (which by the latter part of the twentieth century, due to the influence of the religious right, had become ultraconservative, bordering on fundamentalism) could be shared with as many young people as possible.

By contrast, others involved in the conversation continued to emphasize that the most important aspect of emergent Christianity wasn't primarily about style. For them, stylistic concerns were always secondary to theological concerns, and, more to the point, these folks were interested in reevaluating the standard evangelical message they had received as children in order to cultivate a whole new approach to Christianity. They soon discovered, however, that their newfound faith was actually very similar to the kind of theology that had been valued by lots of other Christians for many years, particularly mainline Christians, and it didn't take very long for "emergents" to start collaborating with mainline voices. In recent years, this collaboration has become quite explicit, particularly as seen in public attempts to pair emergent theological approaches with progressive ones.[10]

It became clear that what was taking place under the umbrella of the "emerging church" wasn't an entirely new way of being church or of being Christian. Rather, the emerging moment helped Christians from a variety of contexts to (1) encounter wider Christian traditions that have come before and (2) consider ways to reappropriate these traditions in creative, authentic, and culturally accessible ways. Because the emerging moment challenged Christians from established communities to also reappropriate their respective ecclesiastical traditions in authentic ways, it's not surprising that throughout this time period a handful of mainline communities began cultivating fresh, emerging expressions of church that prized theological integrity and cultural accessibility.

So an odd assortment of things was happening at the same time: Former evangelicals were developing new Christian communities grounded in progressive theology (including young suburbanites who sold their possessions and moved into poor neighborhoods in order to incarnate radical expressions of discipleship through "new monastic" practices); mainliners were reappropriating their traditions because of the cues they received from emergents; some evangelical expatriates were finding a home in established mainline congregations; and younger Christians as a whole were trying to find a way to move past the narrow version of religious right fundamentalism that had dominated their childhood and adolescence. The Christian landscape had swiftly moved toward what Phyllis Tickle describes as the emerging center, and as such the old categories that easily delineated one group from another group started to wear thin, and a more fluid understanding of church–one that transcends rigid structures–was beginning to blossom.[11]

With all these dynamics at play, it no longer seemed accurate to continue describing the "emerging church" as if it were some sort of separate entity unto itself, treating it like it was something "over there." It became clear that the emerging moment had given birth to a much broader conversation across the landscape of North American Christianity, encompassing evangelicals, mainliners, Roman Catholics, and a variety of other Christian communities as well. The influence of the emergent conversation became so pronounced that it is now much more helpful to describe what is taking place in terms of an action (verb) than an entity (noun). Hence the reason that many have gravitated toward the language of "emergence Christianity" as opposed to the "emerging church," and why several other theorists wish to move away from emerging/emergence language entirely.[12]

A Reformed Church Always Reforming?

It's often pointed out that mainline denominations have mistakenly and superficially understood emergence Christianity as a kind of formula that if implemented properly can result in younger members joining dying congregations, and I agree that this approach is as widespread as it is problematic. But perhaps even more problematic is the way in which established mainline institutions eagerly declare themselves open to the structural critiques that "emergents" or "hyphenateds" have to share, only to ensure that the more radical implications of these critiques do not fully hit home.

To understand the subtleties of this dynamic, it's helpful to recall St. Francis of Assisi's critiques of the Roman Catholic Church (which also hold true for many Protestant churches of today). You'll remember that St. Francis was not a fan of all the glitz and glamour that accompanied the most dominant expressions of the Catholic Church, and he repeatedly charged the church with betraying its commitment to live as Jesus Christ lived, particularly in terms of poverty and nonviolence. Initially, church authorities were very uneasy with St. Francis' order of lay monks (the Friars Minor, or "lesser brothers"), and they refused to recognize the Friars Minor as an order for obvious reasons: Their critiques cut way too close to home. However, over the course of time, the Catholic Church changed its strategy in dealing with St. Francis and his ragtag band of followers, and it has been argued that the change in strategy was not done in order to honor the radical critiques of the Friars Minor, as one might expect, but rather to do the exact opposite. In a surprising turn of events, the Catholic Church officially recognized the Friars Minor as an order, and this is of course what gave the church the ability to say that it had indeed opened itself to the critiques of the Friars Minor (so much so that it created a space for them!). But you can make the case that the very act of creating a space for the Friars Minor is precisely what allowed the church to ignore the order's more radical critiques. *You could go so far as to say that creating this space is exactly what gave the church the freedom to continue doing business as usual.* After all, if someone challenged them on their actions they could say, "Hold on just a second! Don't forget we've also got the Friars Minor! See, we care about poverty and nonviolence!" It's the classic-case scenario of doing something so that nothing really changes.

When established mainline structures "create space" for emergents, they often come quite close to making the same mistakes. In the process, much-needed critiques fall by the wayside, for they too become domesticated and colonized. Therefore, as you read the essays in this book, perhaps instead of asking, "Does emergence Christianity help established structures 'make space' for others?" it is better to ask, "Does emergence Christianity help established structures undergo radical transformation?" The difference is more significant than most established structures care to admit.[13]

Our task today is no different from the one that has occupied Christians for centuries, including the beloved lesser brother St. Francis, who, out of his deep love for the church and the traditions that so formatively shaped him, shared a heartfelt desire for reform within the body of the church:

> [St. Francis] saw such reform as always necessary, given the frailty and sinfulness of a human institution. He and his communities walked a most difficult path: remaining in a sin-filled church while offering her a prophetic challenge. He and the first communities [of the Friars Minor] served as a constant critique to the church, living as they did the gospel without gloss, a witness that called the entire household of faith to do the same. To the church's ostentation, inattention to the poor, neglect of pastoral responsibilities, complicity in the violence of the state, and general situation of decline, the emerging Franciscan movement offered both a strong condemnation and a corrective. It was the communal example of Francis and his followers, rather than rhetoric, which offered the critique and provided the challenge.[14]

It is my hope that the essays in this volume will help you and your ecclesiastical communities faithfully stand between the images of prophet and priest, and in so doing provide communal examples of critique and challenge that are rooted not only in the tradition of a reformed church always reforming, but also a reformed church always transforming. *To the glory of God, and for the sake of the world.*

Notes

[1] Peter Rollins, *The Fidelity of Betrayal: Towards a Church Beyond Belief* (Brewster, Mass: Paraclete, 2008), 130. I am also indebted to Pete for pointing me to the image of St. Peter's Cathedral in Geneva, which I discuss in the introduction, as well as the insight about St. Francis.

[2] Douglas John Hall, *Bound and Free: A Theologian's Journey* (Minneapolis: Fortress, 2005), 22.

[3] I borrow this imagery from Hall. See *Bound and Free*, 18–26.

[4] See Hall, 21–22. For the idea of inheritance (read tradition) not so much as what we receive but rather as a task that we do, see Yvonne Sherwood, *Derrida's Bible: Reading a Page of Scripture with a Little Help from Derrida* (New York: Palgrave Macmillan, 2004), 5.

[5] See Diana Butler Bass, *The Practicing Congregation* (Herndon, Va.: The Alban Institute, 2004); see also *Christianity for the Rest of Us* (New York: HarperOne, 2006), 4.

[6] Rollins, *The Fidelity of Betrayal*, 133–34.

[7] Ibid. See also Michael Naas, *Taking on the Tradition: Jacques Derrida and the Legacies of Deconstruction* (Stanford, Calif.: Stanford University, 2002).

[8] For a more detailed history, see Tony Jones, *The New Christians: Dispatches from the Emergent Frontier* (San Francisco: Jossey Bass, 2008) or Phil Snider and Emily Bowen, *Toward a Hopeful Future: Why the Emergent Church Is Good News for Mainline Congregations* (Cleveland: Pilgrim, 2010).

[9] Perhaps Richard Rorty was right: The term "postmodern" became so overused that it is now too fuzzy to convey anything.

[10] See especially Philip Clayton, *Transforming Christian Theology: For Church and Society* (Minneapolis: Fortress, 2010) and Snider and Bowen's *Toward a Hopeful Future*, as well as recent conferences such as Theology After Google and Big Tent Christianity. For a critique of this pairing, see Matthew Gallion's essay in chapter 8 of this book, "The Postmodern Pan and the ForeverNeverland."

[11] For a comprehensive analysis, see Phyllis Tickle's *The Great Emergence: How Christianity Is Changing and Why* (Grand Rapids, Mich.: Baker, 2008).

[12] It is notable that Doug Pagitt, one of the earliest and most formative voices within the emergent conversation, is interested in moving the conversation past labels such as emerging, emergent, emergence, and so on. See his *Church in the Inventive Age* (Minneapolis: Fortress, 2010). This is also why Andrew Jones's infamous blog post at the end of 2009 declaring the death of the emergent church missed the mark. What Jones failed to recognize is that the impact of emergent, at least in the United States, has become so significant that it has influenced virtually all expressions of church culture and is no longer relegated to voices on the fringes of the church (for better and for worse). If Jones wishes to speak of emergent as "dead," it is only because the critiques and observations at the forefront of the emergent conversation became much further reaching than its early visionaries ever imagined–which is a way of saying that emergent's ethos is much more alive in the church today than ever (almost through an act of *kenosis*), which is perhaps best witnessed by the widespread popularity of early emergent thinkers such as Pagitt and Brian McLaren, whose influence now extends far beyond disenfranchised North American evangelicals.

[13] One of the factors that reinforce this concern relates to the interest that former evangelicals have with progressive theology. On the surface level, this attraction doesn't appear to be problematic at all, especially for mainliners like me who are also drawn to progressive theology. But when you couple the appeal that progressive thought carries for former evangelicals with the eagerness that mainliners have for giving evangelical expatriates a place to explore it, all of a sudden it seems that both emergents and progressives have become a bit too comfortable settling for modern expressions of progressive Christianity. One begins to wonder if the much hoped-for "postmodern" moment in emergence Christianity seems in danger of being lost, if it ever existed at all.

Please don't misunderstand me: I think there are better and worse ways of doing theology, and I wholeheartedly believe that progressive theology is much more helpful for people and the world than fundamentalism and hard-lined evangelicalism. Indeed, I have passionately argued that progressive theology is very good news for emergents, and I continue to believe this is the case. But there is a certain critique that radical postmodernism offers both conservatives and progressives, and when progressive theology becomes par for the course in emergence Christianity then it is easy for emergents and progressives to think they have arrived in the theological promised land a bit too quickly. This can shield mainliners from the more radical implications of postmodernism and in the process allow them to continue practicing the same theology that remains far too wedded to modernism and the problems associated with it. One of the primary reasons I was initially drawn to emergence Christianity was because I believed it offered a vision of reimagining what Christian communities–including progressive ones–might look like if they took the radical implications of postmodern theology quite seriously. I'm not sure that is the case anymore, though I still hold out hope. For an accessible look at the differences between postmodern culture, which emergence Christianity generally responds to, and postmodern theory, which is often glossed over in emergence Christianity, see Carl Raschke's *The Next Reformation: Why Evangelicals Must Embrace Postmodernity* (Grand Rapids, Mich.: Baker Academic, 2004).

[14] Marie Dennis et al., *St. Francis and the Foolishness of God* (Maryknoll, N.Y.: Orbis, 2002), 55.

1

Innovating with Integrity

Exploring the Core and Innovative Edges of Postmodern Ministry

Nadia Bolz-Weber

I am the only one eating a burrito. Everyone else sitting in the basement of St. Paul Lutheran Church in Oakland, California, on this Wednesday night in August of 1996 is pleasant enough. But they are certainly not eating burritos. That would be just me. Yet no one seems to care. Pastor Ross Merkel begins our Adult Confirmation class with a simple prayer and then gets right into it (the "it" being Lutheran theology). It's my third week in a row and I still can't believe I'm spending my Wednesday evening in church. I've somehow gone from ten years without setting foot in a Christian church to three weeks in a row in Adult Confirmation class. That's what happens when you fall in love.

I'm not talking about falling in love with Matthew, my Lutheran seminary student fiancé, although I'm plenty in love with him. I'm talking about the Lutheran theological and liturgical tradition. I fell in love hard and fast. See, I was raised in a sectarian and fundamentalist tradition called the Church of Christ. Not the gay-friendly liberal United Church of Christ. Nope. The Church of Christ, which can only be described as "Baptist plus." When I left at age sixteen I did so with a vengeance and a pesky little drug and alcohol problem. Ten years later, on those Wednesday nights of catechism and confusion, I had been clean and sober for about four years. So when Pastor Merkel said that God brings life out of death and that we are all simultaneously sinner and saint; when he said that no one is climbing the spiritual ladder up to God but that God always comes down to us; when he said that God's grace is a gift freely given, which we don't earn but merely attempt to live in response to . . . well, when he said all this, I already knew it was true. God had completely interrupted my life. I was perfectly happy killing myself until God said, "That's cute, but I have something else in mind." God picked me up from one path and put me on another. I knew everything Pastor Merkel said was true, not because I was choosing to adopt some foreign ideology as my own, but rather because I had actually *experienced* it all to be true. I had undeniably experienced God's grace and now I was hearing a historically rooted, beautiful articulation of what I had experienced in my life, all in the form of Lutheran theology.

It changed everything. At the same time I was in the Adult Confirmation class at St. Paul I was also attending liturgy every week, which was equally as unexplainable. I had never in my life experienced liturgy and it felt like a mysterious and ancient gift handed down from generations of the faithful. It washed over me. I kept thinking, "I want to go back and do those things and say those things again," but I had no idea why.

That's how I fell in love with Lutheranism; and then the Lutheran Church kind of fell in love with me. I was soon asked to take part in several roundtable discussions and to serve on various planning teams. The Evangelical Lutheran Church in America (ELCA) offices in Chicago kept asking me to fly out and talk to them. I became a Lutheran evangelist to these "cradle" Lutherans who had no idea what they were sitting on. But soon I felt an urge to just be an evangelist to my own people because as much as I loved the Lutheran Church, I'd sit on the church pew and look around and think, "No one here looks like me." My friends are not going to ELCA churches. And not because the Lutheran Church is doing something wrong. It's just that in order for my friends to go to a Lutheran church they have to culturally commute from who they are to who the church is and they just aren't gonna make the trip. I just happen to be native to a very particular cultural context: I'm an urban young(ish) adult who is heavily tattooed, a bit cynical, overeducated, kind of artsy-fartsy, and socially progressive. My friends aren't going to show up to a nicey-nice Lutheran church with the friendly chitchat and the pews in a row and the organ music and the awkward formality. Again, there is nothing wrong with traditional church. It's often a faithful and genuine expression of living out the gospel; it's just not an expression that's either native to or conversant with my particular context.

It's a longer story than can fit here, but in the end I felt called to be a pastor to my people. I suspected that if the Lutheran theological and liturgical tradition was deeply meaningful for me then it might, just might, be deeply meaningful for my friends and the other folks in my cultural context.

So while in seminary I started a Lutheran emerging church called House for All Sinners and Saints (HFASS). The term "emerging church" is of course problematic as it is applied broadly to things that are actually antithetical to each other. So when I use the term I like to define it first (which isn't very postmodern of me . . . to actually presume to define a term, but here goes): *Emerging churches are Christian communities that (ironically) emerge out of a very particular cultural context in which the traditional church is largely irrelevant. That context is more often than not urban, young, and postmodern.*

From this perspective, HFASS is nothing more than a Lutheran church that emerged out of the young postmodern context of urban Denver. Many are surprised to learn that we adhere quite closely to the Lutheran liturgy. We are more liturgical than most Lutheran churches I visit as our liturgies include Eucharist, the Kyrie, a chanted psalm, gospel acclamation, Sanctus, and so on. In other words, unlike some Lutheran churches, we haven't jettisoned the liturgy in order to be "relevant"—rather, we've dived deeply into it thinking it might hold some wisdom beyond fleeting relevance. Here's how we describe ourselves: "We are a group of folks figuring out how to be a liturgical, Christo-centric, social justice oriented, queer inclusive, incarnational, contemplative, irreverent, ancient-future church with a progressive but deeply rooted theological imagination." At least that's what our website says.

In many ways we are like any other church. In many ways we are not. The demographic of the church looks a bit different, as 85 percent of the community members are single young adults between the ages of twenty-two and forty-two; so we are a church filled with the kind of people who don't go to church. And there are particularities to that population, which inform the ethos of the community. For instance, postmodern young adults are not as concerned with there being a clear line between reverence and irreverence. There is a humor to our church, which is quite organic and joyful to us, but could be offensive to people from a different cultural context. For example, the logo for HFASS looks like a piece of parchment with a nail in the top, à la Luther's Ninety-five Theses. Our church shirts have this parchment and nail logo on the front, and the back says "radical Protestants; nailing sh*t to the church door since 1517." Had our roots not been critically important to us we never would have bothered to have a logo that harkens back over five hundred years. We believe that we must be deeply rooted in tradition in order to innovate with integrity. So the logo expresses our Lutheran roots while simultaneously affirming that we are reforming that very tradition and also not taking ourselves too seriously in the process. While a more modernist sensibility delineates a clear line between reverence and irreverence, a more postmodern sensibility tends to meld the sacred and profane, the serious and silly. I once heard Tony Jones say that he sees various emerging churches sharing only one thing: a sense of irony.

The use of humor at HFASS illuminates how culturally distinct post-modern churches are from our modern predecessors. Our humor is an important identity marker–expressing our freedom to be the church in ways that make sense to us rather than having to adhere to patterns of behavior determined outside the cultural context in which we live. North American denominationalism has established certain ways of being (dressy church attire, "niceness," formality, Sunday-morning worship time, clergy who are slightly removed and distinctly more pious than their parishioners, organ music), which have perhaps emerged out of a particular cultural context and are now no longer seen as culturally located, but as normative. We have conflated a cultural expression of church with church itself so that any deviation from this norm is seen as, well, a deviation and not simply another of many cultural expressions. This dynamic reminds me of the words "under God" in the U.S. Pledge of Allegiance. These words were not added to the pledge until the early 1950s as a way of asserting the identity of the United States (in opposition to communist nations, which were decidedly not "under God"). Yet even though the phrase was not in the original pledge, and even though the reason for adding the phrase was located in a certain time and cultural ethos of our country and served a function within that context, now, half a century later when asserting our noncommunist identity is no longer necessary, the Pledge of Allegiance is just not the Pledge of Allegiance without it. In other words, something that was added for a particular reason at a particular time is now broadly considered an integral part of the pledge.

One of the most important functions that hyphenated churches (communities like HFASS, which are both denominational and emerging) play in the life of denominations is to illuminate what is central and what is peripheral. Or, as Luther said, what is critical and what is *adiaphora.* By taking the essential practices and theology of the church and dressing them in the native clothing of cultural contexts in which the traditional expressions have been irrelevant, these hyphenated communities not only live out the gospel in their settings but also reinvigorate the denomination by reintroducing them to the possibilities within their own religious tradition.

As an example, HFASS celebrates the Triduum during Holy Week (Maundy Thursday, Good Friday, and a full Easter Vigil). It takes the entire community to pull this off and when the vigil is over and we have come to the resurrection, we have a big dance party–complete with a chocolate fountain in the baptismal font. Because, let's face it, nothing says, "He is risen!" like a chocolate fountain in the baptismal font. I recognize that in many contexts this would be seen as deeply irreverent, even disrespectful. But for us it is delightful. Part of my job as the church planter is to help form the theological identity of the community. Ideally speaking, that identity should be deeply rooted in my theological tradition while simultaneously being informed by the cultural context of the community itself. Herein lies the beauty and importance of denominational emerging churches: the symbiotic relationship in the church between the core and the innovative edge.

I receive countless e-mails from people all across the country—as well as those living in the United Kingdom—who want to express their gratitude for HFASS and how they are inspired by something we have done. (It never fails to feel slightly ironic that people seem to be so inspired by us, seeing that the reality of HFASS often feels wobbly, uncertain, and sometimes deeply frustrating from the inside of things.) During Advent of 2008 we undertook creating an Advent icon (the icon on the cover of this book—Mary with her arms raised, the Christ child still within her). We created this piece of art over the four weeks of Advent during our liturgies . . . but we made it entirely out of Christmas advertising. Since that time, half a dozen churches have sent us photos of their own projects inspired by ours. We also have several "signature events" out in the community, including the Blessing of the Bicycles. It's hard to say how many churches have written us asking if they can use our prayers for their own Blessing of the Bicycles. The ELCA publisher, Augsburg Fortress, has even bought the rights to these prayers and will be publishing them as a resource on their website.

The point is this: Both the idea for the icon and the idea for the Blessing of the Bicycles came from the freedom we have to try crazy stuff. This freedom is a result of being safely tethered to the big ship of the Lutheran Church while having lots of room to play. If we had to make sure that everything we undertook as a community would be understandable and inoffensive to folks from a traditional church, then we would never create things that speak to us and those in our own cultural setting. The irony (and perhaps the beauty) is that, at least for HFASS, the freedom we have to explore and play in the tradition has actually produced many things that people in other settings have found useful, if not inspirational.

If we visualize the Lutheran Church (or any other tradition) as consisting of both the core and the innovative edge, then we can see how needed a mixed economy of church can be for the vitality and survival of the tradition. The core holds the history, the tradition, and the money. It includes the ecclesial structures, the traditional churches that have existed for generations and are dying off, the newer and livelier suburban churches, the seminaries and colleges, and the parachurch organizations. The midsection would be composed of youth, campus, and outdoor ministries—any ministry consisting mostly of younger people. The innovative edges then are emerging churches, multicultural ministries, and any ministry being established outside of the structure of the ELCA, especially by seminarians and laity in response to their context. These edges take the skeleton of the tradition and enflesh it in distinct cultural settings, whether it be immigrant Indonesians or urban punks. The only way for the edges to survive is with the liturgical, theological, and financial resources of the core. The core, in turn, needs the life that is brought back to it from the edges in order to not atrophy. A healthy ecclesial life is a symbiotic system where each sector fills a role and is needed by the other. A simple example is this: HFASS is a community of around fifty-five people who, at the time of this writing, have been worshiping weekly for seventeen months. In that time we have sent three young adults to seminary. In seven years, Church of the Apostles, a Lutheran and Episcopalian emerging church in Seattle, has sent just under thirty young adults to seminary. Will Church of the Apostles or HFASS ever be "totally self-supporting"? Maybe, maybe not. But the ELCA must look at what function these communities play in the whole ecosystem of the ELCA and determine on that basis if they are worth supporting long term. Over the course of seventeen months, HFASS has had five short-term seminary interns, as well as an Anglican intern from the United Kingdom, and we have had to turn down many, many other requests for learning opportunities from seminarians.

The point being that these communities and the ways in which they are living out the gospel is compelling to many people who are looking for where the church is going to be ten, twenty-five, and fifty years from now. My concern for the mainline is that the church doesn't seem to be taking the cultural crevasse between the generations very seriously. The unprecedented rate of technological change in fifteen years has created not a generational gap, but a cultural one. We should pay close attention to the kind of cultural orientation that extends beyond generational boundaries, meaning that someone can think and act like a Baby Boomer and be twenty years old and, conversely, someone can think and act like a Millennial and be fifty years old. According to the Pew Research Center, Millennials are the least likely of any generation before them to care about organized religion, yet they also pray as much as their grandparents did.[1] The truth of the matter is that the institutional church is simply irrelevant to them. Millennials see institutional religion as being quite separate from spirituality and as a result they stay away. As our denominations look back in anger at the image of their heyday in the 1950s and 1960s getting smaller and smaller in the rearview mirror, they have failed to look out the front window. The 1950s are never coming back. The question is not *How do we recapture our past success?* but *What does it look like to be followers of Christ in the here and now? What does it look like to be Christ's body in the future?* Earnest people who love the church and see nothing but it dying all around them often pose to me the first question. As much as I wish I could say otherwise, I simply don't know how to revive the dying church. I don't know what can be done for the countless little churches filled only with older folks: churches that live in a demographic reality that when projected out ten to fifteen years looks grim. These churches are faithful expressions of the gospel, but they are going the way of the dinosaur. So what next? The death of Lutheranism and Methodism and Episcopalianism, and so on? I hope not.

I'm not a cheerleader for postdenominationalism. I don't think our traditions are dying. Perhaps a particular cultural expression of our traditions is dying, but that is a very different thing from saying our traditions are dying. Our traditions have curated parts of the Christian story—including theological viewpoints and liturgical practices—that are like family treasures. The Anabaptists have curated the peace church tradition for us; the Methodists have curated the social gospel tradition for us; the Lutherans and Episcopalians have curated the ancient liturgy for us. These are gifts cherished and lived out by generations of the faithful for the benefit of the whole body of Christ, and they remain incredibly valuable to us. They help us innovate with integrity and become caretakers as well. We would do well to recall Jaroslav Pelikan's distinction between "tradition" and "traditionalism": Tradition is the living faith of the dead; traditionalism is the dead faith of the living.[2] So if we are looking to the future of our denominations, let's not try to relive traditionalisms that worked in the past. Instead, let's be innovative with the traditions that have been passed down to us and consider ways we might be caretakers of them in culturally appropriate ways.

Perhaps the best people to be in conversation with about the future of the church are those of us who are native to Millennial culture and are living out our particular traditions in that context. What is the future of the mainline? I'm not sure. But I think we should be asking the kind of people I am about to introduce you to. They represent communities doing Lutheran Word and Sacrament ministry in nontraditional settings. They are living this Lutheran tradition out by enfleshing it in new places and with new people.

Jodi Houge started Humble Walk Lutheran Church while still in seminary. She describes it this way:

> Humble Walk sprung up in the alleys and yards of this working-class urban St. Paul neighborhood. During my final year at seminary, I invited neighbors and friends to gather for a simple worship at a local coffee shop on Sunday evenings. People showed up—hungry for community and looking for a different way to experience church together. Our neighborhood is teeming with young families, twenty-somethings and first-time home buyers. The Humble Walk community reflects this demographic—most Sundays, half of our worshipers are under the age of seven.
>
> After four months in the coffee shop, we moved to a storefront. We travel lightly as a community—renting space at that storefront for three hours on Sunday evenings. (We own four plastic containers: one for clean dishes, one for dirty, one for worship supplies, and one for toys.) Humble Walk eats well together and often—we have a potluck every single Sunday after worship. Without office space or owning a building, we are forced into public space for every meeting, event, and gathering. We like it this way. We are

very intentional about using our local bars, parks, coffee shops, and yards to be present in this corner of the world. Humble Walk is old-fashioned church (order of worship, plenty of coffee, Word and Sacrament)—and deeply incarnational. Christ is present.[3]

Ryan Marsh is a lay mission developer at Church of the Beloved in Edmonds, Washington, and an adult convert to Lutheranism. After four years of working with Church of the Apostles in Seattle, four partnering ELCA churches north of Seattle called him to explore starting an "outreach to missing generations." He's currently on the slow train to ordination through a distance learning process at Wartburg Seminary. Ryan has a "why not" approach to life and ministry. He describes Church of the Beloved this way:

Church of the Beloved is a four-year-old mission start of the ELCA in Edmonds, Washington. We are made up of many intersecting circles—a worshiping community, a residential Christian community, a community garden, a gaggle of artists, a steady flow of interns, and more young families than we know what to do with right now. It seems like too much to hold together, yet the Gospel of Jesus somehow creates a strong enough thread to drive this beautiful mess. A 105-year-old mansion is the hub for our mission together in Edmonds and it's where we offer classes, concerts, parties, readings, an organic P-Patch, rooms for residing, and other ways of offering the gifts of God's church to our neighborhood. What we do isn't particularly fresh; in fact, it seems pretty ancient, but because the Spirit is doing it now, with us, and in the language of zip code 98026 we have to suspect that God is up to something new . . . again.[4]

Young African American men started Shekinah Chapel in Chicago over fifteen years ago. Yeheil Curry, their second pastor, describes how he came to lead the community and what the church is like now:

Shekinah Chapel is a worshiping community that grew from 30 to 300 members under the leadership of Sean McMillian from 1995–2005. I joined in 1997 when there was about thirty of us. Sean was never ordained by the ELCA, but was very gifted and talented. When he stepped down in 2005, thirty members got together and approached me and asked if I would consider leading. The Synod preferred that an ordained pastor be assigned temporarily, but the Shekinah Chapel leadership resisted and I was granted permission to lead provided that I help move Shekinah Chapel towards becoming an officially organized congregation of the ELCA. From 2005–2009 I led Shekinah Chapel as a lay leader. I was ordained in

April of 2009 and we are now considered an ELCA congregation under development.

Service at Shekinah sometimes includes an element in the liturgy referred to as Libations; a ritual dating back several centuries to the African continent. It is a time when we acknowledge the ancestors–those recently departed and those among us. While only a small portion of the liturgy, this meaningful ritual affirms the importance of the culture that this generation has been separated from. The youth ministry of the church hosts a quarterly interfaith "Holy Hip-Hop" service where they, along with youth groups from several other congregations, fellowship and support each other via praise dance, rap, song, poetry, mime, and the preached Word.

Shekinah Chapel deeply focuses on community service, the arts, and mentoring as a way of living out their mission to "Bring them in, Train them up, and Ship them out."[5]

Emily Scott wanted to create a place where God and God's people sit down and have dinner. Trained as a liturgist and musician, Emily graduated from Yale Divinity School and the Institute of Sacred Music, where she earned her Master of Divinity degree. She started St. Lydia's Table in 2009 as a member of the laity and is now in the candidacy process for ordination in the ELCA. She describes St. Lydia's Table this way:

> St. Lydia's is a Dinner Church in New York City. We gather each Sunday evening in East Village to share a sacred meal, just as the first followers of Jesus did. We are building St. Lydia's together through leadership that draws on the community to support and care for one another. Our liturgy reflects and supports our mission of nourishing and feeding one another at a holy table.
>
> Our life as a community revolves around three central pillars:
>
> 1. Telling Our Story: we gather to proclaim the story of Christ's resurrection, and through it, the daily dyings and risings that comprise the life of faith.
>
> 2. Sharing the Meal: we gather to share a sacred meal, blessed as sacred with an ancient Eucharistic prayer.
>
> 3. Working Together: we gather to cook, set up, and clean, knowing that working alongside one another draws us closer to God and binds us together as the church.[6]

Kae Evensen and Mark Stenberg are copastors at Mercy Seat in Minneapolis, which they describe this way:

> Mercy Seat is a startup church in the urban core of Minneapolis trying to uphold the deepest and most lovely task of the Church: that is, preaching the living Christ. By most parameters, we could

be considered an emergent church, but we don't use that language and we don't fit neatly into any one category. We find our grounding in the ancient liturgies of the Church, renewing them from within, shaping ourselves around Word and Sacrament ministry, our hope staked to the crucified and risen Christ. Can we help it if we dress sort of funny and we happen to be bookish, artsy, and at times a little goofy?

As much as we have in common with those who came before us, we cannot deny the fact that our cultural context has changed considerably over the past fifty years. That means how we speak the message of death and new life has to be framed with new language, and the best of our traditions need to be presented in ways that can be heard. We cannot assume that because we're practicing these traditions within a different context than those who have come before us we are doing it better; we are all simply pointing, like John the Baptist, to the One who loves and graces us all.[7]

While gathering these stories of other Lutheran Word and Sacrament communities on the edges of my denomination I soon realized two things:

1. Out of the seven leaders listed (including me), only two were raised in the Lutheran tradition.
2. Four of the seven of us were not yet ordained when we started our churches.

While new communities with emerging sensibilities within denominational structures cannot be looked to for the answers to all that ails the mainline, they can be seen as signs of hope and new life. When we can identify leaders in our midst who are native to the millennial cultural context, a context that will only take up an increasingly larger space within the cultural landscape of the United States, we can then ask them, *What does it look like to be the church now and in the future?* They have the authority to address this question. The Lutheran tradition is nimble and simply should not be *limited* to an ethnically Northern European, culturally Midwestern expression. Perhaps the future of our traditions lies in the leadership of those who have yet to even darken the doors, those who are still in middle school, those who are passionate about the gospel and are living it out beyond the denominational structures and gate-keeping and systems of approval. The history of Christianity's spread has always been connected to a story that travels: in other words, the parts of the tradition that can be imported into and informed by any cultural context. So let's pay attention to where the Spirit is mischievously breathing anew in places anew. And let's agree to be surprised . . . and hopeful.

Notes

[1] "Religion Among the Millennials," http://pewforum.org/Age/Religion-Among-the-Millennials.aspx.

[2] Jaroslav Pelikan, *The Vindication of Tradition: The 1983 Jefferson Lecture in the Humanities* (New Haven, Conn.: Yale University Press, 1986), 65.

[3] Learn more at http://www.humblewalkchurch.org.

[4] Learn more at http://www.belovedschurch.org.

[5] Learn more at http://www.shekinahchapel.web.officelive.com.

[6] Learn more at http://www.stlydias.org.

[7] Learn more at http://www.nemercy.org.

2

Monocultural Church
in a Hybrid World

Stephanie Spellers

Is the emerging church a whites-only movement? Some savvy observers say so.[1] Perhaps because I'm a black woman serving as priest and lead organizer with an Anglimergent community in Boston, I get peppered with questions like "Aren't they racists? What are you doing with them?" My more skeptical Episcopal colleagues are almost giddy with the news, as if they're grateful to see cracks in the revolutionaries' ranks.

It's sad to realize new forms of Christian community are as prone to affinity-based segregation and insider-outsider power dynamics as older forms. But is it shocking? Not for a moment. American Christian life remains tragically segregated along nearly every line that matters—race, class, culture, language, politics, sexuality. It is true for mainliners. It is true for emergents. And we all need to pray for transformation.

So I will stick it out with emergence. Even with its all-too-apparent limitations, the movement remains one of the best hopes I know of for equipping mainline Christians to embrace the Other and partner with emerging generations and cultures. If mainliners and emergent Christians could harness the gifts in both of our "camps," we might leap forward as reconcilers in a broken world.

Monocultural Churches in a Hybrid World

American life is officially hybrid. Crossing cultures is a matter of course, especially among young people. White and Asian artists rap with skill; Latino and black students dream of becoming CEOs and English professors. Wealthy young people give up their privilege to live in economically bereft communities. Straight young people march in gay pride parades without a thought about whether they'll be mistaken for one of "them." The cultural landscape of America is as multicolored and mixed as it has ever been.

But you wouldn't know it from visiting the average American church. The Pew Forum on Religion and Public Life conducted its "U.S. Religious Landscape Survey" in 2008, and the results made for dour news.[2] Mainline Protestant denominations—as distinguished from those that identify as evangelical, Catholic, or Orthodox—are overwhelmingly whiter, more educated, and wealthier than the general public or those who claim no church affiliation at all.

In mainline Protestant life, we have overwhelmingly yoked our traditions to particular, limited cultural identities, and the numbers prove what we are loath to admit: We are stuck. Lutherans defend Scandinavian and German traditions. Episcopalians love our links to Mother England and prayers in the Queen's English. Presbyterians hearken back to their Scottish cultural roots. Even homegrown Methodists and Baptists often have a hard time breaking out of middle-American culture and life. And our attachment to these cultural identities creates a wall that separates us along class and educational lines, just as it does around racial identity.

Looking back, mainline churches can boast a historic commitment to social justice, reconciliation, and even antiracism, at times standing in the vanguard of cultural and social change. Those days of leading change have passed, and now we are scrambling to catch up. The irony is that, as I have interviewed and consulted with church leaders about the systemic decline of the mainline churches, many say we are suffering because we forgot who we are, chasing trends and watering down our traditions so much that there was nothing left for anyone to believe in or connect with. Research shows we've shrunk because we make up a mostly white, upper-middle-class church, and that particular slice of America stopped growing at the very same time that other racial and cultural groups blossomed.[3] The problem isn't that we let go of our identity. It's that we clung to it too tightly. As our neighborhoods changed, and hybridity became the rule, we came to look like cultural dinosaurs: suspicious of change, judgmental of emerging cultures, and incapable of venturing out to build relationships in the transformed communities around us.

I have heard the great fear among mainliners that emergents and other change leaders will throw the baby out with the bathwater. An equal danger is that we will continue washing the baby in the same tepid, graying water.

Unlocking a Padlocked Tradition

What is also true is that all of us—emergent, traditionalist, mainline, evangelical—have a basic need for what Ronald Heifetz calls a "holding environment": the secure, consistent, dependable, structured relationships and practices that provide an anchor so we can make the adaptive moves necessary to actually deal with change.[4] Ultimately, you can't demonize mainline Christians who protect the concrete practices, songs, stories, leadership structures, traditions, teachings, and, yes, the buildings and art, that have constituted "church." Holding on in this way is, to some extent, utterly human.

Christians speak of an intimate, personal relationship with our Creator, going so far as to call God not only our Father or Mother, but our Brother, Friend, and even Lover. Our faith rests on the belief that God was reconciled with humanity by becoming incarnate among us. "I am in my Father, and you in me, and I in you," Jesus assured his disciples. "They who have my commandments and keep them are those who love me; and those who love me will be loved by my Father, and I will love them and reveal myself to them" (Jn. 14:20–21). Meeting us in the flesh, Jesus transformed our relationship to God. He promised that, as we know him, we could know and hold onto God.

Jesus also transformed our relationship to the stuff of life by dwelling in it. Sacramental communities like the Episcopal, Lutheran, Roman Catholic, and Orthodox churches point to specific acts and physical objects and say these are bearers of God. That, after all, is what a sacrament is: a visible sign of an invisible grace. Baptism and Eucharist are the chief sacraments, where Jesus covenanted to always join us. That was just the start. As we partake in these sacraments, our senses over time become conditioned to perceive the whole world as sacramental, to see the stuff of ordinary life as a potential purveyor for the holiness and grace of God. And so, for sacramental Christians, stuff matters. Stuff can act as a conductor drawing us closer to God.

That impulse has its limits. Church folks, in all our humanity, often cling to our stuff—especially stuff that is wed to culture and aesthetic preference—in a way that breeds segregation and suspicion of difference. While the faith and the gospel of Jesus are forever, our church traditions and practices are designed to facilitate our relationship with God in Christ and our participation in Christ's Way. They were never meant to be frozen by one culture, place, or time. Only God is eternal.

It is a hard lesson to learn, but it was at the heart of Jesus' good news. You can hear him touching our clenched hands and saying, "Do not cling to your own life, to the Sabbath or the shape of your traditions, to the Holy Spirit who blows where she will. Do not even cling to me, for I must ascend." It is safe to imagine what he would say to our churches when we cling to particular cultural forms and particular containers for Christian community. He would tell us to remove the padlock we've placed on our traditions, to do the hard work of discerning how the gospel and shape of Christian community will be translated to meet the contexts and situations in which we find ourselves today.

Is all this just one more impossible teaching from Jesus? Actually, the framers of many of our mainline traditions were also wise and humble enough to embed similar warnings inside the very documents they were crafting. In the preface to the first Book of Common Prayer in 1549, Thomas Cranmer wrote:

> The particular Forms of Divine worship, and the Rites and Ceremonies appointed to be used therein, being things in their own nature indifferent, and alterable, and so acknowledged; it is but reasonable, that upon weighty and important considerations, according to the various exigency of times and occasions, such changes and alterations should be made therein, as to those that are in place of Authority should from time to time seem either necessary or expedient.

In declaring that the "Forms of Divine worship" can and should be changed, according to the local context, in keeping with the core of the faith and scripture, Cranmer set out the warrant for a new prayer book that the English people could call their own. He also laid the foundation for a church capable of bending without breaking when the times changed. Walking in the footsteps of leaders like Cranmer, we might cultivate as deep a concern for translating the good news to meet the diverse conditions and cultures on the ground, as we have for protecting inherited church traditions.

Granted, no single congregation or even denomination can be everything to everyone. No, we can't force people to love and be moved by what simply does not draw them closer to God. Spirituality is subjective, and subjectivity of course depends on social context. But we cannot stop there. Only the most arrogant would claim their church's way as universal, the ideal path to God not only for one group but for all who want to enter relationship with God. I've come to believe it is equally hazardous to say, "Yes, that group of Christians has a valid cultural practice, but it's not ours. They can do that over there. We will continue doing things our way over here. Others will join us because they appreciate what we do and want to take it for themselves." We may think the instinct to separate is a sign of cultural respect—best not to misappropriate another culture with which we are not in relationship. But when we elevate or cling to our own culture in a way that precludes transformative relationship with or deep appreciation of the Other, we are on the road to segregation *and* spiritual suffocation.

That roadblock is the one mainline Protestant churches have thrown up time and again. I used to think it was largely a problem for my own

Episcopal Church. But as I speak with leaders in the United Methodist Church, Presbyterian Church (U.S.A.), Evangelical Lutheran Church in America, and United Church of Christ—and I'm sure it's true among Baptists, Pentecostals, Roman Catholics, and many others—I've come to understand that this clinging is practically universal among faith communities, if not human institutions.

Emerging at Last

How do we live with the freedom, faithfulness, and reconciling love Jesus invites us into? Put differently, How do we actually engage in the spiritual practice of radical welcome: building relationships on the ground, embracing emerging contexts and cultures, and allowing ourselves to be transformed by the gifts, presence, and power of the Other?[5] This is where emergence Christianity has been useful to so many. Engagement with the emergent movement can and has opened us out: out to welcome the Other, out to embrace transformation, out to embrace and be transformed by emerging cultures.

Emergence certainly didn't invent this methodology. I would argue that it is one in a long line of contextual theological movements, including Latin American, feminist, womanist (black feminist), black, Native American, Asian, and queer liberation theologies.[6] I am indebted to these traditions for helping me reclaim and come home to Christianity when I had given up on the whole project. Still, even with those revolutionary forebears paving the way and continuing the struggle, mainline churches clearly haven't embraced the voice and presence of the Other so that people pray differently, sing differently, lead differently, and act differently. Yes, liberation theology opened the door. Yes, plenty of seminarians study it and imagine becoming agents of transformation . . . only to get shut down in their first post. Clearly, we need help living into the change so many Christians claim we seek.

The emerging church movement can draw us back to the practices that Jesus and our mainline traditions have held out to us from the beginning. In particular, we need the movement's tools as we seek to honor our contexts, to embrace the Other, and to restore a tolerance for freedom and flexibility.

Where Are We Now? Contextualization as Anglican and Emergent Practice

In the case of Anglicanism, one could easily argue that our very identity is bound up with being a church in context. In their groundbreaking collection *Beyond Colonial Anglicanism: The Anglican Communion in the Twenty-First Century*, Kwok Pui Lan and Ian Douglas draft one of the most compelling definitions of Anglican identity I know. Douglas begins by laying out this vision:

The advent of the Church of England marked a reconception of the body of Christ on the English shores that was at once profoundly particular and profoundly catholic. This process of contextualization, in which the church becomes grounded in the local realities of a particular people while remaining in communion across the differences of culture and geography . . . is where Anglican identity lies. Anglicanism thus can be understood as the embrace and celebration of apostolic catholicity within vernacular moments.[7]

Professor Kwok follows up with this bold yet tough-to-debunk claim:

Anglicanism was a cultural hybrid from the beginning, and this tradition should be celebrated in our postcolonial world. As a cultural hybrid of Catholicism and Protestantism, the Church of England in the sixteenth century assimilated elements from both traditions to create a very fluid identity.[8]

When we are truest to our roots, Anglican Christians honor and celebrate the catholic, universal, comprehensive, sacramental, apostolic traditions passed down from the earliest days of Christianity, up through the Councils and Creeds, through ever-advancing theological development and conversation with history. But that affirmation happens in "vernacular moments": the particular, contextual moments in place and time that are our reality. Douglas says this is "where God in Jesus meets believers again and again, in all of our uniqueness of culture and contextual specificity." These moments are not "once-for-all points in time, a 'been there, done that' by which the gospel has been translated definitively."[9] They are the place where the gospel is translated and becomes the lively and true word of God among God's people. The Anglican Way is a hybrid, pure and simple.

Unfortunately, thanks to the legacy of colonialism, Anglicans the world over (including in the former colony that is the United States of America) have elided Anglican Christianity with a common English heritage. An even higher pedestal is reserved for our chief cultural icon and source of unity: the Book of Common Prayer. "I love being able to go to any Episcopal church in America, almost any Anglican church in the world, and recognize the liturgy," people have told me with deep affection. "It makes me feel so connected." This is our catholicity in action, and as one who grew up surrounded by independent churches that split over the kind of car the minister drove, I am grateful for a church where we are bound to each other, to the body of Christ in the past, and to the body coming to life in the future. These links matter.

But if our identity and practice is only about catholicity, then it is only half Anglican. Contextualization is the other, sorely neglected half of our Way. In the Thirty-Nine Articles of Faith, an early statement of Anglican doctrine, the church's leaders picked up Thomas Cranmer's lead and declared, "It is a thing plainly repugnant to the Word of God, and the custom of the Primitive Church, to have public Prayer in the Church, or to minister the Sacraments in a tongue not understanded [*sic*] of the people."[10] These leaders were far from radical, but they could not have been clearer about the priority of context and the need to translate the gospel and traditions into the language of the people. Of course English speakers shouldn't pray in Latin. By logical extension, I have to believe Thomas Cranmer and his contemporaries would be more disappointed than flattered to hear Elizabethan English prayers uttered inside a church if the shouts and cries outside are Dominican Spanish.

Emergent ministries, including those affiliated with the Fresh Expressions movement in the United Kingdom, lead us back from temptation by rooting us in context. Bishop Stephen Cottrell, who shepherds Fresh Expressions, writes: "As the Church encounters new cultures and new challenges it seeks to serve the needs of ordinary people and give expression to the gospel in a language they understand: something that meets them where they are and takes them somewhere else."[11] This is not mere mimicry of culture. Cottrell knows the gospel doesn't just affirm, comfort, or entertain people; it engages lives on the ground in order to transform them. This is the goal of contextualization, a listening process that allows us to gear traditions to conditions and life-giving cultural expressions in a context . . . and all so that the gospel might be heard and understood, becoming true food for real people.

Feminists practice contextualization as we lift up images of the divine feminine and struggle for the same equality in Christian community that women experience in the culture at large. Black churches do contextualization every time we set a John Wesley hymn to a beat. American Indian congregations are contextualizing whenever they draw on indigenous wisdom to shape their leadership structures. In his book *Let's Do Theology: Resources for Contextual Theology*, Laurie Green, a liberation theologian rooted in urban, working-class England, argues:

> Christ, at his incarnation, puts himself right inside the cultural context, alongside the people's experience. We must therefore be sure to devise an incarnational theological method that allows for the careful critical reading of each context so that our theology can derive not from abstract assumptions, but is instead substantial, pertinent theology that speaks from, and is relevant to, real people in their specific culture, place and time.[12]

Like these liberation traditions, emerging churches take context seriously. The working definition of "emerging church" that I have found most helpful is simply this: "Emerging churches are communities that practice the way of Jesus within postmodern cultures."[13] In Episcopal and mainline contexts, I usually explain that emergence is not a style; rather, it is a paradigm shift whereby even the most basic elements of Christian practice, faith, tradition, and identity—worship, mission, community, scripture, formation—are translated through a postmodern lens and adapted to come alive in context. And we have no choice but to do this work of translation. "We are in the midst of a cultural revolution," Eddie Gibbs and Ryan Bolger assert, "and nineteenth century (or older) forms of church do not communicate clearly to twenty-first century cultures . . . The church is a modern institution in a postmodern world."[14] If we do not embody the gospel within our postmodern cultures, they argue, Christian community as we know it will not survive the century.

This is not an argument to dismiss church and traditions. For example, the tag for our emergent community in Boston is "The Crossing: where *real church* meets *real life*." In our ministry, we begin with the good news of Jesus and the essentials of sacramental tradition and theology as Christians have discerned them over time (hence, the "real church"). But we share them in ways that honor and come alongside the cultural expressions, sacred experiences, and great longing of urban residents: African Americans; young postmoderns; oral and narrative cultures; and lesbian, gay, bisexual, and transgendered people in our surrounding community today ("real life").

What does this mean for those of us at The Crossing? Ancient chants set to a funky groove that moves our minds, hearts, and bodies deeper into mystery. Gospel reflections preached by laity, not just the priest, so that silenced people discover voice and become apostles. Formation offered in neighborhood small groups, to provide an experience of discipline and accountability to Christian community, and to break out of the aching loneliness and individualism that mark postmodern life. Ongoing mutual partnership with queer justice organizations that rarely link with Christians, because we believe Jesus calls to us from the margins. Eucharist at a truly open table, where real bread becomes the real body of Christ . . . and so do we.

This is how the gospel and traditions come to life in our context. The more authentically we embody the gospel within this context, the more intent we are on joining with the Spirit as she brings new forms of ancient-future Christian community to life where we are, and the more sure I am that we are being good Episcopalians.

Who Is My Neighbor? Embracing the Other as Anglican and Emergent Practice

Episcopalians and mainline Christians long for relationship with emerging communities. We believe that the current state of affairs—racial and cultural segregation a given, entire generations conspicuously absent from the pews—is not God's will for creation. It seems the entire record of scripture could be summarized as God's attempt to reconcile humanity to Godself. The apostle Paul described that mission beautifully when he wrote to the divided community in Ephesus: "[Christ] is our peace . . . he has made both groups into one and has broken down the dividing wall, that is, the hostility between us" (Eph. 2:14–15). The dream of God is to bring us back into right relationship with God, with creation, and with each other.

And yet, the dividing walls spring back up. Emergence Christianity is not immune to this temptation. Our movement's reliance on affinity-based networks that form and morph without direct leadership or intention too easily creates circles of people who "naturally" drift together based on shared life experiences, education, culture, and linguistic background. Unless communities place antiracism or another antioppression commitment at their core, and unless there is a mechanism for a ministry's members to take the rudder and actively turn from the segregated course they are drifting down, we humans quickly fall back into our comfortable patterns. It can be just as tough to drag emergents out of our Eurocentric postmodern philosophical insider talk as it is for mainliners to let go of cozy pews and Bach chorales.

But there are certain practices at the core of emergence Christianity that both emergent and mainline Christians could deploy to nurture communities capable of embracing the Other. For instance, emergent Christians have repurposed the tools of postcolonial mission theory and put them to use in our domestic contexts. Global mission expert Titus Presler spells out some of these insights in his most recent work, *Going Global with God: Reconciling Mission in a World of Difference.* He writes that "mission is ministry in the dimension of difference,"[15] and goes on to explain that mission happens when we bear witness and serve Christ across dividing lines. Emergent Christians couldn't agree more. Leaders in the United Kingdom often group their ministries under the umbrella "mission-shaped church," because these Christian communities are shaped to proclaim and embody the gospel where they are. Clearly, some mission contexts where our conventional mainline church forms speak quite well with little or no significant modification. The heavy lifting begins when we cross boundaries. That is the work that mission-shaped and emergent movements prepare pioneers to engage.

The tools we employ for this work are a missionary's tools: listening, being present, building relationships, and becoming companions within a community, especially across boundaries of difference. Often a congregation or diocese will come to us at The Crossing and ask, "Could we have some emergent worship services to take home?" We laugh. Emerging church isn't worship in a box or in a book. Doing emergence means stepping across a boundary in order to partner with whatever is emerging in *your* context, even—and especially—when it entails moving into a place that your ministry has rarely ventured into before. Doing emergence requires listening and laying yourself open to be changed in relationship with the Other. You are literally tuned to detect what is emerging, what the Spirit is making known, all around you.

Emergence also prepares us to engage the Other because it creatively engages multiplicity, which is a hallmark of postmodern, postcolonial existence. In most emergent Christian communities, we approach the differences others read as a deviation from the norm and from gospel purity, and in them discover proof of God's creativity, presence, and sense of humor. So the scriptures can reveal more than one truth without becoming invalid. The bar down the street can be infused with the sacred when we talk scripture over a cocktail. Dancing in the club gets raised up as transformative Christian practice. We already celebrate the Sunday 9:00 a.m. Rite I Eucharist with its smells, bells, and formal liturgy. Let's also celebrate when a group at the same church launches a Wednesday 9:00 p.m. Goth Mass in partnership with local art students.

Rowan Williams, the Archbishop of Canterbury, blessed all this multiplicity when he issued the invitation to let "a million flowers bloom" in a "mixed economy of church."[16] This shift is nothing short of revolutionary, probably to most mainline congregations, and certainly to most Anglicans. You mean we aren't assuming there is one way to be church, or one group with a unique hold on the "right" way to worship, lead, or act? We're going to creatively engage differences, not paper them over with the pages of the Book of Common Prayer? This is stunning, freeing, good news, especially for mainline churches struggling to proclaim the gospel in a world of difference.

The new monastic movement is also preparing emerging generations to embrace the Other, and it offers wisdom aplenty to the wider church. These (mostly) young Christians live in intentional communities and translate monastic principles for their contemporary contexts. In their contribution to the book *Ancient Faith, Future Mission: Fresh Expressions in the Sacramental Tradition,* Ian Adams and Ian Mosby share the stories of ancient-future ministries like the Simple Way community in Philadelphia, or the Moot Community in London, both of which have gone out of their way to enter into solidarity with the economically and the spiritually poor people in their cities. It's classic monastic practice. "Monastic communities have traditionally been good at moving into new settings, often places where others fear to go, and lovingly engaging with local people. Almost all of them embrace the monastic tradition of offering hospitality to the stranger, traveler, or visitor."[17] These new monastics, like their forebears, know how to move out of their comfort zones, sink roots in a community, stand in solidarity with the least of these, and welcome the stranger as Christ.

This prophetic, ancient-future witness has humbled and challenged me. These earnest and faithful emergent Christians could help those of us tucked into comfortable mainline Protestant *and* emergent life to reclaim the tradition of engaging the Other as Christ and engaging difference as a gift from God.

Please, do come alongside and engage with the Other. But don't do it to expose a new community to our "better" way of being Christian. Become companions because God is always revealing more truth to us, and we know and live it best in fellowship with each other, and especially with the Other.

A Big Tent and a Big Mess: Freedom and Paradox as Anglican and Emergent Practice

I don't know if there is a mainline denomination messier than the worldwide Anglican Communion and Episcopal Church, the expression of Anglican life based in the United States. But we are ambivalent about all this freedom and unruliness, which may explain why we are also the church known for perfect presentation, much of it rooted in our role as church of the empire and of the ruling and owning classes.

The die was cast in the sixteenth century, early in our church's life, when Queen Elizabeth I reportedly announced, "I do not wish to make windows into men's souls." As long as people gathered for Christian community and communion, she wasn't concerned with their beliefs about precisely what was happening at communion. What she was concerned about was bringing peace to her fractured nation and empire. For that reason, even as she granted broad freedom on matters theological, she enforced an Act of Uniformity around matters liturgical. Believe what you want, but use this Prayer Book.

The framers of the Episcopal Church in the United States restored freedom to its former glory. Then again, our church was established in 1789, the same year the first U.S. Constitution was ratified; in the same location, Philadelphia; and by many of the same men. Those leaders took Thomas Cranmer's Preface to the original Prayer Book and pushed it to its logical conclusion:

> It is a most invaluable part of that blessed "liberty wherewith Christ hath made us free," that in his worship different forms and usages may without offense be allowed, provided the substance of the Faith be kept entire; and that, in every Church, what cannot be clearly determined to belong to Doctrine must be referred to Discipline; and therefore, by common consent and authority, may be altered, abridged, enlarged, amended, or otherwise disposed of, as may seem most convenient for the edification of the people, "according to the various exigency of times and occasions."[18]

And so continued our journey as a church equally committed to freedom and order. What tipped the scales toward order? As the British Empire expanded, and American revolutionary spirit gave way to institution-building impulses, both needed an orderly Anglican church. Today, especially when it comes to liturgy and church practice, Anglicans have overwhelmingly aligned order, perfection, and sober bearing with holiness, while freedom and flexibility look like a throwback to the formless chaos before God brought order to creation. Perfection and order—highly valued commodities in European and American culture—are truly next to godliness.

I see in that deep yearning for perfection and formality a gesture of humility and respect toward the awesome and almighty One we worship. Yet on the ground, our "frozen chosen" attitude makes it much harder to link with and value the diverse cultural expressions emerging in our neighborhoods and around the world. The question is, how could our orderly traditions meet and be woven with different, more flexible cultural expressions? Could we seek partnership with the Other, instead of domination, assimilation, or rejection? Could we build bridges and build our tolerance for greater freedom in the areas of worship, leadership, and identity? Is there any way for us to lean into the comprehensiveness that is also at the core of Anglican identity, and lean away from our need for control and sobriety?

With the help of emergence, I truly believe our mainline traditions could finally decouple perfection and holiness, and increase our tolerance for a free, fluid, multicultural, contextually meaningful, faithful, and sacramental church. Karen Ward, pastor and abbess for the Church of the Apostles in Seattle, has served as midwife to one of the fullest expressions of Anglican and emergent (or Anglimergent) identity in the United States. She shares her dream of a more fluid, hybrid church in this way:

> I was convinced that Anglo-Catholic ritual, practice, and sacramental mysticism—when brought into dialogue with contemporary art, culture and media, and in the context of a welcoming and "culturally fluent" community—could provide space and place for postmodern seekers to fall in love with God, form community with one another and then practice extending God's love to the surrounding neighborhood.[19]

I love Karen's witness, for it tells me the balance can be struck. The either/or mentality has always set out win/loss scenarios: You must either love freedom and chaos *or* love structure and rigidity, love what's fresh *or* love tradition, love the gifts of your marginalized culture *or* love the gifts of upper-class Anglo-American culture. This dualistic approach no longer applies in an emergent paradigm. Technically, it does not apply in an Anglican paradigm either. Early leaders in the Anglican fold urged the church to "keep the mean between the two extremes, of too much stiffness in refusing, and of too much easiness in admitting any variation from it."[20] Our Anglican Way stands between impulses—ever reforming, ever remembering—and always recognizes that we need the witness of both sides if we are ever to grasp the gospel in its fullness.

Every Christian must ultimately discern how to effect this balancing act. Clinging to tradition and order because they are part of our identity, because we feel safe inside the structure, because we respect our ancestors—these are not reasons to block change. At the same time, freedom for its own sake, chaos just to watch the sparks fly, bowing at the altar of contemporary culture—these are not values in their own right. Both freedom and order are tools—like any other element of human life—that we employ to move deeper into the heart of God, further along the path of Jesus, and out into love and care for community and creation. Whatever contributes to the flourishing of creation and the proclamation of the gospel, whatever increases peace and reconciliation between communities that were once at odds—these are the litmus tests that matter.

Emergents understand this boundaried practice of freedom, contrary to what others might imagine about us. Liturgist Isaac Everett serves as Minister for Liturgical Arts and Outreach at The Crossing in Boston and as the cofounder of the transmission community in New York City. Isaac works in several denominational settings. He has served in plenty of truly "free" spaces and actually finds it harder to operate with that blank slate. Like other emergents, he likes starting with the gifts of tradition—ancient hymns, Latin mass settings, the psalms, the liturgical *ordo*, the Book of Common Prayer—and then mining, exploring, flipping, and weaving to see how these traditions speak afresh today. He may need to push the envelope and incorporate electronica or salsa. He may work with a team of prostitutes and artists to bring an Easter Eucharist to life at a nightclub in New York. But it's out of deep love for tradition and a desire to interact with the order, not a careless whim to jettison it and have absolute freedom.

Our freedom is disciplined by our calling. We are free to take up the goodness of tradition and blend it with the goodness of the world, for the purpose of serving and enacting the reign of God. Anything that does not serve that end can't just be maintained, however long it has been beloved and lauded. Likewise, any practice that clearly leads to the flourishing of God's reign deserves consideration and possibly even celebration. Abbott Stuart Burns, superior in a Benedictine community, said it so well: "We need to be free to explore fresh ways of hearing the gospel imperatives for the situations in which we find ourselves now; new ways of hearing the radical things Jesus was trying to say in his day, which people weren't ready to hear, and applying them now, to where we are."[21]

* * *

Opening in these ways, mainline and emergent Christians would all find ourselves in shocking, revelatory new relationships. We would cross boundaries—lines of race, class, gender, identity, language, sexual orientation, education, some lines of our own choosing, some because the Holy Spirit compelled us. We would embrace the Other and also find authentic and fresh ways of embracing our own traditions. We might lose our lives, our old ways, our assumptions, our privilege. But we'd surely take up new life in Christ.

Notes

[1] Soong-Chan Rah, *The Next Evangelicalism: Freeing the Church from Western Cultural Captivity* (Downers Grove, Ill.: Intervarsity, 2009).

[2] Pew Research Center, *U.S. Religious Landscape Survey: Religious Affiliation: Diverse and Dynamic* (Washington, D.C.: Pew Research Center, 2008), 79. For precise breakdowns along racial, educational, and economic lines, see especially 75–85. Available online at http://religions.pewforum.org/pdf/report-religious-landscape-study-full.pdf.

[3] Kirk Hadaway, "Facts on Episcopal Church Growth" (New York: Episcopal Church Center, 2008), 3.

[4] Ronald Heifetz, *Leadership without Easy Answers* (Cambridge, Mass.: Harvard University Press, 1994), 22.

[5] See Stephanie Spellers's *Radical Welcome: Embracing God, The Other, and the Spirit of Transformation* (New York: Church Publishing, 2006).

[6] For additional reflection on the link between liberation theology and emergence, see Stephanie Spellers's "Emerging from the Underside," in *Radical Grace* magazine (January/March 2010–Emerging Christianity issue), 20–21.

[7] Ian Douglas and Kwok Pui Lan, eds., *Beyond Colonial Anglicanism: The Anglican Communion in the Twenty-First Century* (New York: Church Publishing, 2001), 35.

[8] Ibid., 56.

[9] Ibid., 39.

[10] "The Articles of Religion (1801)," in *The Book of Common Prayer* (New York: Church Publishing, 1979), 872.

[11] Stephen Cottrell, "Letting Your Actions Do the Talking: Mission and the Catholic Tradition," in *Ancient Faith, Future Mission: Fresh Expressions in the Sacramental Tradition*, eds. Steven Croft, Ian Mosby, and Stephanie Spellers (New York: Church Publishing, 2010), 51.

[12] Laurie Green, *Let's Do Theology: Resources for Contextual Theology* (New York: Continuum, 2010), 13.

[13] Eddie Gibbs and Ryan Bolger, *Emerging Churches: Creating Christian Community in Postmodern Cultures* (Grand Rapids, Mich.: Baker Academic, 2005), 44.

[14] Ibid.

[15] Titus Presler, *Going Global with God: Reconciling Mission in a World of Difference* (New York: Church Publishing, 2010), 49–67.

[16] Rowan Williams, foreword to *Mission-Shaped Church: Church Planting and Fresh Expressions of Church in a Changing Context* (New York: Seabury Books, 2010), ix.

[17] Ian Adams and Ian Mosby, "New Monasticism," in *Ancient Faith, Future Mission*, 28.

[18] See *The Book of Common Prayer* (1979), 9.

[19] Karen Ward, "A Story of Anglimergence: Community, Covenant, Eucharist and Mission at Church of the Apostles," in *Ancient Faith, Future Mission*, 166.

[20] *The Book of Common Prayer* (Oxford, England: Oxford University, 1662), 7.

[21] Abbott Stuart Burns, OSB, "Concluding Thoughts," in *Ancient Faith, Future Mission*, 173.

3

A New Day Rising in the Church

Elaine A. Heath

It was a scorching July afternoon in Dallas, Texas–a fine day for a field trip for my class in missional ecclesiology for multicultural contexts. My students and I hurried across the asphalt to the beautiful old building marked with a sign in English and Spanish asking visitors to use a gentle touch with the doors. We had come to tour Grace United Methodist Church, a historic downtown church whose members in the early twentieth century had included mayors, governors, and many upper-class families.[1] With white flight in subsequent decades, however, the church began to decline. It was nearly at the point of closure in the 1980s when a new pastor was appointed, Rev. William Bryan, who offered the congregation an opportunity to reimagine itself in mission with its now wondrously diverse neighbors. At the time Rev. Bryan arrived, a fledgling low-income preschool was the only missional arm of the church into its neighborhood.

Because of Rev. Bryan's effective relationship-building efforts with longtime members while introducing the seeds of change, the congregation caught the vision and they launched their first outreach to immigrant adults. The slow but certain turnaround began. Today Grace UMC is a numerically small but vigorous congregation that is home for many immigrants and refugees, as well as lifelong octogenarian members. Proud of its commitment to the full inclusion of LGBTQ members, Grace is a church with a historically liberal theology that has become missional to the core. It has much in common with the revitalized mainline churches that Diana Butler Bass describes in *Christianity for the Rest of Us*.[2] Emergence for Grace

UMC has meant engaging a process of living back into its own neighbor-hood and reclaiming some of the early missional impetus of Methodism.

Upon entering the weathered doors of the church, we met Dr. Diana Holbert, the lead pastor, who gave us a tour and introduced us to many of the staff from the nonprofits that are housed in the church. These include Refugee Services of Texas (an agency that brings refugees from around the world to Texas and helps them find housing, medical care, ESL classes, and employment), the Agape medical clinic (a four-day-a-week clinic for low-income families living in the area), a twice-a-month legal clinic, and the Open Door (a low-cost preschool for area families).

Grace UMC is an example of a congregation "replanting" itself on its own campus in an "abandoned place of empire," to use a phrase common in the new monastic movement.[3] Because of white flight and growing poverty in its neighborhood, the church and its remaining congregants had become a white island in the middle of a multicultural, economically distressed community. The missional transformation of Grace UMC required pastoral and lay leaders to work together over the long haul to cultivate a missional ecclesiology in the congregation, through preaching, teaching, and leadership development. It meant reimagining how to use the church buildings, including the old parsonage, in ways that reached out in mission with their neighbors, and it meant befriending their actual neighbors. There was and is nothing flashy, quick, or gimmicky about Grace UMC becoming a missional congregation. The worship is traditional, with liturgy, an organ, a choir, and a pastor who wears a robe. The building, like the neighborhood, is in need of much repair. But the congregation has never been a more faithful witness to the gospel.

It is vital for my students to hear the story of Grace UMC and meet some of the leaders of its remarkable missions precisely because Grace is very small (by Dallas standards) and theologically left of center. Its revitalization took place slowly, without being overly reliant upon one charismatic pastor. The tendency for many pastors and seminarians over the age of thirty is to think that in order to become evangelistic and missional a church has to become evangelical, which they think means aligned with the political and religious right. This simply isn't true. More literally understood, an evangelical church is one that bears the gospel faithfully to the world, through prayer and action, presence and deed. It incarnates good news to its neighbors in such a way that many of them, too, welcome and enter the kingdom of God. So we could say that Grace UMC is deeply evangelical, according to that meaning of the word.

Diana Butler Bass proposes that the kind of renewal that is taking place in mainline Christianity in North America transcends the old labels of "conservative," "moderate," and "liberal." For this reason she has dropped the words "emergence" and "progressive" to discuss what is happening in favor of "generative."[4] I find this word a rich descriptor, because it conveys the life-begetting, holistic evangelism that characterizes such faith communities.

Students (and the rest of us) need exposure to a diverse array of possibilities for mission and evangelism through new church starts and old church restarts, especially in "abandoned places of empire" so that they will understand that emergence is not bound to one denomination (or lack thereof!), to one theological stream, or to one generation. The future viability of Methodism will require a comprehensive vision for possibilities. It will require a missional, monastic, and generative imagination.

Emerging Theological Education

Valuable as our field trip was that blistering summer day, what made this class truly extraordinary were the students themselves, and the work they are doing to help develop and lead a different model of emerging faith community: New Day Dallas.[5] Christian Kakez-A-Kapend is from the Democratic Republic of Congo, Ceciliah Igweta hails from Kenya, and Filipe Maia comes from Brazil. These three students are powerfully gifted and called not only to a vocation in theology but also to local church leadership in multicultural contexts. They are the face of global emergence in the church, and they have been vitally important to the growth and depth of our experimental microcommunity.

New Day Dallas started a little over two years ago with a handful of students and friends. We wanted to create an alternative form of church that drew from the best insights and practices of the missional church movement, the emerging church, and the new monastic movement, as well as from our own Methodist tradition.

Early Methodism was in many ways a lay monastic, missional movement.[6] We have in our own heritage a wealth of theological and practical resources that can help us to be a vital church in a postdenominational world. For those of us who are Methodist hyphenated Christians, "postdenominational" means "post-treating-the-denomination-like-a-corporation-that-should-look-and-act-like-the-federal-government-or-a-big-business-or-a-competitor-with-other-churches." We have not given up on the theological treasures of Methodism. We are returning to them from a decomposing version of Methodism that Mr. Wesley would likely abhor. We believe Methodism is called to be a humble servant of God's one holy, catholic, apostolic church, a beloved and important member of the multifaceted body of Christ. We hyphenated Methodists keep remembering that Methodism began as a holiness movement within the Anglican church. Methodism became a denomination almost against the will of our founder. Part of what we feel the Holy Spirit is doing today is calling us Methodists back to our roots as a holiness movement, one that integrates a disciplined spiritual life with incarnational ministry in the abandoned places of empire.[7]

So we envisioned New Day Dallas becoming a laboratory for our students and others to learn how to start and lead missional microcommunities. Thus New Day Dallas is a triply hyphenated church–Metho-missional-monastic-generative.

The anchor church for New Day Dallas is Lover's Lane United Methodist Church, a large congregation with a long history of strength in recovery ministries in north Dallas.[8] New Day is considered a satellite or affiliate congregation of Lover's Lane, where one of our lead team pastors is on staff.

We began our New Day worship gatherings at the Wesley Foundation House, an old home that, like the Velveteen Rabbit, through much use has become threadbare, beloved, and Real. The Wesley house is near campus, and we meet there every Sunday evening from 5 p.m. to 7 p.m. for a communal supper and worship. Our lead team, consisting of several bivocational pastors who are multiracial, multigenerational, multicultural, and both genders, follows a rule of life together and shares the leadership of our community's worship and mission. The lead team meets twice a month for an old-fashioned Wesleyan covenant group, checking in with each other on our specific practices of our rule of life, and praying for one another. Our structure is extremely simple, and we want to keep it that way.

New Day Dallas partnered with the Southern Methodist University Wesley Foundation, which is the United Methodist campus ministry; its director, Rev. Andy Roberts, now serves as one of the pastors on our lead team. We also enjoy a warm friendship with the SMU chaplain and his staff. Collaborating with campus ministry gives us more opportunities to invite students to experience this alternative model of church and to consider a vocation in missional ministry.

Our primary mission is one of hospitality and friendship between students and refugees who come to live in Dallas. Upon arrival in Dallas many refugees are initially placed in neighborhoods like Vickery Meadow, a densely populated, three-square-mile area of low-income apartments. It's a tough neighborhood plagued with crime, a situation that is causing some of the refugee agencies to explore other alternatives for housing. But with limited resources available, the options are lacking. Most of the refugees who are part of New Day Dallas are from Africa and live in Vickery Meadow, but our community includes people from around the world. It is not uncommon for half a dozen languages to be spoken around our table.

At the time of this writing, New Day Dallas is in the process of relocating from the Wesley Foundation House to an apartment in Vickery Meadow that will make it easy for our immigrant friends to walk to worship and other ministries we host. In addition to our Sunday-evening gathering, our community is increasingly involved in teaching English to refugees, helping with afterschool programs for immigrant kids, and wildly fun soccer matches. There is always plenty of laughter.

We would be hard pressed to find a more abandoned place of empire than among refugees in Vickery Meadow, most of whom are here because of war, most of whom bear the lasting scars of colonialism, and virtually all of whom live in poverty. My students and I are profoundly impacted by the faith and communal spirit of these friends. We are being reevangelized to deeper levels of the gospel by their witness to Christ in the midst of incredible dislocation. As we break bread around our table and share our stories, we encounter Christ, something that prompted one of our friends to dub New Day as "the church of one table."

Our community is beginning to reach beyond our "one table," with several more microcommunities starting this year, anchored in various other churches and Methodist missions in and around the Dallas/Fort Worth Metroplex. Our dream is to inspire the imagination of the United Methodist Church to embrace new forms of missional faith communities, the kind that are led by teams of bivocational pastors and that are focused on mission rather than bricks and mortar. We believe that this kind of new faith community development is going to be necessary to the evangelistic health and vitality of the church of the future.

Part of what is emerging in hyphenated Methodism is a reimagining of contextualized theological education. Much of what we have been doing in mainline seminaries for the past fifty years was designed to equip pastors to lead the church of yesterday. Retooling for our current and future needs is going to require much more engagement between the seminary and the church and our diverse missional contexts. We are going to have to decentralize theological education more, using distance learning strategically, and offer many more immersion experiences in healthy, missional communities so that students can engage in holistic learning. Mentoring, apprenticeships, and other learning opportunities beyond the walls of the academy are going to be increasingly necessary in order to prepare students for the rigors of missional ministry, especially in regard to starting new faith communities in abandoned places of empire.

For this reason, three years ago some seminary students, friends, and I started a new monastic immersion program called the Epworth Project. During its pilot year three students shared a rental house in a mixed-income, predominantly Hispanic neighborhood, followed a common rule of life, and engaged in ministries of hospitality in their neighborhood. The students helped to formulate the plan for the future of the Epworth Project by experiencing the gifts and challenges of intentional community, as well as engaging in academic research in the theory and practice of new monasticism. Their participation was invaluable in helping us develop a strong plan for the future. Two of these women, Megan Davidson and Amy Proctor, now serve as house pastors in the Epworth Project.

From that tiny beginning we have grown a network of four houses and an apartment, and we launched the Missional Wisdom Foundation, a private nonprofit corporation, to support the Epworth Project and several other new initiatives in missional theological education.[9] Students live in the houses rent free, share the cost of utilities, follow a rule of life including a daily office, engage in monthly hospitality nights in their neighborhood, and offer a minimum of four hours of missional service each week in their neighborhood.

This year there will be twenty people in the Epworth Project houses, including seminary students, undergraduates, and a couple of staff members from one of the anchor churches. It is clear that this is a form of theological education that engages the hearts and minds of a growing number of students who feel called to a more rigorous life of discipleship and mission. The combination of academic rigor in the classroom, intentional community shaped by rhythms of prayer and hospitality, and missional work is shaping a powerful, generative imagination in these students. The Epworth Project is, when you think about it, a challenging course in missional leadership development.

Each Epworth Project house is named for a Christian leader whose life and teaching reflects some of the core values of the Epworth Project. The houses are anchored in missional congregations in diverse parts of the Dallas/Fort Worth Metroplex. The Oscar Romero House is within walking distance of La Fundición de Cristo (Christ's Foundry), a Hispanic mission church started in a low-income apartment complex eight years ago in west Dallas. Most of the students who live in the Romero House are part of the ministry of Christ's Foundry. The Phoebe Palmer House in Fort Worth is connected to White's Chapel UMC campus ministry, The Lab, and the Texas Christian University Wesley Foundation, so the students living there are involved in both campus ministries and local missions. The William Seymour House is located in a racially and economically diverse neighborhood in Plano, with a dual connection to Northpointe Church[10] and New Day. Students there are involved in ministry with at-risk children. And the Dietrich Bonhoeffer House is next door to Grace UMC in downtown Dallas, the church I described at the beginning of this chapter.

While I have focused this discussion on specific examples of what we are developing in the Dallas/Fort Worth Metroplex to cultivate missional, monastic, and emerging forms of church within the United Methodist Church, especially in relation to theological education, there are many signs of emergence around the nation. New monastic houses for students are popping up around Duke University, Wesley Theological Seminary, and elsewhere. I regularly hear from Methodist sojourners who have read *Longing for Spring*, who write or call to tell me they have decided to form a small order, a small community, or some other new expression of church from West Coast urban centers to the suburbs of Maryland and small towns in Ohio. Some of these are "permaculture" communities with a daily office. Some are spiritual formation communities with an outreach to homeless people. And some are just ordinary Methodists living in ordinary homes, but with anything but an ordinary view of the church. A new wind is blowing.

I also hear from longtime Methodists who have been part of an alternative vision of church for decades, who are excited to see what is now emerging. These prophetic voices include Mary Stamps, who founded the Methodist-Benedictine community, St. Brigid of Kildare, in 2001, in Collegeville, Minnesota,[11] and a number of people who have been part of the Christian Ashram movement initiated by Methodist evangelist E. Stanley Jones in 1930.[12] The integration of a disciplined spiritual life and social action resonates with their own vision and praxis.

Emergence is also evident in the way that United Methodist churches, districts, conferences, and other official institutions are inviting the likes of Brian McLaren, Doug Pagitt, Phyllis Tickle, Jonathan Wilson-Hartgrove, Shane Claiborne, and Richard Rohr to resource events focusing on the massive cultural and ecclesiological shifts in which we find ourselves. In October 2010, I was part of a conference organized by the Texas Methodist Foundation for bishops, chairs of boards of ordained ministry, and other denominational leaders to focus on what we in this book are calling "hyphenation." We will in particular explore the increasing number of young adults who pursue a theological education with no interest in traditional, ordained ministry but a deep commitment to a missional life. The question before us is not "How can we make them turn around and go back to the way we have always done church?" but "How can we equip and empower them to answer their call?"

Challenges to Ordination and Appointment Systems

One of the biggest obstacles at this time for United Methodists who participate in what the Holy Spirit is doing through emergence is an ordination system that no longer fits our missional context. That is, every person who is planning to be ordained as an elder and receive full membership in an annual conference (the level of ordination necessary to have full voting privileges and to enable one to rise to significant levels of leadership, including bishop) must also plan to receive his or her full-time income and benefits from the local church. People aspiring to be elders cannot plan to be bivocational, working as a pastor of small, possibly impoverished faith communities while earning a living doing something else. The only exception to this is for people like me who are already ordained as elders who, at some point after having served in local churches, are appointed beyond the local church to an extension ministry such as teaching at a seminary. Cases where persons are ordained as elders and immediately sent to extension ministries are extremely rare.

What this adds up to is that with almost no exceptions you cannot pursue ordination as an elder while openly planning to be a bivocational pastor (a missionary who plants and leads small, emerging, new monastic, missional faith communities) in the abandoned places of empire. While you are going through the lengthy ordination process you have to let the Board of Ordained Ministry know that you plan on going to a church where people can afford your full-time salary, pension, and a hefty health insurance policy in addition to whatever costs they have for a building, utilities, and programming. New church start strategies are heavily influenced by this reality, so that even though there are a few exceptions, much of the focus for new church starts ends up being among middle-class people so that they can pay for their elder.

We also have something in the UMC called "guaranteed appointments," so that every ordained elder is guaranteed an appointment to a full-time job with benefits. Our annual conferences (each of which is presided over by a bishop) even have temporary subsidies to cover the pastor's guaranteed minimum salary and benefits, if churches for a brief time cannot afford the full amount for their pastor who is guaranteed an appointment and a minimum salary. As every bishop in the UMC will tell you, these practices are simply no longer sustainable.

While these interlocking ordination and appointment systems were developed with an eye for justice so that elders could receive a living wage with benefits, and be appointed to churches without respect to race or gender, and have freedom to preach prophetically about difficult subjects such as racism, what we now face is a system that makes it impossible to serve bivocationally as a pastor in abandoned places of empire *and* get ordained as an elder. You can serve bivocationally as a "local pastor," but that means you do not have the same voting and leadership privileges as elders and lay delegates in our annual and general conferences, which means you are restricted from shaping the direction of our denomination. Local pastors do not become district superintendents or bishops. So if you are an innovative, missional, creative, bivocational local pastor who is good at planting and leading emerging faith communities in the margins of society, you will never become a district superintendent, never become a bishop, and never be able to offer to the ailing UMC at large the ecclesiological medicine it needs in order to become healthy again.

There is one more piece to this troubling puzzle. We also have qualified, gifted, called, fruitful candidates whose elder ordination is delayed because there is nowhere to send them for the required, guaranteed, full-time appointment, because so many United Methodist churches are shrinking and closing. These candidates are rarely told that the reason for their deferment is that there is no room at the inn, but it seems clear that this is what is going on. Sadly, this is one of the big reasons that young candidates leave the denomination and go elsewhere, and that some young seminarians decide not to pursue ordination in the first place.

The great frustration at this time is that the more innovative and socially entrepreneurial the candidate is, the more suited to generativity, the more at home working in the margins of society, the more interested in bivocational ministry, the less likely it is that she or he will ever make it through to ordination. Without ever having planned for this outcome, then, our ordination system and our guaranteed appointment system work hand in hand to actually prohibit some of our most gifted young adults from answering their call to missional, monastic, and generative ministry within the United Methodist Church. Small wonder that we are having a hard time attracting young adults to ordained ministry in the UMC these days, and keeping the ones who are focused on emerging, missional work!

So it is that across the nation our bishops, chairs of boards of ordained ministry, seminary deans, and clergy are wrestling with how to change the systems in order to accommodate necessary movement without compromising the sanctity of ordination to word, sacrament, and order. Meanwhile, under the radar, out on the margins, and right under our collective noses increasing numbers of Methodists are answering God's call to create new faith communities that use nontraditional leadership structures, in order to go and make disciples. Most of them don't care if they ever get ordained. What they do care about is living the gospel in the manner of the early Methodists: faithfully, holistically, as good news in a broken world.

A Hyphenated Future

Here we are then, Metho-monastic-missional-generative Christians, loving our heritage, loving God's church, frustrated with institutional rigidity, working within, around, and outside of official structures in order to say "yes" to God's call.

Whether emergence comes in the context of an old, historic congregation like Grace UMC reclaiming a missional ecclesiology and practice, or through the development of new microcommunities in places like Vickery Meadow, or through exciting new forms of campus ministry or a number of other models, it is essential for the United Methodist Church to grasp and respond to the massive cultural changes in which we find ourselves. It is a day for us to go beyond the walls of our buildings and our cramped imaginations in order to participate in the unfolding work of the Holy Spirit. A new day is rising.

Notes

[1] Grace United Methodist Church website, http://www.graceumcdallas.com.

[2] Diana Butler Bass, *Christianity for the Rest of Us: How the Neighborhood Church Is Transforming the Faith* (New York: HarperOne, 2006).

[3] For more about the new monasticism, including the meaning of "abandoned places of empire," see Jonathan Wilson-Hartgrove, *New Monasticism: What It Has to Say to Today's Church* (Grand Rapids, Mich.: Brazos, 2008).

[4] Diana Butler Bass, *A People's History of Christianity: The Other Side of the Story* (New York: HarperOne, 2009), 12.

[5] New Day Dallas website, http://www.newdaydallas.org.

⁶ For an introduction to the importance of new monasticism for United Methodism see Elaine A. Heath and Scott T. Kisker, *Longing for Spring: A New Vision for Wesleyan Community* (Eugene, Oreg.: Cascade, 2010).

⁷ For a recent postcolonial theological analysis of church and empire, see Joerg Rieger, *Christ and Empire: From Paul to Postcolonial Times* (Minneapolis: Fortress, 2007).

⁸ Lovers Lane United Methodist Church website, http://llumc.org.

⁹ Missional Wisdom Foundation website, http://www.missionalwisdom.com.

¹⁰ Northpointe Church is an Assemblies of God congregation, making this our first ecumenical Epworth Project house. United Methodist students living there assist with the church's excellent ministry to at-risk children during the week, and take part in the worship and fellowship of New Day Dallas on Sunday evenings.

¹¹ Saint Brigid of Kildare Monastery website, http://www.janrichardson.com/saint brigidmonastery.html.

¹² United Christian Ashrams website, http://www.christianashram.org/Pages2/ESJones 2.html.

4

Why Luthermergent?

Because We Always Have Been and Better Be Now and Forevermore, or We Probably Aren't Really Lutheran

Nate Frambach

"So, what you're saying about these emerging church communities sounds really great, but how do we integrate some of this stuff into the life of our congregation?" This is a fairly generous paraphrase of a question I've had posed to me countless times in a wide variety of venues composed mostly, but not exclusively, of Lutheran audiences. I have been party to the emerging church conversation for many years now as a curious and hopefully careful observer and curator. I have spent significant time learning from those who populate emerging church communities—at learning parties and Internet cafes and pubs and coffee shops, in their homes, at worship gatherings, in community. At the same time I'm also a company guy, a teaching theologian at one of our denominational seminaries (Wartburg Theological Seminary in Dubuque, Iowa). Like many others, I have spent a lot of time with ordinary church people "on the road," exploring points of resonance and dissonance between emerging church communities and more conventional church life in order to pursue a faithful and culturally relevant response to a fundamental ecclesiological question: What does it mean to be church today?

The subtext of the mostly heartfelt, well-intentioned question stated earlier is in actuality a keen and accurate instinct, palpable yet often difficult to quantify or easily articulate: We've lost our bearings as church. As Brian McLaren noted many years ago, "If you have a new world you need a new church. Guess what? We've got a new world."[1] Caught somewhere between allegiance to the structures (strictures?) of wooden denominationalism and the current, trendy, culturally fueled pull of the "quick fix" for the ecclesial and missional quagmire in which many churches find themselves, many church people are hungry, even desperate for renewal but have no idea where to turn. Denominations and seminaries, once the "go-to places" for both leaders and congregations, are now simultaneously resource rich (e.g., intellectual capital) and resource poor (e.g., significant financial challenges). Beholden to modern administrative and educational structures no longer viable, these institutions are in the process of retooling and reinventing themselves for the time in which we live. At the same time, the lure of the quick fix is strong today.[2] Programmatic, prepackaged, "easy button" approaches to renewal and revitalization are a dime a dozen. Ecclesial charlatans offer trendy, glitzy, "toolbox" approaches peddled at garden-variety conferences and seminars that serve as a model or formulae that others simply need to "tweak," or, at worst, replicate and adopt (not to be confused with adapt, because adaptive rather than adoptive work can actually become culturally authentic even if it is not indigenous to a particular community).

In my estimation, what is taking place in emerging church communities does not represent the newest passing fad or the current trendy "quick fix," although it is often perceived as such. The emerging church impulse has leavened a much larger and more important conversation about a renewed and reinvigorated missional ecclesiology for the North American context today. Yet what is actually taking place is more than leaven to a conversation. Emerging church communities might be the best "exhibit A" around when it comes to embodying a radically indigenous, missional, communal approach to the Christian faith in the midst of culturally comfortable Christianity.

This is a *semper reformanda* (always reforming) moment in the history of God's church. The moment in history in which we are living has birthed a new wave of missional Christian leaders with bold, creative, and fairly orthodox sensibilities about what it means to be church in a culturally authentic manner. They are bright, curious, faithful Christ followers who are willing to speak with their own voices about "the faith that was once for all entrusted to the saints" (Jude 3), from their own traditions and communities of Christian practice, with integrity, passion, and, at times, an appropriate dose of moxie.

Although the background for many of these Christian communities (and their leadership) is the modern evangelical denominational ethos, they represent, in reality, the "generous orthodoxy"[3] of the historic Christian faith. If these communities are denominationally linked, they typically live on the fringe of the denomination. Karen Ward, Abbess of the Church of the Apostles in Seattle, has used the image of dinghy and mother ship to reflect the relationship between emerging church community and larger church body. Denominationally linked or not, many of these communities forge and maintain multiple ecclesiastical relationships—often expanding and redefining *in practice* more modern, conventional notions of ecumenism.[4] Although intriguing and perhaps even inspiring, denominationally linked emerging church communities often get under the skin of their denominations by resisting the templates and structures through which the denomination "does its business."

In short, most emerging churches are particular subsets (communities) of Christians exercising theological imagination—not so much rethinking as reliving Christianity against the backdrop of (for lack of a better phrase) postmodernism. Culturally comfortable Christianity is built on modern scaffolding, the supports for which are crumbling. Consequently, culturally comfortable Christianity is standing on cultural and social tectonic plates that are shifting underneath. The people of God who populate conventional (e.g., mainline) churches, judicatories, and national offices are trying to find their land legs so that a fluid, emerging landscape can be navigated during a time of profound transition.

Subsequently, many mainline church communities, Lutherans among them, are being poked and prodded by emergents to pony up, mine the riches of their tradition, and engage in the hard work of contextualizing ministry for today. For Lutherans I believe the challenge is twofold. In the first place, along with many other modern, "mainline" denominations (in a process akin to a long-term gradual erosion), we have become willing participants in culturally comfortable Christianity, the evidence for which, as I highlight and describe later on, is mounting well beyond academic circles.[5] Second, we suffer from a kind of theological and ecclesial amnesia. We've either lost track of or lost our passion for the core elements of the Lutheran witness to the Christian gospel. Many Lutherans today seem to have a difficult time translating that which we believe and profess into Christian life and practice. The primary task before us in response to this ecclesial and cultural confusion is not the need to discover or create anything *new* but rather to *remember, retrieve,* and *practice* that which is deeply embedded in our theological and ecclesial DNA.

A few years ago, Karen Ward and I were invited to participate in a theological conference entitled "Church at the Cross Road: The Emerging Church." When I first saw the flyer advertising the conference I immediately thought, "Yes! They've got it right." The conundrum in which the churches find themselves today is at its core a missional and ecclesiological challenge. What does it mean for "the church" to be church today? This seems to be the most urgent question. Emerging church communities are attempting to *live* this question, thereby resisting the temptation to allow it to remain simply a good question. These communities are also resisting the temptation to create more or new rules whereby navigation might come easier. Rather, emerging church communities are doing the poetic work of renarrating the religious landscape; they are producing new stories, an outgrowth of their willingness to practice faithful innovation. In a time of transition, can the churches live in a tension: moored to our collective past as the people of God and yet freed to experiment and take risks for the reign of God?

I suggest that Lutherans, among others, have always been "mergent," particularly in this North American context. Fidelity to the Lutheran witness to the Christian gospel and the *semper reformanda* impulse central to what I consider the core ecclesiology of the Lutheran reformers means ever and always "mergent" or likely not Lutheran at all. Following that, I suggest that the "mergent" impulse was certainly operative earlier in the history of this country in which Lutheran immigrants migrated their faith into various frontier contexts. This argument contains an implicit challenge (particularly to Lutheran audiences but not exclusive to them) that I intend to render explicitly clear: All too often Lutherans have understood (and still do understand) this "mergent" impulse in theory and theology, but not always so well in practice. My deepest hope and desire is that the emerging church conversation and the witness of emerging church communities will compel mainline denominations to *remember, retrieve,* and *practice* that which is deeply embedded in our theological and ecclesial DNA—particularly our commitment to the priesthood of all believers and the ministry of the baptized—thereby resisting and escaping the allure of culturally comfortable Christianity.

The phrase *paradigm shift,* although overused, seems an accurate description for the acute changes experienced by Christian churches that attempted to navigate the twentieth century. Underlying these changes was a massive shifting of tectonic plates—what Graham Ward calls a "cultural sea change." This should come as no surprise; the church had a place, had *its* place in Christendom and then lost this place. In short, during Christendom, the Christian church as an institution had a culturally supported, central place in the public life of this American society. There existed an accommodating, intimate relationship between the "church" and the predominant culture of the larger society. As a result, this relationship led to an environment in which these two entities, "church" and "culture," were functionally one and the same. For some time now, however, we have not been able to talk about culture without using the plural, "cultures." We live within what some have called a "pluriverse" of cultures determined by geography, race, ethnicity, class, worldview, and the like. All of us inhabit and are shaped by a variety of cultures at the same time. Given the impact of some large, powerful realities—secularization, cultural and religious pluralism, globalization, the massive advances in technology that created the digitally enhanced world we now experience in this Infomedia age–the "church" (and here I refer to the Christian churches) has been decentered. Under increasing pressure from these aforementioned powerful realities, the cultural underpinnings that once supported the church swept away (shifting of the tectonic plates), and the church practiced some ecclesiastical free agency that swapped its central place in public life for a prominent place in the private domain of life.

At the same time, this decentering of "the church" and the emergence of the perverse secular theology of consumer capitalism has led to yet another iteration of "Christendom Christianity": what I referred to earlier as culturally comfortable Christianity. If clericalism equates ministry with the ordained ones and thereby deprives the whole people of God of their ministry, then culturally comfortable Christianity has turned the people of God into consumers of religious goods and services and church leaders (read primarily clergy) into religious entrepreneurs who dispense said goods and services. Christianity has become a "church" that one attends and sup- ports (which is then extended to the level of judicatory and national office), rather than a way of being human in the world patterned after the life of Jesus, as interpreted through that tradition's witness to the Christian gospel. Culturally comfortable Christianity has discovered an accommodating, "hand-in-glove" relationship with consumer capitalism in order to market, reach, and proffer the very best religious goods and services. By contrast, culturally *authentic* Christianity employs the interpretive tools of theology to provoke and inspire the people of God to mine the riches of their tradi- tion and engage in the hard work of contextualizing ministry for today.

The changes in the sociocultural and ecclesial landscape are difficult to grasp, and maybe even harder to digest for many of us–particularly members and leaders of the so-called mainline churches in North America. Tribes like the Lutherans, Presbyterians, Methodists, and Episcopalians specifically enjoyed the benefits of establishment and protection under the cover of Christendom and have bought into culturally comfortable Christianity. For these churches the paradigm shift outlined previously is extremely challenging. Navigating this emerging missiological landscape will involve discerning and experimenting with approaches to ministry that will radically challenge many present understandings of what it means to be the church today. Even more so, it will involve remembering, retriev- ing, and practicing the core elements of one's faith tradition in a way that is both faithful and culturally authentic for ministry today.

If we are to be true to our historical legacy as Lutheran Christians in these United States–a people possessing a strong missional impulse coupled with a knack for navigating new frontiers–then we must wrestle with this missional paradigm shift. Why? Because it defines the North American religious context in which we are called to live God's mission today. The challenge before us is, at its core, a missiological challenge.

Wilhelm Loehe (1808–72), founder of a new Lutheran body in the United States (the Iowa Synod), as well as the institution where I teach (Wartburg Theological Seminary), was noted to say, "Mission is nothing but the one church of God in motion."[6] In capsule, this phrase reflected a missional ecclesiology that served Loehe and his missionally-minded cohorts well in the particular frontier context (mid-1800s in these United States) to which they came as Christian missionaries. Loehe, a pastor from Bavaria (Germany), is today regarded as a spiritual father by Lutherans of three continents–North America, South America, and Oceania.[7]

> Wilhelm Loehe's most lasting contribution to the church was not a literary one, however, but a living one. A dedicated churchman, he became a forceful supporter of missionary endeavor . . . The isolated community of Neuendetteslau became the hub of a missionary movement that encircled the globe . . . During Loehe's lifetime America was the chief object of his concern . . . His interest in North America was aroused in late 1840 when he chanced to read a pamphlet containing appeals for help from overworked Lutheran pastors ministering to German immigrants on the American frontier. Deeply moved by the accounts of the hardships of the Germans in the New World and their obvious need for spiritual care . . . Loehe's words (writing, preaching, and teaching) were the spark that ignited a great missionary activity on behalf of the Germans in America.[8]

By 1849 Loehe had been instrumental in the establishment of a missionary society, the *Gesellschaft für Innere Mission*, which by this time was capable of carrying out the necessary work by itself. The missionary work begun almost single-handedly by Loehe was taken up by scores of dedicated men and women and was ably carried forward.[9]

Today, in this new, emerging frontier context in which the churches of North America find themselves, a missional ecclesiology must emerge *in practice* that is more deeply Trinitarian and eschatological: more organic and fluid *as it lives*. The question that will drive such an emergence is, "What does it mean to be the church *as we live*?" Not as we think or remember or long for, but as we *live* as the people of God. Mission in this new frontier context is the way a people sent by a sending God live every day, on mission, as they risk living for the reign of God and bear witness to the gospel of Jesus Christ "24/7," as many are apt to say. The work God has done in Jesus Christ cannot be undone; it is *pro nobis*, for us. It is this central proclamation of the Christian faith to which the Holy Spirit continually points us, and, in turn, to which we are called continually to point others. What matters first, and perhaps most, is *who* we are–a people created, chosen, cleansed, claimed, and called by God in Christ–and we are who we are, for better or for worse, all the time, not just on Sunday mornings or Wednesday evenings. On the new wilderness roads emerging everywhere all around us, being "on mission" looks strikingly similar to what happened on that much older wilderness road in the Acts of the Apostles (8:26ff). Someone is sent, and goes, to an unexpected place along the Way, and is encountered in a deeply mutual and relational way by an other in whose midst the Spirit works mutual transformation.

Lutheran Christians in the United States have *at least* two fundamental foci in our DNA–a people sent to and always living in particular places that are historically conditioned. There is this strong missionary impulse to bear witness to the Christian gospel "Lutheranly," remaining faithful to the primary accents of our Lutheran heritage: the doctrine of justification by grace through faith and the centrality of a theology of the cross; a deep commitment to the efficacy of the word of God as both law and promise; an understanding of the human as *simul justus et peccatur* (at the same time justified and sinful); a profound sensibility about the priesthood of all believers; and following, a clear understanding of *vocatio* (calling) as the primary means of the ministry of the baptized.

This missional impulse with its theological scaffolding is coupled with a built-in sensibility about learning to navigate the realities of frontier living by attending to, analyzing, and interpreting the context for ministry. The missionary work of Wilhelm Loehe and his colleagues is evidence that many of our Lutheran forebears knew well how to migrate their faith into a new place. They became bilingual, both literally and figuratively–learning a new language as well as the customs and mores of new people. They learned not only how to survive in, but how to adapt to, a new environment, all the while holding on to the core elements of the Christian faith indispensable to their beliefs and way of life. Perhaps many of our forebears were culturally savvy before adapting to a new place was considered savvy. Regardless, we must affirm, celebrate, and build on these dual commitments–the strong missional impulse and the knack for navigating new frontiers. However, we must also fess up to another reality: The landscape has changed. Many emerging church communities have confronted and embraced this reality and are challenging mainline denominations to *remember*, *retrieve*, and *practice* that which is deeply embedded in our theological and ecclesial DNA in order to navigate the missional, frontier landscape today.

I have identified a constellation of primary accents of the Lutheran witness to the Christian gospel. In all of these core elements, the emerging church conversation and emerging church communities are poking and prodding mainline, conventional Lutherans to wake up and with renewed energy and passion remember, retrieve, and contextualize these commitments for the practice of ministry today. While I cannot fully address all of these commitments in what remains of this essay, I wish to highlight one: the priesthood of all believers, which includes the ministry of the baptized.

In many and various ways, some of which are quite insidious, much of the Christian church in North America still lives in bondage to its clerical captivity. This runs contrary to a major theological and ecclesiological impulse in the Lutheran witness to the Christian gospel–the priesthood of all believers. As Loren Mead commented about Lutherans a few years ago while visiting the seminary at which I teach: "You have the right theology. How do you get the right behavior and practice?"[10]

According to Leonard Sweet, clericalism–the class distinction between clergy and laity (that is, the professional and the amateur)–is "one of the most insidious distinctions ever developed by the church." We live in an age when there is no longer a culturally assumed and approved benefit of clergy:

> The church is ruled by a clerical minority that carries on about institutional matters of deep interest to the clerical minority (ordination issues, language of the liturgy, etc.) rather than the true concerns of most church members . . . The clerical era of the church is apparently nearing an end as the people of God reject the class separation. Many church members think it is time to deemphasize clergy as well as "dechurch." The driving force of the church must be the "laity," not the "clergy." The pastoral leadership of baptized ministers is missing in the oldline church today . . . The postmodern church apparently will not tolerate the beloved "benefit of clergy" . . . This distinction between do-it-all clergy and do-nothing laity is evaporating in favor of new definitions of shared ministries and full-time ministry. Soon only two categories of leadership will be discussed in the church–"baptized ministers" and "ordained ministers." In fact, if one is interested in actually doing ministry, one shouldn't get ordained. Ordination authorizes a baptized minister to educate and train other baptized ministers in the art and science of ministry . . . All Christians are ministers.[11]

It should be said that this critique of clericalism is not simply one of the latest fads being wordsmithed by a theological futurist such as Sweet. Well over twenty years ago it was none other than Joseph Sittler, whom Martin Marty referred to as our sage and our seer, who shared a similar concern in responding to a question about the uniqueness of the ordained ministry:

> The church insists on preparing a designated cadre to see to it that the constitutive story is told, and that the nurturing sacraments are administered . . . This is a way of defining the ordained pastorate of the church that does not elevate it above the laity, but gives it a particular job among the people of God.[12]

The bottom line is the same: Equating "real ministry" with the ordained deprives the whole people of God of their ability to conduct ministry and exercise the priesthood of all believers. Lutherans know this but seemingly have a difficult time breaking the bonds of clericalism, escaping from the complacency of culturally comfortable Christianity, and authenticating and mobilizing the ministry of the *laos* today.

Laos refers to the whole people of God, not merely those who are not "professional." Christian ministry is given to the whole of God's people. In the vision of the people of God that flows from the cross and resurrection of Jesus Christ there is no "special" priesthood. Jesus Christ is the end and fulfillment of special priesthood. The reality that the *laos* is a priestly people (cf. 1 Peter 2) has absolutely nothing to do with ecclesial or culturally supported rights and privileges. Any notion of rights and privileges is likely a by-product of the professionalization of clergy during modernity based on training, expertise, and status. Rather, the biblical referent is the conviction that all are called to serve in gospel ministry for the well-being of God's world. Although congregational leadership must be expansive and shared, those called and authorized specifically for the task of leadership—ordained, consecrated, commissioned, or otherwise—give structure and guidance to the ministry of the community "to equip the saints for the work of ministry, for building up the body of Christ" (Eph. 4:12).

Christian scripture clearly understands all ministries as a gift of the Spirit. Ministries are never a right, but always a gift. The "gift lists" in the Pauline letters (Rom. 12:6–8, 1 Cor. 12:4–10, and Eph. 4:11–16) include nineteen various ministries. These ministries neither depend on nor derive from any office of congregational leadership. Rather, they are the birthright of the baptized and engendered by the work of the Holy Spirit.

This core commitment to the priesthood of *all* believers, to the ministry of the *whole* people of God, has to do with the very identity and nature of the church, which has particular import to congregations as local theological cultures. One helpful way to explore the identity and nature of the church is to ask about its mission—what it is about, what it is *for*. From the perspective of my own tradition represented in the Evangelical Lutheran Church in America, with essential support from the Holy Scriptures, the ecumenical creeds, and the Lutheran confessional writings, I refer to Article VII of the Augsburg Confession, which states: "It is also taught among us that one holy Christian church will be and remain forever. This is the assembly of believers among whom the Gospel is preached in its purity and the holy sacraments are administered according to the Gospel."[13]

This means that what is often and quite casually referred to as "the church" is not so much a place (i.e., building) as it is an event: the happening of the gospel. While in principle I believe this to be true, I fear that the operative interpretation for Lutherans causes us to fixate a bit too much on church or congregation as *place*. God's mission in the world that the gospel announces, driven by the Holy Spirit, is a deployed rather than an employed mission. It is the public ministry of the whole people of God: Calling, gathering, enlightening, and sanctifying people for life in Christian community is the ongoing missionary activity of God the Spirit.

An "assembly of believers" need not be confined to a building, correct? Perhaps you have heard it said that "the church" is to be "*in* the world but not *of* the world"? If this is true then it represents only two-thirds of the equation, to the extent that it coheres to and reflects the nature and identity of God: *in* the world and not *of* the world yet decidedly *for* the world. A fundamental premise of the Christian faith is that the world belongs to God (cf. the First Article of the ecumenical creeds). Everything "in heaven and on earth" belongs to God; God has claimed it all, and in the future God has promised that the whole creation will be renewed and transformed. The Triune God of the Christian faith is a God for the world and a God for people.[14] The Christian gospel is grounded in the event of Jesus. This grounding is the basis for the confession of God as well as for the experience of the Christian community. The gospel is always directed–it is "good news to . . ." or "good news for . . ." Hence the church is that happening of the gospel in and through community for the sake of healing, hope, and redemption in God's world. Could it be that what happens *through* the "assembly of believers" is just as important as what happens *in* the "assembly of believers"? We need church communities today that are rooted deeply in God's Word of promise through Christ and yet more nimble, agile, and mobile in terms of how they understand their "place" in God's world.

The emerging church conversation and emerging church communities are influencing mainline denominations precisely by challenging them to be who they are–to remember, retrieve, and practice the core elements of the Christian faith that constitute their particular *charism* and witness to the gospel. Perhaps more than anything, these communities are not only asking but seeking to live an operative question: What does it mean to be *who* we are *where* we are? What does it mean to be the church *as we live*? Intentional, sustained attention to *who* we are and *where* we are generates communal conversation and critical reflection that become part of the air we breathe. People not only come to accept it–they expect it as well. The question is never answered; it is continually, even relentlessly pursued, and thus mitigates against complacency. This process can keep a community honest and on edge, fostering openness and curiosity.

The first Reformation returned the Word of God to the people of God. A second reformation, under way at this present moment, is seeking to return the work of God to the people of God as the *laos* come to understand and act on the belief that they are called, gifted, and empowered as ministers of the gospel. Trying to go in the out door translates into, "How can we employ more laity as church workers?" There is a dicey, seemingly innocuous but potentially dangerous assumption here–that all viable ministry happens inside the church walls. There is a better question, I think, that amounts to sending people out the out door: "How can the people of God—gifts in one hand, creativity in the other—be sent by God as apostles to impact God's world for Christ?" The challenge before us is to send God's gifted people out the out door and see their primary ministry assignment as *being* good news wherever God places them: homes, schools, workplaces, communities, marketplaces, civic clubs, even a kiosk at the farmer's market. Unleashing the giftedness of all the people of God is a key to being church today, living God's mission, and exercising mobile leadership in the spirit of Jesus. Lutherans (among others) would be wise to take heed, take risks, and remember, retrieve, and live into God's vision for the *ecclesia* in God's world today.

Notes

[1] I heard Brian say this, among other times, at an event at the Lutheran Theological Seminary in Philadelphia on March 24, 2007.

[2] Cf. *A Failure of Nerve: Leadership in the Age of the Quick Fix* (New York: Seabury Books, 2007) by Edwin Friedman for a compelling case about the temptation toward the quick-fix approach that runs rampant today. Although specific to issues surrounding leadership, the broader analysis and critique is cogent and helpful.

[3] A phrase coined by Brian McLaren, now the title (before the colon) of his book *A Generous Orthodoxy* (Grand Rapids, Mich.: Zondervan, 2004).

[4] The growth in the emergent network—whose tagline has been "a growing generative friendship among missional Christians"—is evidence, at least in part, of this propensity. Join the conversation at http://www.emergentvillage.com.

[5] The nascent research findings of the National Study of Youth and Religion documented in Christian Smith's *Soul Searching* (New York: Oxford University, 2005) and *Souls in Transition* (New York: Oxford University, 2009) narrate this with painstaking detail. For additional information see the National Study of Youth and Religion website, http://www.youthandreligion.org.

[6] Wilhelm Loehe, *Three Books about The Church*, trans. and ed. by James L. Schaaf (Philadelphia: Fortress, 1969), 59.

[7] Ibid., 1.

[8] Ibid., 17–19.

[9] Ibid., 24–25.

[10] Loren Mead, public forum conversation, Wartburg Theological Seminary, September 2001.

[11] Leonard Sweet, *FaithQuakes* (Nashville: Abingdon, 1994), 142–45.

[12] Joseph Sittler, *Gravity and Grace* (Minneapolis: Augsburg Publishing House, 1986), 52.

[13] Augsburg Confession, VII:1, in Theodore G. Tappert's *The Book of Concord* (Minneapolis: Fortress, 1959), 16.

[14] Cf. David Bosch, *Transforming Mission: Paradigm Shifts in Theology of Mission* (Maryknoll, N.Y.: Orbis, 1991). This seminal work has already become a classic in the field of missiology.

5

Satanism in the Suburbs

Ordination as Insubordination

Christopher D. Rodkey

The greatest weapon that the mainstream evangelical and "mainline" liberal churches have used against any semblance of genuine or radical theology sweeping into their leadership is the pseudosacramental scandal of ordination. Anyone who has been through an ordination process understands that, on one hand, churches need to have a mechanism to discourage unsuitable individuals for ministry, but on the other hand, too often the most gifted and interesting of candidates for ministry are anathematized, thrown out, or, at worst, spiritually castrated.

I am not being hyperbolic. Go to any gathering of young adults in the mainline church or to any "emergent" meeting and you will hear these stories—sometimes these narratives become legendary in the halls of divinity schools. It's not pleasant to talk about because the way that churches often treat those of us who have been denounced is as deflowered whores whose diminished fire for the Spirit flames the eros of the unstable personalities who find themselves on ordination and pastoral examination committees. The raison d'être of many of our "calls" to ministry would seem to be to reify boundaries and limitations.

Yet these pastors, administrators, and bishops are the first to cry foul about clergy shortages, the notion that most seminary students want nothing to do with pastoral ministry, "clergy incompetence," and the most outrageous of them all–the rumor that there is a specific shortage of white, heterosexual males seeking ordination.[1] Lilly Endowment money is pouring into mainline conferences and seminaries to specifically address these issues, while the obvious problems remain and reside within the ordination processes and procedures of most mainstream churches.

Hell's Bells

Surely, I have my biases about this matter. I felt a call from God when I was a teenager as a result of one of those weeklong service immersion trips. I prayed for a woman at a hospice and when I opened my eyes the world appeared to be quite different and a small voice began pushing me into thinking about being a pastor.

Like most young people discerning a call, I did not have many places to turn for guidance. I was afraid my parents and friends would think that I was crazy. While I highly respected the youth pastor and associate pastor at my church, there was always something about the senior pastor that bothered me. I was invited to be on the board of the church as a teenager, and there I witnessed just how political the senior pastor had to be. I was not afraid of the preaching aspect of being a minister; it was the slickness with which I saw the senior pastor operate that totally turned me off of the pastorate.

The church also became more conservative. Comparatively speaking, when my family first started coming to the United Methodist Church, our experience was that the Methodists were much more liberal than the Evangelical Congregational background into which I was baptized. At the Methodist church you didn't bring your own Bible to church! But over time, "creation science" was regularly discussed, and photos of aborted children became part of our youth group discussion time.

Then there was the night where we had an all-church gathering to talk about the rise of Satanism in our local community. The speaker was a man who claimed to be a police officer who talked about ritual sacrifices and witch gatherings in the area. He had the photos to prove it–but he would only show them to us with parental permission. We watched a documentary film called *Hell's Bells*, named, of course, after the AC/DC song, where a man with an electronically altered voice claimed to be a warlock and that his powers were real. One of us asked our youth pastor if this stuff was real. He thought about it, and said, "You have a choice to make in this life. You can practice black magic or white magic. We are in the light of Christ in this church." The older people passionately applauded, surely sticking one to the Devil; I suppose he had it coming.

This medium is not the proper place to speak in detail about my experiences applying for ordination, and many people I have told the story to tell me they don't–or *won't*–believe it. To make a long story short, because I did not have a spoken faith that sounded evangelical to my home church's committee, they eventually said "no" to me as an ordination candidate.

They even sent me a letter saying that I am clearly not to be categorized as an "Orthodox Christian."

My "examinations" by ordination committees were purely gestures of vague "evangelical" identity. I would be asked a question such as, "Chris, is Christianity an easy faith or a difficult one?" My response was "There could be no more difficult faith than Christianity." The answer that they apparently wanted to hear was that Christianity is an *easy* religion because *all one has to do is ask Jesus into one's heart.* My existentially informed approach to Christianity as extremely narrow path somehow got construed into a "liberal" position. Clearly, I read too much Kierkegaard in college and not enough John Hagee.

It might sound trivial to speak in this way now, but up to this point in life I had experienced no greater personal pain than being cut off from the church that had nourished my call to ministry and confirmed me as a teenager (*God forbid* that anyone, especially young people, take their Confirmation seriously!). The pain was not just private but very public—I was twenty-three and I was already officially a heretic. Meanwhile, the United Methodist Church's University Senate (the denomination's accrediting body that approves appropriate seminaries for their students) de-accredited my seminary, the University of Chicago, along with Harvard, Union, and others, as a move to weed out "liberals" and as a political gesture after de-accrediting Gordon-Conwell Theological School, a conservative seminary, a few years before.

At bottom, the entire ordination process was demoralizing, insulting, and spiritually nauseating. And this was intentional: The man who signed the letter declaring me not Christian was my former Sunday school teacher. I filed complaints with the district superintendent and the bishop. The district superintendent called the senior pastor to ask if anything had been done wrong. When the senior pastor said no, the district superintendent called me back and said that his investigation was complete.

This is a true story. It is a painful story for me. But most important, *it is not a unique story.* Mine is only one of many variations of similar struggles among young adults in mainline churches today.

Satanism in the Suburbs

Only twice through the ordination process in the United Methodist Church was I told specifically what my theological errors were. First, I was told that I did not have an adequate understanding of Creationism—specifically, I do not find any relevance to be had in a scientific or pseudo-scientific understanding of the creation. Second, my senior pastor informed me that I needed to have a substitutionary theology of atonement.[2] In explaining this, he used the old analogy of the olive oil press to describe the messy bleeding out of Christ for our sins, substituted in our place. My position was that while I find this view to be a valid theological possibility, despite the racist and sexist issues that surround it, substitutionary atonement was far from the *only* valid option. While, of course, my "errors" were mostly smokescreens for other political positions that I held (this was the late 1990s and early 2000s, when white, conservative heterosexual Methodists became obsessed with homosexuality as a public fetish), the proclamation of these errors is telling.

My senior pastor challenged me to go back to my seminary library and read up on theologies of the atonement and return to him in a more enlightened state. An element of his error here is that I am fairly certain that when he knew I was in seminary in Chicago, he just assumed it was Moody Bible Institute and not the University of Chicago Divinity School; as such, the libraries held very different kinds of collections on this subject.

Of all the theologies of atonement I encountered during this time, it was the "radical" one that appealed to me most deeply. I had read Thomas Altizer's writing in college (I discovered his *Gospel of Christian Atheism* on a night in which I found myself locked in the underground level of the college library), so I was familiar with the way in which he prioritized *kenosis*, the radical outpouring or self-subverting nature of the Incarnation, as a primary metaphor for describing the metaphysics of God in history.

As such, according to Altizer, the act of Godhead speaking creation is a *kenotic* act of self-dismemberment. The primordial totality of Godhead is broken in creation, and a dialectical process of transcendence bleeding into creation begins, breaking the "absolute hymen" of absolute transcendence into creation itself. The final act of kenosis from transcendence occurs in the Incarnation of Christ, through which Godhead continues a "forward and downward" movement–and further so in the ministry, crucifixion, burial, and resurrection of Christ. The resurrection is a symbol of an *actual* disbursement of Godhead into the human flesh of every hand and face, and as such the epoch of the Holy Spirit begins in the present *eternal now*.

The ethical implications of this theological metaphysics fascinate me the most. In the present, the Holy Spirit is what pierces the nothingness of our current situation; genuine acts of love and charity and radical acts of justice bring about the Holy Spirit against the spiritual forces of wickedness. The onus is upon the Christian person, and preferably in community, to interrupt the banal, current nothingness by taking on Christ, that is, by *doing* "kenotic acts," taking on the kenosis of Godhead for oneself. Taking up your own cross.

For the purposes of this essay I am oversimplifying the radical position for the sake of easily communicating it, especially for those who may be unfamiliar with it. Nonetheless, the bottom line is this: The radical understanding of atonement demands of the Christian believer to first understand that atonement is linked to a kenotic metaphysics that begins with creation, is disclosed to us in the Incarnation and Resurrection of Christ, and continues with the reality of the Holy Spirit in the Christian community in the present. Second, and most important, atonement is not a static, single historical event, but an unfolding dialectical process to which the Christian testifies not by passively preaching or observing, but through actively bearing witness.

In other words, in this radical position, we may dynamically *participate* in the atonement. To simply claim to have felt, experienced, or historically "know" of the atonement and evocatively convince others that they may "know" of the atonement—which is a goal of evangelical preaching as a "fundamental" of the faith—is an *apprehension* of the active and continuing presence of Godhead in our current situation. This preaching then is the negation of any conception of Godhead in the present. Furthermore, to worship this static Godhead whose actions seem to have died at the closure of the revelation of scripture is to worship a dead and lifeless God.

In addition, not only is this dead and flaccid God no longer existing, this dead God was not the God who speaks in scripture and continues to speak, because this God has *ceased* to speak. This God of evangelicalism is the God of alien, absolute transcendence, a God with superhero strength who "can do anything." It is the primordial Godhead that *once did exist*, that is, prior to Genesis 1 (and Proverbs 8) and renders the metaphysical language of John 1–"in the beginning was the Word"–to exclusively be about the fixed words of scripture rather than a truly amazing and fantastical story of Godhead pouring Godself out into creation and, finally, into us. This God primordially *once existed* but *ceased to be* at the moment of creation, at the breach of absolute hymen.[3] This Godhead fundamentally changed, and can only be known as *changing* through history. Any theology of the incarnated *logos*, or Word, must admit the perpetual dynamism implicit in the Christian story.

The continued worship of the dead and flaccid God perpetuates a culture of death and a spiritual situation where men and women "lust for death." Mary Daly calls this "necrophilia," a "sado-state" where a God that does not exist, or no longer exists, is corporately worshiped on such a world scale that the evil and harm of this Holy Ghost (or "spectre of sublimation") become ritually real and enacted. In traditional Christianity with a static Godhead, Daly writes that the "dogma of 'The Incarnation' is not only sublime; it is a paradigm of male sublimation . . . indeed it is the supremely sublimated male sexual fantasy, assuming fantastic proportions." Daly concludes, "It is mythic Super-Rape." In other words, the Incarnation as enacted by a static, transcendent God where "warped words/ideas made 'flesh'" ritually "legitimates the rape of all matter," including and especially those without power or voice within this theology's implied ecclesiology. Out of this theology, Daly suggests, "nuclearism, chemical contamination of the earth, planned famine, torture of political prisoners, torture of laboratory animals, obscene medical experimentation" are "all . . . discharges of male instinctual energy" legitimized through static theology.[4]

While this may seem a bit extreme, we hear traces of this kind of think-ing from our most conservative sectors of society. For example, it is not uncommon to hear arguments made from religious or political authorities in the present time that "if Islam just went away, we would not have war." In the film *Islam: What the West Needs to Know*, this argument is even illustrated using a world map, blaming every act of genocide and war in the world on the religion of Islam–a religion that very directly rejects any notion of radicalized Incarnation to protect the primordial alien transcendence in the deity Allah.[5] This is the same deity who evangelical politicians became fond of proclaiming to be the same God of Christianity after the 9/11 terror attacks on the United States. To this end, the doctrine of the Incarnation is largely absent from most evangelical thinking today, with the Incarnation relegated to being celebrated in our most pagan celebration of material reality, Christmas. But along with this story is glossed over the tension between "pseudoparthenogenesis"[6] and pagan rape implicit in the scriptural Advent narratives. Mary is left to be the ideal subservient girl, her virginity perpetuated so as to idealize her against the whores of the world and the whore of the world itself. And this theology is ritually enacted by American churches at the end of every Advent, placing their most attractive teenage virgin on display in Christmas pageants.

This traditional Christianity is not really Christianity at all: This "Christianity" is the negation of anything that is genuinely and radically understood to be Christian. The situation recalls the writings of our mystic William Blake, whose poetry unmasks the Jesus of orthodox Christianity to have been Satan all long. It would seem that evangelicalism's preoccupation with Satanism in the suburbs–culminating in Carl Raschke's embarrassing book, *Painted Black*, which gave mainline churches academic credibility for their fears[7]–was more of a sibling rivalry than an actual threat or a serious theological claim. The necrophilial culture of traditional Christianity is a testament to this statement: In the ten years that have passed since I was rejected as an ordination candidate in the United Methodist Church, my former senior pastor was removed from the ministry (but returned under a new bishop); another local clergyperson with whom I had met as part of my ordination "process" was recently convicted of child abuse and rape; and a former college professor and Benedictine priest, who implicitly judged me for my theological liberalism, has been accused of one of the most disgusting cases of rape (including priests passing a child between abusers) that one can imagine.[8] This behavior is not only perpetuated by the church and its Satanic theology, but it has in the past been tolerated–at least until the public relations issues related to these cases forced churches to self-promote themselves with "child safety policies," policies that catch our churches up with the broken systems latent within our schools and communities–in institutions that are modeled after and, in some ways, are nurtured by the necrophilia of Christendom.

Radicalism and Emergence

When I first heard of emergence Christianity and the "emerging church" I felt that I had finally found a group of young adults who were growing increasingly dissatisfied with the institutional church. My impression was that the "emergent" rebellion was more institutional than theological, and suddenly publishing ventures began and it seemed that any white male in his thirties with any remotely successful church-start ministry was writing books, blogging, podcasting, tweeting, and one-upping others in the technological maelstrom of the last decade. The lines became blurred about what is "emergent" and what is "emerging," and later "emergence"; the term "radical" was used unreflectively and liberally; a few Bible colleges joined the trend; and then came a major backlash of ridiculous polemical books such as *Why We're Not Emergent: By Two Guys Who Should Be*–indicating that if you're a male young adult, college educated, tech savvy, and Christian, you *should be* attracted to this emerging movement, because it's "cool," but apparently it was not evangelical enough.[9] (The last chapter of this particular book is titled, tellingly enough, "Why I Don't Want a Cool Pastor," which preoccupies itself with the *image* of emergent Christianity: Moby, the name dropping of postmodern theology, and *The Matrix*.)[10]

Tony Jones, in his book, *The New Christians*, gives a genealogy of the emergence movement from his perspective. I heard him speak at Princeton Theological Seminary, where he began his lecture by giving his own history within mainline Protestantism, saying, "I feel that I need to establish my mainline 'cred.'"[11] Still, to me, the emergence movement seemed like just another failed attempt at evangelicals trying to be "relevant," even publishing magazines such as *Relevant*, which ripped off the aesthetic of the countercultural periodical *Outburn* and became media outlets for Christian rock artists to sell their products to marginalized evangelicals in their mid- to late twenties. But the polemics continued from the more conservative branches of evangelicalism, and mainline church publishing houses and seminaries were more than happy to give a "big-umbrella" welcome to young people now calling themselves "postevangelical."

I am attracted to the *ethos* of the emergence movement because it seems to be embodying what Paul Tillich called the Protestant Principle–that the gospel will always be new and relevant, always re-inventing itself, even if it means leaving the church and establishing something new.[12] When Phyllis Tickle proclaims that the emergence movement is the social move that the Christian church makes every five hundred years,[13] I do not necessarily disagree that something significant is happening in the shifting tectonics of the church today. Instead, however, our situation may be that we are really just now feeling the full effects of the tremendous shifting that began in the Copernican Revolution, the Protestant Reformation, Nietzsche's declaration of the death of God, the technological devastation of the two World

Wars, international pain spiraling out of colonialism, and the advent of the Internet. This is to say we are still struggling with modernism, and emergence is one of many attempts to continue the Christian faith in a changing modern world. The radical theology of Thomas Altizer, Gabriel Vahanian, Mary Daly, and others that began in the late 1960s was also a response to this same modernism, forty years before emergence Christianity appeared.

Journalist Ray Waddle has suggested that it was the theology of Altizer and his public presence in the media—on the cover of *Time* magazine, an appearance on the *Merv Griffin Show*, even being the subject of an academic essay by none other than Billy Graham—that led to the new megachurch evangelicalism of the 1970s and to the hippie Jesus movement.[14] Both of these movements were fundamentally theologically conservative but were relabeled "evangelicalism"; yet these are the movements within evangelicalism that emergence Christianity seems to be most directly rebelling against.

As such, signs of radical theology remain latent within emergence Christianity. Aside from a few authors who have engaged directly in radical theology who are well liked and well read within emergent circles—Peter Rollins, John Caputo, and Carl Raschke, for example—emergence Christianity as a continuation of the Protestant Principle remains its most radical contribution. Like the radical theologians of the 1960s, the potential for a secular, postecclesial theology once again becomes a real possibility. Mary Daly even delivered a famous sermon in 1971, the first sermon delivered by a woman at Harvard Chapel, titled "The Courage to Leave," where she ended the sermon by stepping out of the pulpit and leaving the chapel, with many of the students following her.[15]

Conversely, emergence Christianity has within many evangelical and mainline churches become a catchphrase for their young adult ministry, a contemporary worship service with "edgier" rock music, or even a worship service with divergent worship elements such as Taizé worship with digitally projected video. A local Presbyterian congregation near me has an "emergent" service that is reminiscent of what one might have experienced at Willow Creek Community Church's "seeker service" in the early 1990s, but it seems that the labeling of the worship service as "emergent" *has a primary social function within the church to separate generations from worshiping with each other.*

I suggest that the homogeneity in much of what is called "emergence" among both evangelical and mainline churches is that, at bottom, emergence Christianity has not led to a fundamental and radical shift in thinking Godhead newly or differently, at least not on a large scale. But what *is* promising within the movement as a whole is a willingness to *think Godhead* quite differently and to make ecclesiologically *incarnational moves*, even if these shifts are not fully radical or radicalized. Along these lines, for example, Raschke, in *GloboChrist*, outrightly accuses Brian McLaren of not fully engaging the radical ends of his own incarnational ecclesiology in *A*

Generous Orthodoxy.[16] To borrow a cliché from McLaren's title, the orthodox is still very orthodox—but it is little more than a relabeling of *orthodoxy* to render it a bit more *generous.*

The best example of this relabeling is in a lesser-known book, Jarrett Stevens's *The Deity Formerly Known as God.*[17] Despite this promising title (which reminds me of William Hamilton's truly radical *On Taking God out of the Dictionary*),[18] Stevens explains early in his book that it "is an attempt to recapture the spirit and power of J. B. Phillips," namely, Phillips's 1952 work, *Your God Is Too Small,* yet Stevens simply talks about bad images of God (such as a cosmic policeman) to more preferable ones.[19] Most telling is Stevens's "good" image, "Lord of the Boardroom," where Stevens compares the power and transcendence of God with the power of a corporate CEO as "God's 'otherness.'"[20] This "generous . . . King"[21] is the primordial transcendence of a God who, in the radical theology model, no longer exists and is a shadow of any possible conception of a God who abides in the flesh of the weak. While I can appreciate some of Stevens's thinking in his book, the final image of God as "Equal-Opportunity Employer" takes the cake, disclosing that Jesus "assures . . . that all who have given in to God's economy will be rightly rewarded in heaven" along with a personal narrative justifying the Protestant work ethic.[22] Rethinking images is a good start, but the conclusions must go beyond relabeled images, especially when the preferred images are not completely deduced or even particularly new. Rather, they become yet another piece of evangelicalism's social mechanism of patting the white middle and upper classes on the back.

Ordination as Insubordination

All churchly doctrines and practices are now primed to undergo radicalization if Godhead is radically and dynamically rethought in the contemporary situation. Ordination is as good a starting point as any for our radical thinking to take shape ecclesiologically, as so many of us who flirt with or appeal to "emergence" Christianity are trying to be ordained, have been denied ordination, or are ordained.

First, we must accept that ordination usually operates, on a practical level within mainline churches, as a *mechanism to promote control,* of both the ordained and the nonordained. In episcopate-based polities, such as the United Methodist Church's, one is guaranteed employment so long as one is fully ordained and in good standing with the bishop. It is not to the political advantage of the ordained to be the ones whose names are placed on committee minutes approving exciting, challenging, or even intellectually gifted pastors; nor is it to their advantage to accept as clergy those who might call them out for being too comfortable with their entitlements and ministerial complicity. Those who challenge these structures are anathematized as "Satanic" or "Not Christian" and are weeded out;

consequently, the insubordinates are often the individuals best suited for the ministry of the ordained.

Second, this control also supports a *division of labor* within some churches' structures. Designations as "lay ministers" or "lay clergy" have long historical traditions in some denominations, but today they function on paper to largely separate those pastors who went to seminary from those who, for any variety of reasons, did not. Yet in practice there are scores of "licensed" and lay ministers who are seminary graduates who choose not to be ordained or whose ordination application processes are perpetually in limbo.

These individuals are usually paid less, pastor the problematic or historically suicidal churches where many ordained pastors would refuse to work, or work with "less desirable" (and sometimes *imaginary*) populations—children, youth, and young adults. This model is very common for youth and young adult pastors who survive working under easily threatened senior pastors for more than a few years. These associate or "special-population" pastors often work without benefits and sometimes see doing this as "paying their dues" until more substantial employment opens up for them. For example, I was allowed to pastor a United Methodist church even while I had been declared "Not Christian" by the denomination's own institutional processes. This indicates on one hand a lack of reliance of the church on its own language, theology, and structures, and on the other hand, an overreliance by the denomination's broken ordination system to fill empty pulpits by stratifying its labor.

Third, we must acknowledge that an important Protestant doctrine is the priesthood of all believers. In congregational-polity churches often the pastor is seen as a hired hand who functions as a priest of *memorialism*—that is, the pastor lives the ideal Christian life so the congregation does not. It could be said that in episcopate-polity churches the pastors are more like itinerant workers—for example, the United Methodists have long used the terminology of "itinerant preachers." Yet this attitude toward ordained clergy that is generally unofficial but widely practiced is one of the most discouraging aspects of ministry for many pastors—namely, they are paid to be the professional Christians in a *substitutionary* arrangement for the congregation itself. Their lives *atone* for their constituents'.

As a radical movement, we must root ourselves in the innovations of the concept of ordination bestowed upon us by the Radical Reformation. Ordination is to then be understood as an extension of our common baptism, directed toward the public: "living to become for others the bread of life."[23] The "Other" of the nonchurched, we must acknowledge, is not accessible without evangelism that values members of the church body who speak the language, live and work with, and culturally habituate with *others* spiritually located in a postecclesial world. Ordination can be a sacramental practice that encourages the *whole body*, including those members on the "fringes," to be empowered and formally authorized for the work of the Great Commission—not just token individuals to reach out to the "young families and children" who dress formally and live in the suburbs and who represent the population most churches claim they want to attract. Luther, at his most radical in the tract *Babylonian Captivity of the Church,* gave this advice to prospective ordinands: "If ye wish to live in safety . . . do not seek admission to these holy rites, unless ye are either willing to preach the gospel, or able to believe that ye are not made any better than the laity by this sacrament of orders."[24]

If we are to take seriously any radicalized notion of Godhead, and along with it a radicalized doctrine of resurrection and Pentecost, the priesthood of all believers must be rendered to be a genuine and actual priesthood, kenotically given to the church. As such this ministry of all flesh reflects the dialectical and kenotic Godhead, which it is called to enact. All flesh enacts and reenacts the apocalyptic movement of Godhead in scripture by gathering together in communities of care, singing, reading, interpreting, reflecting, praying, composing, responding, and radically acting. All flesh re-members the dis-membered Body in Eucharistic actions. All flesh blesses new members by ritually washing new flesh with the water of the world—the world that traditional Christianity has instructed us to reject, reduce, and abuse.

What, then, of ordination? Ordination is a ritual act of *transfiguration,* which recognizes and calls certain individuals to a life of Christian service with a specific ministry to the church. What is radicalized here is what I mean by "Christian service"—this is the *transfiguration* in my definition. If an ordained life is to reflect the dialectical, kenotic, and negating nature of Godhead, as disclosed through the Incarnation and resurrection of Christ, a life of Christian service functions *to perpetually challenge and subvert the church* so that a *self-negating and authentically self-critical ecclesiology may be enacted and practiced.* As a rite of the church, I propose that ordination, as an extension of the baptismal priesthood of all believers, is a *healing act* of the church's inability to recognize her erasure of her primordial *liquor amnii.*

Ordination, then, is *insubordinate:* Ordination implies having a *prophetic* role. The ministry of the ordained is not necessarily limited to established leadership roles, as its ministry is to the *dis*establishment. The ordained are not necessarily called to preach from the pulpit—regardless of emergent critiques of "the pulpit"[25]—but rather the ordained speak *to* the pulpit, and *against* the pulpit when necessary. To steal Peter Rollins's pun, the ordained preach the Gospel of the Insurrection,[26] that God liberates us from those things that hold us in bondage, and the ministry of the ordained is to "open a window for the Spirit"[27] that blows how it so chooses, especially when the ministry of the church seeks to promote its own hierarchy or structure. The ordained are willing to speak with great voices of Christian history whose ordinations were not recognized, as with Søren Kierkegaard, who proclaimed, "I would rather put a wax nose on the face of God than have anything to do with this 'Christianity.'"[28]

For those of us who flirt with or are directly involved with "emergence," this notion of ordained ministry—whether recognized or not—has been *our* role within the mainline denomination. The Good News is that some of the mainline denominations are now thirsty for something new and different, and some (though some more than others) are now primed to change from the inside out, and simultaneously shift their theological thinking about God, and seek changed lives and changed communities. Most of these churches are small and unable to domesticate these activities to certain groups within the congregation, as is happening in evangelical churches, where one often hears statements such as "This kind of radical thinking is OK *there*," pointing toward the youth or young adult rooms of their building, even building *separate sanctuaries* for the younger age groups. Smaller churches are forced to do things inter- or pangenerationally and as such are satiated for revolution from the inside out. They are ready for the ordained to bring their insurrection.

For those of us who are theologically radical, believing in a diachronal Godhead who is *still speaking* and still pouring out into the present moment, the mainline church is perhaps our best home. As many left the "mainline" churches in the late 1960s and early 1970s searching for relevance, declaring these denominations and their God to be dead—our Good News is again that in every death there is a resurrection, and that the once-mighty mainline churches are now in a severely weakened state. We emergents understand the appeal of weakened structures, and it is here in these "oldline," mainline churches where we may genuinely follow a Christian descent that unmasks the majority of our American churches' bad habits as too comfortable, too *easy*, and exhibiting an idolatry of corporate American selfishness.

We boldly expose these bad habits, this idolatry of corporate American selfishness, as a form of Satanism. We proclaim loudly that Satanism has indeed found its way into suburban America, but Satanism does not threaten suburban values; rather, it threatens to *perpetuate* them. Indeed, Satanism *feeds* on the dark forces of the mainstream American church, which only strengthens with every new youth center, coffee shop, and bookstore erected. They have their own radio stations and they have large music festivals where their children are programmed. They often make their teenagers worship in special centers where they are enticed with video games and bad rock music. They call for a biblical "Christianity" that is not biblical in any genuinely apocalyptic sense; that is, a "counterapocalypse" against a truly radical understanding of the kingdom of God.[29] We must now acknowledge that Satanists are everywhere and they have outnumbered the Christians in the United States. The cross we bear, friends, is to reject this spiritual wickedness and to reclaim the very fringe of religious experience.

Notes

[1] This was definitely my experience during my short tenure within the Methodist system; a Methodist district superintendent directly told me that as a "white male heterosexual" I was an ideal candidate within the conference's appointment system because of an overwhelming number of small churches who would not accept any other kind of pastor. Most of these congregations were, of course, the most backward thinking within the absolutely sick system. Congregations within the United Methodist Church are, generally speaking, guaranteed pastoral appointments by paying their apportionment money to the local conference.

[2] As defined as an essential doctrine in the famous and heavily influential essay by Franklin Johnson, "The Atonement," *The Fundamentals*, ed. A. C. Dixon and Reuben Torrey, vol. 6 (Chicago: Testimony, c. 1915), 50–63. The essay begins with the sweeping statement "The Christian world as a whole believes in a substitutionary atonement . . . The Christian world . . . accepts the substitution of Christ as fact" (50).

[3] D. G. Leahy, *Foundation* (Albany, N.Y.: SUNY, 1996), 392ff.

[4] Mary Daly, *Pure Lust* (New York: Harper, 1984), 75.

[5] *Islam: What the World Needs to Know*, directed by Bryan Daly and Gregory Davis (2006).

[6] Daly, *Pure Lust*, 76.

[7] Carl Raschke, *Painted Black* (New York: Harper, 1990).

[8] This latter case is discussed in Randy Engel's *The Rite of Sodomy* (Export, Pa.: New Engel, 2006), 828–30.

[9] Kevin DeYoung and Ted Kluck, *Why We're Not Emergent: By Two Guys Who Should Be* (Chicago: Moody, 2008), 14–15. Here, DeYoung offers a confessional *that despite all odds, he has overcome the temptation of "emergence."* The irony of books and articles such as this is that the authors nearly always employ the same argument—namely, that emergence Christianity is neither what "we" are nor what "we" define the overarching narrative of "Christianity" to be, therefore, it is wrong—which is largely the kind of exclusivity with pretentious epistemological assumptions that emergence Christianity, even in its more conservative forms, is rebelling against within evangelicalism.

[10] Ibid., 225–36.

[11] Tony Jones, presentation at the Princeton Theological Seminary Youth Ministry Forum, April 30, 2008.

[12] Paul Tillich's negating vision of the church as "the fight of religion against religion" is succinctly described in his *The Irrelevance and Relevance of the Christian Message*, ed. Durwood Foster (Cleveland: Pilgrim, 1996), 51ff.

[13] Phyllis Tickle, *The Great Emergence*, 16, 19, 21–22, 27.

[14] Ray Waddle, "Megachurches Arise from Death-of-God Theology's Ashes," *The Tennessean* (April 2, 2005), 2B.

[15] Cf. Mary Daly, *Outercourse* (New York: Harper San Francisco, 1992), 139.

[16] Carl Raschke, in *GloboChrist* (Grand Rapids, Mich.: Baker, 2008), 160–61. I explore Raschke's criticism of McLaren more in my review of *GloboChrist*, in *Journal of Cultural and Religious Theory* 10, no. 3 (2010): 148–50.

[17] Jarrett Stevens, *The Deity Formerly Known as God* (Grand Rapids, Mich.: Zondervan, 2006).

[18] William Hamilton, *On Taking God out of the Dictionary* (New York: McGraw-Hill, 1974).

[19] Stevens, *Deity*, 13; J. B. Phillips, *Your God Is Too Small* (New York: Macmillan, 1953).

[20] Stevens, *Deity*, 112.

[21] Ibid., 116.

[22] Ibid., 164.

[23] James McClendon, Jr., *Doctrine: Systematic Theology*, vol. 2 (Nashville: Abingdon, 1994), 369.

[24] Martin Luther, *First Principles of the Reformation or the Ninety-Five Theses and Three Primary Works of Dr. Martin Luther*, trans. Henry Wace and C. Buccheim (London: John Murray, 1883), 235. Luther also objected to the sacramentality of ordination by virtue of the absence of a healing or forgiving function in its administration as a rite (Hans Hillerbrand, *The Division of Christendom* [Louisville: Westminster, 2007], 390).

[25] See, for example, Doug Pagitt's *Preaching Re-Imagined* (Grand Rapids, Mich.: Zondervan, 2005).

[26] See especially Peter Rollins' book, *Insurrection: To Believe Is Human, to Doubt Divine* (New York: Howard, 2011).

[27] Martha Grace Reese, *Unbinding Your Heart* (St. Louis: Chalice, 2008), 36, 80.

[28] Søren Kierkegaard, *Attack Upon Christendom* (Princeton, N.J.: Princeton University, 1968), 169.

[29] Here I use the "counterapocalyptic" language of Catherine Keller; see her *God and Power* (Minneapolis: Fortress, 2005), 40–41. It is worth pointing out that in the ecclesiological vision of *Why We're Not Emergent: By Two Guys Who Should Be*, discussed earlier, DeYoung and Kluck's apocalyptic Christ of the *parousia* must be "deeply theological" (248). This is counterapocalyptic: DeYoung and Kluck point toward an apocalypticism in a very narrow sense that would seem to trump, if not *parody*, John of Patmos's perpetual astonishment over the multitude of heaven in Revelation 7–8.

6

Net-A-Narratives

The Evolution of the Story in Our Culture, Philosophy, and Faith

Carol Howard Merritt

I stood on the National Mall with my husband, Brian, and daughter, Calla. We had just finished eating at one of the Smithsonian cafés and Calla was telling us about her school project on Helen Keller. After we finished listening, Brian pulled out his iPhone, hit the YouTube icon, and tapped in "Helen Keller." And there, in that wide-open space, we watched a black-and-white film from the thirties of Helen Keller, standing with her great teacher, Anne Sullivan. We enjoyed the moving pictures, as Keller and Sullivan told the story of how Keller learned to talk with her mouth. Eighty years later, we watched them on my husband's phone.[1]

I couldn't help but look down at my nine-year-old at that amazing, yet ordinary, moment. *We were watching a film from the 1930s on a cell phone. The movie only took seconds to retrieve.* This is the kind of world that Calla is growing up in. How would she navigate these amazing shifts in culture? What will it be like when she is an adult?

I imagine how exciting it must have been for Helen Keller to be captured on that black-and-white celluloid, telling her story in a whole new form. Since that film was first produced, technology exploded, along with the ways in which we communicate our narratives. We have seen an incredible evolution in the ways that we entertain ourselves, educate one another, and communicate with friends. As our denominational churches stand in the midst of this, we serve as a prophetic witness as we thought-fully reflect cultural changes, vehemently react against them, or actively ignore them. What should be our faithful response? Hyphenated Christians typically react by diving into new developments; we learn to navigate the innovations and dangers while we struggle in the midst of them.

So many things are emerging in our culture and religious movements that it is often difficult to wrap our heads around all of it. Yet as mainline church leaders engage postmodern culture, one thing is clear—we cannot ignore what is happening with our narratives. Technology has allowed us to tell our stories in a new way, and with the innovations, we see the pro-liferation of stories in our individual contexts. While the computer used to be a station in our home, a place we visited for a short segment of our day, now we carry computers in our hands, and with them, we stay con-nected to the Internet on a constant basis. The web has become ubiquitous (at least for those of us on the positive side of the digital divide). In our tiny pockets, we keep our web-ready computers, music collections, photo albums, and book libraries, all compacted with our cell phones. Many of us stay wired throughout the day, even at lunch in the wide-open space of the National Mall. As new tools emerge and social media sites spring up, a new generation of people engages more with the Internet than with traditional entertainment and news sources like television.[2]

The shifts in culture and technology are rapidly evolving, and those who are part of postmodern religious movements understand that we are not just being amused and informed on the web, but something deeply spiritual is happening as well—especially as we tell our stories. Our stories have moved from grand, sweeping narratives to individual accounts, told in a particular context. In the following pages, we look at the narrative shifts in the larger culture, explore how they reflect postmodern philosophy, and observe the ways in which hyphenated Christians respond.

The Cultural Frame

Why is a new generation engaging more on the Internet than with television?[3] It's not just the media that keeps us engrossed; it's also the mes-sage, and flowing through all these sources is a narrative. Stories bubble up on blogs, they course through the pictures and notes on Facebook, and even pulse in the random updates on Twitter. By the time you hold this book (whether it be in digital form or paper and ink), we may not be using these particular means of social media, but we will still be telling our stories in some fashion, because the story has become so important in our postmodern culture.

Narratives have become vital in this information age, because we can get facts so quickly and easily. Research is no longer locked in a high ivory tower; we no longer have to stretch in order to reach the data. Now, with the extraordinary organization and retrieval prowess of Google, facts, information, and research can be acquired and pursued with ease. Alongside that access, we began to see the rise of the personal narrative.[4]

I suppose it's no wonder. For a short time, we lost the place where we could tell our own stories. There was no space for us to draw out the mundane details of our lives, and present them with a context and an emotional impact.

When I was a child, stories fed me. I spent hours breathing in the damp humidity on the porch of my grandmother's house in South Carolina. After picking ears of sweet corn, we shucked the layers of coating and stripped the silks off. Pulling the strands from the tender kernels became one of those rare jobs that I was better at as a little girl. As my tiny fingers tugged on the white threads, my grandmother, aunt, and mother talked about our relatives, always leaving the juiciest parts of the history out, and allowing my imagination to work. The women of our family were masterful storytellers. With their exaggerations and wit, they could craft a mundane scene into something so funny that we would end the afternoon aching with laughter.

My grandmother entertained with fresh vegetables and old tales. I longed for those short intervals when she sat and I could hear from her. I wanted to know why she struggled with her sisters, how her church was doing, and what kept her praying that week. As I untangled those delicate silks, I unraveled the intricate details of my personal history. The bonds that held us together thickened as they tugged on and sorted through the secrets of their lives. On muggy afternoons, our family created community through words and laughter.

Then, over the years, things changed in the way our grandmother entertained. Slowly, the space to listen and hear the stories became crowded, because the television took center stage. Not only among my relatives, but also all over the country, our family and community tales migrated to Hollywood. Our narrative-hungry culture paid wonderful actors to tell our stories. Men and women reflected our lives back to us through carefully crafted episodes, with intricate plot lines. With the advent of air conditioning and television, we moved inside from our porches, and shared the screen with our parents and siblings.

It worked for a while. Community often flourished among my generation of thirtysomethings, because there were only a handful of stations, and most programs catered to the entire family (or there was not as much concern about what was appropriate for children to watch). We could all talk about "the" show that was on that night—whether it was *M*A*S*H* or the *Cosby Show*, what happened on the screen could be shared with most of our friends.

Then, when fighting over the remote control got old, we bought more TVs and started gazing at television on our individual screens, until watching was no longer a family affair. The MTV generation began to enjoy music videos, while their parents tuned into CNN. Channels and episodes metastasized; producers created each new story line for a particular demographic, and our TVs became catered to each gender and generation. In the process, we relinquished the communal aspect of our storytelling. The individual screens lost a bit of magic, because the next day, when we tried to talk about "the" show, we found our friends were watching something else entirely.

Now another shift is occurring in the narratives surrounding us. In a new generation, we are turning off our televisions and pulling the plug on the sitcoms, dramas, news, and commercials. We are taking back our stories and recreating that neighborhood porch online. As we post our everyday musings and profound thoughts on blogs, connect with old classmates and loved ones on Facebook, and discover new friends and news items on Twitter, we are telling the stories of our lives. Often they come in shattered bits and fragments, and yet the insights are pieced together into a mosaic that makes up a larger picture. The short updates reflect who we are. In the process, we reflect the postmodern tendency to reject the metanarrative in order to present a narrative that is true to our context and personal experience.

The Philosophical Frame

If we refocus for a moment, and move our frame from a cultural analysis to a philosophical one, we can see that this popular shift of stories is similar to the transition from modernism to postmodernism. Postmodernism has been described as "incredulity towards the metanarrative," or suspicion of the grand story that points to a universal truth.[5]

Why would postmodern women and men be skeptical of a grand story that points to a universal truth? Georg Wilhelm Friedrich Hegel (1770–1831) was a modern philosopher who looked at the historic dimensions of thought. He was fascinated by the many contradictions that surrounded him and wanted to emphasize the Spirit as a great movement of history that compels us forward. Hegel held to the general sense that history would progress and evolve.[6] Hegel's philosophy dominated our thought, and his theories fit well into our Christian understandings of hope.

Yet, over a hundred years after Hegel died, we witnessed World War II and the Holocaust. In light of men and women being carried off to concentration camps, where Jews, gays, lesbians, and mentally ill or disabled men, women, and children were burned en masse, people began to see the sweep of history in a different manner. When the United States dropped atomic bombs on Nagasaki and Hiroshima and utterly destroyed over 150,000 civilians, we became aware of the evil that we could cause. As children learned drills to hide under their desks in a flimsy attempt to shield them from an attack, as warfare developed, and our technology became more and more brutal, philosophers and theologians began to question their unbridled optimism. They became skeptical of that grand story that promised a better future for each generation.

Postmodern thinkers see Hegel's wheel of history moving forward, but they realize that the wheel is crushing many people in the process. Progress may be possible, but it isn't inevitable. Postmodern Christians pause and pick up the troubled person. We brush the dirt off of them, and listen to their stories. We do not assume that things will always get better as we move forward, because the evidence of history too often goes contrary to that optimism. That confident view wipes us clean of our responsibilities and encourages delusions. We can no longer pretend that our destructive power in warfare and over the environment is moving us to some positive end. If we do, we lose sight of the sin that we commit. In our moment in history, we know that we must question that grand narrative.

To use another metaphor, when I think of the narrative shift from modernism to postmodernism, it reminds me of the time I went to Turkey, and I admired the incredible mosaics of the early church. The glistening shards made up extraordinary interiors, and the orchestrated tiles worked together to fashion incredible pictures. The postmodern Christian is like one who visits a beautiful mosaic in Turkey, and stops to look at each piece. She realizes that the metanarrative is like a mosaic—the larger story is made up of intricate, detailed smaller stories. But she is not so worried about making sure that there is a synthesis in all the pieces; rather, she is more interested in the parts. She doesn't assume that every story will have a happy ending; instead, there is some trepidation, some realization that the big picture is constructed of shattered parts, and those broken bits need to be examined in their own right. The truth of postmodernity comes into focus as we look at each shard, as we listen to each story, with its sharp edges and broken bits, as well as its evocative color and deep beauty.

Our technology reflects our philosophies. Our stories have found new resonance in the particularities of blogs, Twitter, and other means of social networking. These mediums allow us to present and see the context of each other's everyday lives. We are not only entertained by the staged and scripted stories that are being told to us on our flat-screen televisions, but we have taken those screens, and now we are telling our own stories with them. We have broken up that large storyline into shattered updates, and created "net-a-narratives." The short status reports can be full of emotion and wisdom and they can be a place where we can account for the good news in our own particularities. We share our vacation photos, report on our business travels, and meet our spouses over the Internet. Not only that, but we use those individualized flat screens to create community in our broken world. Through blogs, social media sites, and podcasting, as we reveal information and passions, giving our profiles a context and emotional impact, we connect with one another.

We used to build strong communities through our families, careers, and social institutions. But now young adults have to move away from their families of origin in order to get an education and a career, average job tenures last a mere 2.7 years, and social institutions are often (for one reason or another) less inviting to a younger generation. As a result, we yearn for connection, community, and a tribe. Many of us have learned to form community online. Through social media, we took the flat screen—that beacon of solitary entertainment—and made it into a source of human connection by telling our particular stories. Of course, people do not use social media exclusively for communicating narratives. Its applications seem endless, engaging us with practical communication, opinion writing, business marketing, political commentary, and cultural analysis. Yet its storytelling function can often be found moving alongside these things, weaving through them.

The Faith Frame

Culturally, we can see the importance of the individual narrative as we move from the television screen to the computer screen. Philosophically, we understand the shift to skepticism of the metanarrative. What do these shifts look like when we peer at them through the frame of our faith? How do hyphenated Christians embody these changes?

Many Christians feel threatened by the idea that the metanarrative is breaking down, because they feel that this thought imperils the story that binds our beliefs. "If there is suspicion of the larger narrative," they ask, "then what about the good news of Jesus Christ? If there is no universal Truth, then what are we saying about God? Have we lost hold of what makes us Christians?"

For me, as a postmodern Christian, the good news is not just in the story that happened a couple thousand years ago; it is the ways in which that story becomes lived out in individual lives and current communities. Often there is beauty in those shattered pieces. Other times, there is a horror that we cannot ignore.

The particularities of context become important, as we examine the gospel in light of a man who was lynched in the South or as we look at it in the context of a woman who has been brutalized in her own home. These figures might have been overlooked in a Hegelian view of history; they might have been seen as mere casualties, crushed by the wheel of fate in the forward movement of our metanarrative and the work of the Spirit. But the postmodern Christian stops, and with trembling hands, she wrestles with her faith in their presence. Through the call of social justice, she hears the voices of those long silenced—and stops to listen for the cries of the oppressed, needy, and disadvantaged. In our small shift in history, we have been able to open our ears to liberationist and feminist perspectives, and in the process, our own beliefs, histories, and context gain understanding and emotional depth.[7]

Even if we believe that God is the truth, we also have the humble recognition that "our thoughts are not God's thoughts and our ways are not God's ways." We realize that we "see through a glass darkly" and we will never be able to apprehend the fullness of our immense and awesome God. The best that we can do is to understand God in our own particular context, through our own stories. We can point to the ways in which we see the reign of God in our lives.

Often in our emerging faith communities, we invite ways to tell these stories of our lives. We bring the broken bits and pieces of ourselves, and share them with one another.

When we work within many of our denominational settings, our churches look back on that post–World War II era, when our Sunday school attendance and membership were at their height. We were constructing Christian education buildings all over the country, and our church members looked good on Sunday mornings. In decades past, it felt as if the church has been about a shiny newness that we bring with us into the sanctuary—the flattering dress, the glistening shoes, and the sparkling teeth. Our churches flourished in a White Anglo-Saxon Protestant society. Our congregations were like the Rotary Club, the Shriners, and the Garden Club—they were centers of civic duty and there was a sense in our larger culture that people ought to attend them.

Now, as that WASP culture has become less dominant in our country, church attendance is no longer an expected norm and younger men and women are seen as oddities when they reserve time for worship. Pastors see the shiny backs of those empty pews on Sunday morning and realize that something just as profound was happening in the twelve-step meetings in the basement while we were upstairs in the pretty sanctuary. In those groups, they were not dusting themselves off to show their newness: People were sharing their broken selves. They were presenting their shattered lives in order to form a different sort of community.

Emerging movements began to learn from these groups that inhabited our spaces for the last seventy years. Hyphenated Christians began to realize that there is something sacred, not just in *the* Story but also in *our* stories. In silence, with prayer, and through liturgies, we worship together. We explore the ways in which God is present in our spiritual journeys, we look back and see how God aided us in our decisions, or how certain people reflected the hands and feet of Christ in our lives.

The stories not only emerge in our physical communities, but also with our online tribes. It would be easy for us to look at these narratives that spring up in this ever-evolving world of social media and dismiss it as a fad. We could ignore religious movements that form online, declaring them shallow distractions that hinder the "real" work of ministry. We could argue that community only comes from face-to-face communication, and online interactions take away the flesh-and-blood aspect of the body of Christ. For hyphenated Christians, this approach would be disingenuous. Technology and social media have become a way of being for us. They have become extensions of how we think, communicate, and form community.

Not only has technology become an extension of our social and spiritual lives, but hyphenated Christians realize that the narratives unfolding through social media can be a response to our cynicism. We also acknowledge that there can be something faithful in those fractured stories. There is the beautiful hope that God is still working and the Holy Spirit is still moving throughout our particular moment in history. Through our online communities, we are compelled by that Spirit to bring our broken bits together, listening to one another, and caring for each other.

It would be possible to take all of these tools and use them as cheap advertising platforms in order to buttress the same sort of churches that we've always had. Or we can realize an opportunity to move deeper and learn how to engage with people more authentically, allowing the tools to help us create community. In a new generation, we can understand that social media allows us to provide pastoral care for the man who needs a way to ask for prayers at two o'clock in the morning or for the woman who relocates for her job every two years. This web of friendships can provide support even in the times and at the places the church cannot be geographically present.

When we do something as simple as hold our smartphones in our hands, we know that our culture is shifting in an exciting and sometimes terrifying fashion. We change the ways in which we share our stories, reflect our philosophies, and attest to our faith. Within our denominations, it is often the hyphenated Christians who experiment and explore in the midst of these changes. Whether we gather in emerging communities or tell our stories online, we are presenting the broken bits of ourselves. We are revealing our stories, in our particular context. We are creating beautiful mosaics.

Notes

[1] See "Helen Keller & Anne Sullivan (1930 Newsreel Footage)," YouTube video, posted by transformingArt, http://www.youtube.com/watch?v=Gv1uLfF35Uw.

[2] Deloitte Research, "Millennials View Their Computers as More of an Entertainment Device Than Their Television: State of Democracy Survey 2009," http://www.deloitte.com/view/en_LT/lt/press/lt-press-releases-en/49e5bf2733101210VgnVCM100000ba42f00aRCRD.htm.

[3] Pew Research, "The Millennials: Confident. Connected. Open to Change," February 24, 2010. Pew conducted a thorough and extensive study of men and women ages 19 to 29 and found that the increase in technology usage is the defining factor for these young adults. http://pewsocialtrends.org/assets/pdf/millennials-confident-connected-open-to-change.pdf.

[4] Daniel H. Pink, *A Whole New Mind: Why Right-Brainers Will Rule the Future* (New York: Riverhead Books, 2006), 103. Pink observes, "When facts become so widely available and instantly accessible, each one becomes less valuable. What begins to matter more is the ability to place these facts in *context* and to deliver them with *emotional impact.*"

[5] Jeffrey C. Alexander and Steven Seidman, *Culture and Society: Contemporary Debates* (Cambridge: Cambridge University, 1990). Jean-François Lyotard defines postmodern as the "incredulity toward metanarratives" in his chapter "The Postmodern Condition."

[6] Georg Wilhelm Friedrich Hegel, *Phenomenology of the Spirit* (New York: Oxford University, 1979), 479–93.

[7] Often those voices can feel overwhelming. For instance, as I'm writing this, I'm reminded that the smartphone that I held on the National Mall could have caused systemic injustice in its manufacturing. Companies pay low wages to factory workers and the batteries cause great damage to the environment. So even the tools that we use to make our social justice work more effective can perpetuate injustice. See, for instance, Clifford Coonan, "Tenth Worker at iPad Factory Commits Suicide," *The Independent*, May 26, 2010, http://www.independent.co.uk/news/world/asia/tenth-worker-at-ipad-factory-commits-suicide-1982897.html.

7

The Imperative of Imagination

Nanette Sawyer

When I pray, I imagine. I imagine that there is a God who loves me and who wants to hear my prayers. None of us has ever seen God (1 Jn. 4:12) and yet my imagination helps me know a God who is beyond knowing. Imagination can do that. It can make tangible the intangible. Someone said to me recently, "Without imagination, can we even be in relationship with God?" I believe that God is always in relationship with us, but our experience of that relationship is based on who we imagine God to be, as well as our interpretation of our feelings and perceptions. People who imagine God to be primarily angry and wrathful, for example, have a very different experience of God than those who imagine God to be primarily compassionate and loving.

Faith as Vision

Some might suggest that if I am *imagining* a God who loves me, then this God is therefore *imaginary* and that any consolation I might feel is a false consolation. But faith is about the shaping vision we have of the world. Faith is not about believing something irrational and trying to convince ourselves that it is rational. It is not about consoling ourselves away from the harsh realities of human finitude and vulnerability. Faith, our shaping vision of the world, is what guides how we engage the world. It affects how we approach other human beings, events, the material world, and the natural environment. If the sense of being beloved is part of our shaping vision of the world, this has a significant effect on how we behave individually and communally. When this brings consolation, it is real consolation, based on our many relationships with each other and our sense of place within the cosmos. It is not false consolation, based on the not-true; it is consolation based on what we have created in community and how we interpret human existence.

While imagination can bring consolation, it can also be used to create suffering, to delude the self and others. It can paint a picture of a world in which evil is winning and despair has the upper hand. Imagination allows us to stereotype people, to see them as our enemies and as threats when they are not. It can be used to create more inhumanity and to develop greater cruelty. Once twisted upon itself in these ways, it can carry masses of people to their deaths. Imagination can be very dangerous. It can destroy the fruits of the spirit: love, joy, peace, patience, kindness, generosity, faithfulness, gentleness, and self-control (Gal. 5:22–23).

Whether the imagination bears the good fruits of the spirit or destroys the fruits of the spirit is not based on the question of whether God is imaginary or "real." I have atheist friends who hold beautiful shaping visions of the world. Whether God is in or out of this shaping vision is not the key question. Some religious people have shaping visions of the world built around fear, shame, anger, and destruction. Some atheists have shaping visions of the world based on loneliness, meaninglessness, and mechanistic physicality. Yet many atheists and theists share worldviews rooted in visions of compassion, possibility, human community, transformation, hope, and love. The label (theist, atheist) is less important than the content of one's vision. We may judge all of these visions based on whether they are bearing good fruits or not.

To avoid the danger of imagination gone awry we must always continue to assess the fruits that come through the use of our imagination. Assisted by imagination we create meaning–we develop our shaping vision. Based on our shaping vision we choose how to spend our time and where to direct our energy–we take action. What are the fruits of our actions? Are they the fruits of the spirit? Or do they destroy the fruits of the spirit?

The content of our vision of the world is what changes our commitments, our actions, our interpretations of events, and the nature of our relationships. This shaping vision is a core component of our *faith*. It's what we believe. We hold it to be true. Everyone holds a shaping vision of how they think *things are*, whether theist or atheist, Christian or Jesus followers, Muslim, Jewish, Hindu, Buddhist, or Humanist. Human imagination plays a significant role in the development and the maintenance of our shaping vision.

My particular faith includes a couple of other elements in addition to my shaping vision. My faith includes an element of trust in a God who loves me. These two aspects of faith, vision and trust, are related, as my shaping vision includes a God who loves me. My trust in that God then flows naturally out of that shaping vision. A third element of my faith is fidelity to God through Christ. Again and again I choose to turn toward God and Christ. Fidelity, as a concept, is based in this kind of repetitive choosing to practice devotion and to develop a particular relationship. My fidelity is also related to my shaping vision and my trust. I envision a God who loves me and I am faithful to that God; I trust in a God who loves me and that trust causes me to desire and commit to fidelity. *Vision, trust,* and *fidelity* come together to create a particular *faith.* So we can ask ourselves: In what do we trust? Toward what do we direct our fidelity? Our answers to these questions flow out of the shaping vision of existence that we imagine to be true, and they can all be assessed based on the fruits they bear.

Imagination and Transformation

The involvement of imagination in and of itself does not tell us what is true, nor suggest that we are engaging in the realms of the false. Imagination *can* lead to the imaginary and it can be very destructive if rooted in fear. On the other hand, fear of imagination's creative power can cause us to shut it down completely rather than apply it toward the good and the beautiful. If imagination is bearing the good fruits of the spirit–love, joy, peace, patience, kindness, generosity, and so on–it is contributing to the betterment of the world in a very real way.

God has given us this power–the power to imagine–and through imagination, the power to create meaning and to effect real change and tangible transformation. The power of imagination is what makes it both scary and exhilarating. Human will, our will, and our decisions about how to direct our imaginations play a tremendous role in how its power will be wielded in the world.

Imagination can help us understand in new ways when we open ourselves to possibilities we haven't yet considered. It gives us access to the *"eureka!"* moment, when the light suddenly clicks on in our minds. Imagination can help us learn from the past, by imagining into the experience of those who have come before us, seeking after their passion, their brilliance, their struggles, their successes, and even their mistakes. Learning is not only based in imagining, of course; we need to seek information as well. But applying our imaginations can help us internalize what we learn by helping us to integrate information into our own worldviews and daily habits of mind and body. In these ways, imagination can help us connect with those who are different or distant from us. It can help us become more compassionate toward others by helping us bring their stories and experiences into our awareness and into contact with our own lives.

Healing can also be experienced through the thoughtful use of imagination. Through it we can connect with places that are beyond words in us, which are not logical or rational but are rather shaped by images and symbols. We can tap into these places and draw them out into the light through music, art, poetry, movement, and story. Story can help us remember, retell, and heal our own experience, often by bringing it into contact with other stories. As Christians, we can look to the story of Christ as one significant shaping and healing story. On the other hand, some of us are actually healing *from* damaging interpretations and applications of this same story. How do we tap into the healing elements of this particular story—how might we receive its transformative power in our hearts, minds, and lives?

Imagining a New Church

When I was invited to begin my current ministry as founding pastor of Wicker Park Grace, I had no idea what to do. Everyone knew this was the case, since no one knew exactly what they were asking me to do either. "Do something different" was the charge; go outside the church and into the neighborhood; drink five hundred cups of chai latte with people from the area; engage young adults who are not engaging the church.

Although fresh out of seminary and ordained for this position, I did have some experience with community organizing in my first career working on a college campus in the student life department. To start a church, though? We weren't even sure it was going to be a church, per se. We wanted to be in relationship with people who wouldn't come to church, people who had negative experiences of church in the past, or who just couldn't connect with a traditional church.

I began by meeting people, getting to know them, gathering for "spirituality" discussions in teahouses and coffee shops. Whatever was to be developed here needed to come out of relationships with the people themselves. My task as leader was to get to know them, but also to get to know God and myself better. I was pushed outside my comfort zone often, never knowing what the next step would be until I was taking it. And sometimes it was a misstep.

I questioned myself and my capacity to create something new when I didn't know where we were going, didn't know what the finished product would look like. I had been trained to "be" a pastor, a preacher, a liturgist, a theologian, a historian, and a caregiver—all in the generalist sense. Do a bit of all these things on the weekly schedule, show up in church on Sunday morning, preach the word "rightly" and voilà. Pastor.

But I had none of that structure. I showed up in a preselected neighborhood with an empty day planner, an introverted personality, and a desire to share God's love with people in the way it had been shared with me. It had transformed me. I had blossomed. But it took almost forty years of life before that happened to me and I wanted to help others have that experience right now! I had a passion to convey the truth, depth, and breadth of God's love to people who had experienced rejection, injustice, or narrowness in the church into which they could not fit. Yet here I was, with no road map, no tried-and-true method to guide the way. I had to imagine it; I had to create it. And that was scary. Exhilarating, but scary.

Not only was I called to use my imagination to create new ways of being together, being church, I had to reimagine my self and my role as pastor. There was no Sunday bulletin to prepare, no liturgy to write at that point (that has since changed). My work was all about relationships and the contents of our imaginations as they related to God, Christ, the church, and our multireligious world.

Meeting with people in coffee shops in the early days involved telling and listening to a lot of personal stories. It wasn't long before I realized that our stories help us connect. Sharing our stories is a way to share ourselves–they are expressions of our multifaceted identities. In telling stories we recreate them in the presence of each other; and in listening we imagine our way into the experience of another, as their words and gestures paint pictures in our minds. Personal storytelling is an act of creativity through which we may be changed if we are open to a truthful encounter.

This creative sharing is most evocative if grounded in the authentic self, in the deepest parts of ourselves, where God knows us by name and calls us out into the world. I am *uniquely myself.* Each human being has this quality of uniqueness. It is our identity, made up of the particular giftedness that God has placed in us, as well as the particular experiences that life has given us. And yet I, the unique individual, also share a second core identity with all humanity: I am a *beloved child of God* and every individual is also a beloved child of God. I associate this love with the image of God, which rests in each human being.

In addition to this shared identity I have a third identity as a *follower of Jesus.* I have "clothed" myself in Christ, as the apostle Paul says. I wear him and he covers me, so to speak. I internalize his stories and his teachings. These stories become part of my story, part of my shaping vision of the world. This third identity is one that is shared with others, but not with all humanity.

These three aspects of my identity, or three identities, are significant in my role as a shaper of the church: *unique individual, beloved of God, clothed in Christ.* Who I am uniquely and the particular gifts I bring have a profound impact on my capacity to imagine and the kinds of community I long to create. My self-understanding as a beloved child of God and my belief that I share this core identity with all human beings significantly shapes my ideas about the nature of the future church. For example, I believe that love is not contingent and it is universal; there are none who are outside the love of God. The theological implications of that are very important. My third identity, as one clothed in Christ, means that I am shaped by the Jesus story and that my vision of community, the world, and my role in it are all shaped by the Jesus story as well.

The place where these three identities intersect is the point from which great creativity in reimagining the church can spring. In order to bring the fullness of each identity to bear, it is vitally important to tell the truth about who we are and how we have come to be where we are today in each of our faith journeys. God is speaking to the world through each of us. If we can't bring authenticity to our expressions of faith and community (a.k.a. church), then the meaning we discern and the stories we tell will be ungrounded and untrustworthy.

A Dynamic Faith

People create meaning in many ways, then share and further shape that meaning through communication. The forms of meaning creation include language, movement, image, and sound. As we share and shape meaning, we continue to create it through our interactions and our responses to one another: when we tell stories about what happened to us today or yesterday, when we explain what we hope for in the future or what our dreams and desires are. We are living stories, ever changing, future trajectories shifting with each new decision we make and each new action we take: creating lives and shaping one another's lives. Stories encounter stories and change the shape of lives.

Once, in the early days of Wicker Park Grace, someone asked me, "Why are *you* Christian?" On that same night I was asked about the resurrection; the Bible; women's roles in the church; and the controversy over gay, lesbian, bisexual, and transgender people being fully included in the church (they were for it). It was my authenticity and honesty, my wrestling openly with language to convey my thoughts and feelings about all these things that really made a difference.

When I got home that night, I had an e-mail in my inbox waiting to be opened. In part it said, "Before our discussions I naively thought that Christianity was a one-dimensional theology with minor shifts in beliefs across denominations; and I definitely thought that it did not coincide with my own world view. However, after each discussion I feel a deeper connection to Christianity as a dynamic faith and feel an overwhelming sense of well-being and connection."

Her use of the word "dynamic" struck me in a profound way and I realized that she, like many people, had never been given permission, let alone invited, to bring her whole, complex, ever-evolving self into active engagement with Christian ideas. What we were doing in the coffee shops was engaging our imaginations, wrestling with ideas, groping around for language that might tell a meaningful story that heals and opens hearts. In truth, Christianity has always been a dynamic conversation, with many different voices vying for primacy. Theological libraries document the diversity of thought and interpretation developed in this search for meaning, yet Christianity, as this young woman learned, has earned a reputation of being a "one-dimensional" faith.

Recently, an evangelical pastor visited Wicker Park Grace on a night that we were doing Bible study. His experience, which he shared with me over dinner a few weeks later, helped me articulate what we are doing in our process of study. We include Bible study twice a month during our regular Sunday gatherings. As pastor, I feel that my role includes teaching historical and narrative context around a scripture and framing difficult questions about theological issues suggested by the text. The community then discusses these questions in small groups before coming back together for a brief sharing in the large group. I act as facilitator, sometimes offering a variety of theological interpretations that have been suggested throughout history, simply to help get the conversation going. We affirm, right from the beginning, that there have been a variety of interpretations on most stories and topics, and that we most likely reflect that diversity in our own gathering.

This process is highly valued by the community, many of whom have never been given a "safe" place to ask their deepest questions or to disagree with a particular interpretation. The freedom to do this allows them to construct meaning from the inside out. Their theology is stronger because it is rooted in the truth of who they are, what they believe, and what they are concerned about. The biblical story, the God story, and the Jesus story are all filtered through their own life stories—and in this way they become internalized.

When the visiting pastor and I had dinner a few weeks later, he shared how surprised he was that I facilitated the Bible study without telling the community what the correct understanding of the text was. He had been taught that this was the role of the pastor—to give the correct interpretation so that people would not go astray and to protect the creed of the church. I see a couple of problems with that method of teaching. It gives too much power to the pastor, who is also fallible, after all, and it does not acknowledge that participants have a direct relationship with God (without needing a priestly go-between). It also backfires as a method of developing shared understanding because it places people in the position of merely accepting or rejecting a particular idea without really engaging in or exploring it. Asking someone to accept or reject an idea has a qualitatively different effect than asking them, "What does this mean? How can this be understood? Where does this intersect with your life?"

What the visiting pastor said he learned that night at the Bible study was that God could protect God's self, and didn't need the pastor to do that. He experienced God speaking through that open-ended Bible study. One young woman in his small group offered an interpretation of a text with which he had always struggled—and he felt that her interpretation was better than any he had ever come up with!

Giving permission to honestly wrestle with the biblical texts encourages each person to encounter the stories through the lenses of their own lives. Because we expect a diversity of interpretations to come out, there is a freedom to authentically ask the hardest questions and strive for meaningfulness through the process. The imaginations of each participant are engaged and God has more hearts and minds through which to speak.

Entering the Story

A couple of years ago at Wicker Park Grace we used the season of Lent to create an encounter between that very old story of Jesus and the very contemporary stories of members of our community. Using the framework of the Stations of the Cross, we gathered a group of artists in our community to retell the story of Good Friday.

The artists met and discussed the spiritual and theological significance of each station and the different representations of them. Each of the fourteen stations represented a moment on the day of Jesus' crucifixion. Together, they tell the story of that day. (After Easter, we added a fifteenth station, representing the resurrection.) We looked at the Stations of the Cross that other churches had created and reflected on the interpretations that several artists had made. Each artist in our community selected one or two stations that they found compelling and agreed to create a piece of visual art engaging that moment of the Jesus story. The remaining stations were designed to be community art projects, bringing larger numbers of people into the process in ways that even nonartists could be comfortable participating. For example, Station five represents Simon of Cyrene helping Jesus carry his cross. We invited people to make simple plaster casts of their own hands and we placed these hands into the sculpture. In relation to this station, we asked the questions: How do we live out this story today? How do we help relieve injustice and suffering in the world?

On Good Friday, we prayed the stations. We had them arranged throughout the art gallery where we regularly worship, and we went on a prayer pilgrimage through the series, reading scripture and reflecting on related questions at each station. Engaging the imaginations of the people in this way brought the Jesus story more powerfully into our own lives. Many of us were deeply moved. Afterward, I asked one writer, Nick Croston, to reflect on his experience. He wrote this:

> Heritage is very important to me, but is it really so important to preserve the heritage of a religion I disassociated and distanced myself from seven years ago? . . . On the day we opened the Stations of the Cross, though, the music, light, and contemplative quiet of the exhibit impacted me in a way that no religion ever had before. As I walked and looked at the Stations, I let my atheism simmer as the highly metaphorical artwork made me think, for the first time, about how Jesus must have felt. I wondered how painful a crucifixion must have been, and about the crushing anger and sorrow Jesus' friends must have endured. As I entered the burial chamber which was the fourteenth Station, I was swept in a whirlwind of

sorrow as the music, sight, and the prayer of a Jewish woman for her tormentors lifted and crushed me at the same time. For a short span of time, I was not an atheist. I was a Jew who had borne witness to every lash of the whip, every hit on the nail's head. I had seen the death of a man who I thought would rid my people of the Romans. I choked up. I was speechless.

In Nick's experience of the stations, the intangible was made tangible. What had seemed like a distant story, unrelated to his own experience, was made real to him in a new way. The metaphorical artwork engaged his imagination and allowed him to make connections he had never made before. He could relate. Nick *entered the story* and was changed by it.[1]

Fostering Spiritual Artfulness

Transformation happens when we engage creativity and imagination. People tell me they are interested in what I do and what we do at Wicker Park Grace, but they ask me, "What can *I* do? I'm not an artist." They say, "I don't have artists in my community." They say this, I think, because their skills are different from mine. They can't do what I do (they think), or what that painter does, or what that poet does. That may be true, but it's the wrong question to be asking. I can't do what they do either, not the way they do it. I'm not them! People are different and have different gifts. Discovering, developing, and honoring our own uniqueness, passions, and particular gifts is fundamental to tapping into our own creativity.

Every person has the capacity for imagination, but it manifests itself very differently in each one of us. Some people are more visual, and some are more tactile. Some may find their intuition to be strong, while others ground their experience in the physical senses. Some may find themselves most open to possibility through ideas and concepts, while others are most transformed by emotions. On some level, fostering our own creativity is about learning who we are and accepting that. Discovering what is beautiful to us, what is powerful, and what inspires us can help us create and share with the world that God is sharing with us.

Consider what it is that inspires you. Ask yourself: Why am I a Christian (if you are)? What is it that is compelling to me about the Jesus story? What inspires me in the world? What gives me hope? How do I encounter that? Through words? Concepts? Nature? Color? Laughter? Engage your dreams because that is where your imagination is enlivened. Do you dream of a world founded on compassion, where random acts of kindness happen all the time? By imagining into your shaping vision of the world you will actually be developing and strengthening that vision, and this will make it easier for you to share it with your community.

What people are looking for is someone who authentically tells the truth about their experience, someone who shares their hopes and dreams as well as their uncertainties and fears. Exploring our imaginations and expressing what we find there does require courage, because expressing what is true for us makes us more vulnerable. What we are expressing may be judged unworthy, or the way we are expressing it might be criticized as unskilled. In the face of such possibilities, many people don't take the risk.

To counteract this requires creating a culture within our communities in which permission is given to embrace experimentation. We "test" things to see if and how they work. Spiritual artfulness is about the process, not the product. Practicing imaginative experimentation is a way to discover and to encounter the holy. It could be practiced through Bible study, which encourages exploration and asking hard questions of the text and of ourselves. It could be engaged through writing, visual arts, music (creation of sounds and rhythms), or movement. But it's so much more than these commonly understood forms of art. Spiritual artfulness is about opening ourselves to possibilities that we haven't yet considered. It's about being transformed by the imaginations of others, by being open to their unique insights, and to the way that God speaks to and through them.

Jesus saw things that others didn't see. He had a shaping vision of existence he called the reign of God. Others have called it the beloved community. Imagine a world in which everyone knows that they are beloved. That is a significant element in my faith, the shaping vision I hold in my mind, as I go through my days. I have faith, I hold this vision, even though the world doesn't look like this now and may never look like this completely. My faith causes (or empowers) me to live in that direction, to move toward that vision as best I can.

While I hold to my vision of the beloved community, I also hold an openness to the many things I have not yet discovered and don't yet understand. Scripture says that "now we see in a mirror, dimly, but then we will see face to face" (1 Cor. 13:12). The Greek here has the connotation of a riddle. Now we see like seeing a riddle. Riddles require metaphor and imagination, not systematic outlines of the way things are—because we don't know how things are. It's a riddle. All we have is our current best guess, our current assessment of what seems to be. Riddles require us to consider many possibilities in order to find the best possible solution to the riddle.

Part of the challenge of the riddle of life, though, is that once we think we find an answer, the question changes. Some of the answers Jesus offered don't apply to the new questions we're asking today. What the reformers said in earlier periods of church history no longer works well. We have to keep imagining our way forward. Jesus once said that there were things he wanted to tell us, but "you cannot bear it now." The Holy Spirit would continue to teach us, he said (Jn. 16:12–13). The Holy Spirit can speak to us and teach us through the power of imagination.

Imagination necessarily involves thinking about more than we already know, things that may not (yet) exist, or that might even be wrong, in order to discover new insights, new interpretations of traditional stories or concepts, and answers to the new questions we are being asked in our contemporary context.

Imagination opens up possibility, but sometimes we do not dare to imagine something as beautiful as God. What if our imagination leads us astray? Sometimes we deaden our hopes and dreams. We judge ourselves and one another. The fear that we may be led astray by the imaginary may cause us to stop dreaming dreams of hope, or to demand that others limit their imaginations. If we do this, we risk destroying our own future, destroying possibility, hope, and human hearts.

To create a community that welcomes and fosters spiritual artfulness, get in touch with your hopes and dreams, your *greatest* hopes and dreams, the ones you are afraid to dare to dream. Be bold because God and God's love are dreams of that magnitude. You are a beloved child of God. God's love for us is bigger than our minds can grasp. We have to imagine our way into it.

Note

[1] High-quality images of all the stations are posted at Wicker Park Grace's blog, http://www.wpgrace.blogspot.com. After Easter, in order to complete the story, we added a fifteenth station representing the resurrection. More and more artists are doing this as a reminder that the story does not end with death, but with new life. You can take a virtual prayer pilgrimage by visiting this blog site and reading the artists' statements and the scriptures associated with each station. Take a few moments to reflect on the questions posed with each piece of art, and consider the stories that artists have brought into conversation with the Jesus story. You may find that you enter the story, too, or that the story enters you in a new way.

8

The Postmodern Pan and the ForeverNeverland

Matthew Gallion

Understand that to write a book and revoke it is something else than not writing it at all; that to write a book that does not claim importance for anybody is something else than leaving it unwritten.

—Søren Kierkegaard[1]

It is fairly popular in some circles of philosophy and theology to talk about something often dubbed "postmodernism." For some, the word carries heavy connotations about the "reality" of knowledge, one's ability to perceive and interpret, and, perhaps most important, the great enemy of all things good: Certainty. This villainous Certainty can be viewed as the Captain Hook of the postmodern Neverland. It is old and crusty, it lacks imagination, and, most damnably, it cannot fly. It is the "modern Epistemology," the thought of dead-and-buried thinkers like Kant and Descartes, who believed in silly trifles like "absolutes" and "universals" and the like. The gleaming hook of this Certainty slices through thoughts, latching firmly onto "Truth" and leaving the tatters of the Absurd in heaps on the ground. And much to Hook's chagrin, the postmodern Pan floats lightly overhead, crowing and cackling, taunting and torturing the poor, Certain Captain Hook. "Why can't that silly youth follow the rules of the world?" the angry Hook wonders endlessly. "Doesn't he realize how the world works as I have mastered it? Little children cannot and should not fly." Hook's thoughts, while certainly reasonable, do nothing to affect the impenetrable and stubborn imagination of Pan. Not in Neverland and certainly not in the on-and-on land of philosophical discourse.

The lost boys and girls, the Wendybirds, and the Tinkerbells, who dearly love the Pan, find the world of Neverland enchanting. It is the place where dreams come true, a place of sights and sounds beyond belief. And the smells! The air is rich with indescribable sensations. It is a land of freedom and beauty, a land that many little lost boys and girls, Wendybirds, and fairies have always dreamed of. Barely have their feet scraped the ground when the Pan jumps up and begins a game of make believe. The lost boys and girls have found the land of their imagination, but the Pan's imagination always goes further. Even Neverland is not enough for the boy who never grows up. Instead, he chases the twinkle in his own eye, through the material and toward *the* impossible.

Domesticating Neverland

Evangelicalism, which is a very certain kind of theological and ecclesial movement, has a history of irritating people. In what is, to date, the most thoroughly researched and scholarly overview of the emerging churches, Eddie Gibbs and Ryan Bolger trace a common evangelical heritage from many who consider themselves a part of the emerging church movement. Specifically, Gibbs and Bolger note the influence of Dave Tomlinson's book *The Post-Evangelical.*[2] While one of the hopes of many in the emerging church is to escape such labels,[3] many in the earliest conversations associated with emergence strongly resonated with Tomlinson's ideas. Descriptions such as "postevangelical," "postdenominational," and "post-Protestant" were tossed around and eventually deemed inspiring though mostly unhelpful. In other words, many former evangelicals who hoped to apply the "postmodern" critique to the current state of the church became "post-posts," preferring to try to move beyond negatively defining themselves by what they do not value.[4]

For some, emergents seem to be "angry evangelicals." One might even see them as "postevangelicals" who have found "postmodernism" as a way of moving fundamentalist foundationalism slightly to the left (perhaps to more comfortably accommodate an increasingly liberal social milieu, especially among younger generations). In other words, some evangelicals found aspects of postmodernism appealing as a means to critique the evangelical theology and ecclesiastical practices they inherited, but didn't want to become members of what they perceived to be stodgy, old mainline congregations. For one thing, mainline congregations come across as being too bureaucratic. For another, they're often theologically vacuous and programmatically boring. Mainline congregations often struggle vehemently to maintain whatever programs have the longest histories without having any idea why such programs are necessary. It reminds me of a story that Peter Rollins tells:

> There once was a wise teacher who would go to the temple every evening to pray with his disciples. By the temple there was a stray cat who would wander in every evening during these prayers and disturb the peace. So, each evening before prayers the teacher would tie the cat to a tree outside before entering. The teacher was old and passed away a few years later. His disciples continued to tie the cat to the tree each evening before prayers . . . Eventually the cat died and so some of the disciples purchased a new cat so they could continue the ritual. After a hundred years the tree died and a new one was quickly planted so that the cat (by now the eighth-generation cat) could be tied to it. Over the centuries learned scholars began to write books on the symbolic meaning of the act.[5]

So some emergent Christians, finding tiresome programs and activities in established churches to be silly and unfaithful to Christian tradition, "discovered" postmodernism and boldly declared themselves free from the entire system.[6] Postmodernism became the Neverland for these wandering orphans who no longer had parents and resisted the foster care of mainline institutionalism. It was a magical place where imagination ruled supreme. They were free to make up their own rules for every game.

But the thing about Neverland, which emergents haven't quite figured out, is that it doesn't exist. Even after you follow the second star to the right and burst through the last batch of clouds to see the glowing green island below you, you're never *really* there. As soon as you land on the dusty forest floor, the Pan is ready to pretend that you are somewhere else. To paraphrase several of the most notable thinkers in postmodern philosophy: The Big Secret to the mystery of Neverland is that there is no Big Secret. It is not the goal of imagination as much as the continuous and never-ending journey into it that makes Neverland so special. It might be more accurately called the "ForeverNeverland," the land of the always escaping, or, as Jacques Derrida might call it, the land of "the trace." As a significant number of participants within emergence Christianity continue to tinker with the bells and whistles of postmodernism, I can't help but wonder just how "postmodern" these attempts really are.

"Postmodernism" is an unfortunate term for several reasons. For one thing, it is amorphous and without certain meaning. While this is characteristic of postmodern thought itself, it makes it equally slippery. For those who enjoy a certain precision of language, this elusive term dashes swiftly down the proverbial rabbit hole. The elusion of the postmodern has created space for many critics to denounce it as nothing more than an illusion that leads to relativism and nihilism.

Another unfortunate side effect of the term "postmodern" is the limiting way in which it is defined in relationship to "modernism." The project of the scapegoat known as the Enlightenment is often described in terms of Kantian epistemology that idealizes reason and the human ability to comprehend the inner workings of the metaphysical cosmos and the "realities" of universal truths. This Kantian epistemology led to a separation of science and religion: the former being reasonable and the latter being dismissed as superstitious.

Modernism is primarily obsessed with its own objectivity, and the "postmodern" critique challenges such notions of objectivity. Put more simply, modernism considered itself the pinnacle of human intellectual achievement, and postmodernism dared to challenge such claims. It moved beyond the modern affair with reason into a much more muddled sense of "reality" (if one can use such a term). Postmodernism, then, challenges and hopes to move beyond the limited constraints of modern thought, yet in the process it found no easier way to identify itself than by limiting itself to the term that it attempted to escape. By doing so, one might suggest that the postmodern is simply the other side of the modern coin, being nothing but another pretentious academic methodology that prattles on and on with its exclusive vocabulary and complicated theories.

Still yet, there are those who understand postmodernism to be something much more than an elusive illusion or a "hyperadvanced 'New New Criticism.'"[7] For these thinkers, the legacies of postmodernism and of deconstruction are a way of reading, of thinking, of living that pushes back against the modern epistemologies that relegate religion to the realm of the ridiculous. These thinkers bring into question the authority of human thinkers to dismiss the "nonrational" with such flippant ease. For these thinkers, deconstruction "desecularizes" and makes religion a viable topic of discussion in philosophy and critical theory.[8] In other words, the postmodern is the (holy?) ghost of the divine, the nonrational, and the impossible that brings into question and subsequently sublates human attempts to objectively explain the complex relationships between God, the self, and the world.[9] The postmodern is the Pan that leaps into the unreachable nowhere of imagination as soon as the Darling children of modernism find Neverland—for the beauty of Neverland is that it can never be found, even though it perpetually calls.

Jacques Derrida is the philosopher most famous as the pioneer of poststructuralism and postmodernism. Derrida, who questioned the meaning of "signs" and language in questions about God, the world, and the self, saw two ways of "erasing the difference between the signifier [what religion might call the finite] and the signified [what religion might call the infinite]": The first is simply establishing (or, as Derrida puts it, "reducing or deriving") a meaning for the sign; the second is to "put into question the system in which the preceding reduction functioned."[10] This second way is the basis of what will later become widely known as "deconstruction." Derrida explains what he means by highlighting language of the trace, a point that is central to postmodern expressions of religion (at least those influenced by Derrida):

> As rigorously as possible, we must permit to appear/disappear the trace of what *exceeds* the truth of Being. The trace (of that) which can never be presented, the trace which itself can never be presented: that is, appear and manifest itself, as such, in its phenomenon. The trace beyond that which profoundly links fundamental ontology and phenomenology. Always differing and deferring, the trace is never as it is in the presentation of itself. It erases itself in presenting itself, muffles itself in resonating, like the *a* writing itself, inscribing its pyramid in [the French neo-logism] *différance*.[11]

This theoretical terminology is displayed in the fleeting gleam in the Pan's eye, the dreams and imaginations that appear and disappear. It is the ForeverNeverland. Once one has landed in Neverland contentedly, once one has grasped Neverland, discovered it and known it, Neverland immediately slips away. To be in Neverland is to lose Neverland. This doesn't negate Neverland's lure, but makes it more brilliant, more compelling, more praiseworthy. The ForeverNeverland is what we desperately long for, hope for, "pray and weep" for, and as soon as we think it has arrived we have diminished its beauty and domesticated its call.

The New Liberalism?

I am not sure that the emergent church is all that postmodern. As a movement, it seems quite content to have found its "new" set of answers that are just as certain and foundationalist as the conservative and "modern" fundamentalism it hoped to escape. They seem to have set up camp in Neverland, pillaging the magical forest for firewood and settling in nicely. Unlike the pirates or (even worse!) the silly grown-ups back in London, emergents have no problem with flying boys or invisible food—they resent "modern" kinds of resistance to the impossible. But when the Pan wants to pretend he's elsewhere, emergents are quite content with Neverland and are well aware of limits of imagining.[12]

Perhaps it is entirely foolish to suggest that one can quantitatively or qualitatively measure the level of "postmodernism" in any school of thought or sociological movement. Perhaps that is the point. Nothing is postmodern because the postmodern is the perpetually escapable impossible. It is the trace that Derrida argued was always missing and always calling. When one believes they have grasped the trace or found Neverland, it is precisely at that moment that the trace is gone and the magic of Neverland is nullified. Our pursuits of the boy who never grows up, of the trace, of the gift, of *the* impossible, are always just the beginning.

Within my own journey, the illusiveness of the Pan is precisely why I feel so compelled to raise such questions about emergence Christianity. It was emergence that introduced me to Neverland, and it was the Pan that I met there that draws me "further up and further in," to borrow an expression from C. S. Lewis's Aslan. I hope it is clear that I love what the emerging conversation has offered the church and how it has opened up conversations about the never-foreseen and always-hoped-for future. While part of what I am saying might sound critical, it will hopefully be understood as it is intended: a critique done out of love and friendship—made possible only because of emergence—coupled with the recognition that I often find myself much too settled in Neverland as well.

While some postmodern philosophers and theologians may use the language of "emergence," it is important to note one strong distinction: They hope for the "sublation" of dichotomies such as liberal and conservative so that such perspectives might give birth to something much more (radically) constructive, if not altogether new. From a theological perspective, postmodern theorists are equally disturbed by conservative "either/or" conjunctions as well as liberal "both/and" conjunctions.[13] In *The New Christians*, which adamantly claims to be written from a postmodern perspective, Tony Jones expresses a somewhat similar frustration with both sides of theological and political debates, and he critiques the right for the same reasons that several postmodern theorists do (for certainties that lead to violence and hatred, rigid dogmatism, good old-fashioned bigotry, and so on).

However, Jones limits his critiques of the left to bureaucracy and institutionalism. And while these things may be problems on the left, the right has the same problems as well. Jones's inability to critique the left's theology portends to his unspoken embrace of it. As such, his arguments against the left become very weak and unsubstantiated, representing a straw man that largely exists in Jones's own mind. Jones tries to make his argument against the left by suggesting:

> Potential mainline preachers have to pick a flavor of Christianity early on in their careers—Presbyterian, Methodist, Catholic, Quaker, Baptist—the list could go on and on. Like ice cream, these are the main flavors, but there are also all kinds of exotic variations—Baptist Chip, Baptist Swirl, Low-Fat Baptist Lite, and Double Baptist Chunk. The pastor then becomes a one-flavor guy. He goes to *that* seminary, learns *that* theology, buys into *that* pension plan, and goes to *that* annual trade show. This is not to disparage the erstwhile pastors—they really have no choice; they don't get to pick a new flavor on a whim. That's how the system of getting to be a pastor is set up; those are the rules by which the players are bound to play.[14]

This critique of the "left" is hugely problematic. First, as a critique of the *left*, it is striking that Jones's favorite example is Baptist, a denomination usually situated fairly comfortably on the right. Second, it is not even true. I currently work with a mainline pastor who was, until she moved to our current church, in a different denomination. She made the transition fairly easily. There were hoops, but they were not overwhelming. Most important, the caricature of seminaries on the left that are supposedly spouting off one particular theology endlessly is inaccurate. One could make a fairly convincing case that most mainline Protestant seminaries are more likely to present a diversity of theologies. Indeed, at a mainline seminary, students are generally required to engage historical theologies as well as more contemporary streams such as feminist, womanist, liberation, process, and queer theologies, just to name a handful of examples. It is typically the theologies on the right that are known for defending one particular interpretation of Christian theology, not those on the left. Jones's critiques of the left are weak, and the rest of his work falls in line with most "progressive" or "liberal" expressions of Christianity.

In *The New Christians,* Jones's first "dispatch" sounds surprisingly like classical liberalism: "Emergents find little importance in the discrete differences between the various flavors of Christianity. Instead, they practice a generous orthodoxy that appreciates the contributions of all Christian movements."[15] I can't determine whether this is a move toward postmodern relativism of some kind or liberal tolerance. Either way, it appears that Jones's emergents, as well as their version of "postmodernism," simply make them more "liberal" than their evangelical counterparts. While many do maintain a strong sense of spirituality and mysticism (something sometimes lacking in more liberal denominations, as Jones and other emergents rightly point out), they also tend to explore more progressive theologies, such as process theology or open theism. They tend to be open and inclusive of gays and lesbians.[16] Some have publicly endorsed Democratic politicians or even attempted to run for office in the Democratic Party. While these perspectives aren't problematic in and of themselves, it is disingenuous for *The New Christians* to criticize theologies on the left when in fact such theologies represent the operating theological perspective among a vast number of emergents, including Jones.

To make this point in another way, Jones recently endorsed attempts by Philip Clayton and Tripp Fuller, a professor-student team from Claremont School of Theology, to make "progressive Christianity" the popular theology in American life. In *Transforming Theology*, Clayton writes:

> There are increasing signs that the rigid opposition between these two sides [conservative and liberal] is beginning to abate. Younger Christians across the spectrum of churches are no longer willing to be pigeonholed into one of the two camps . . . These are signs of an exciting return to "big tent" Christianity. No one is urging that we create one mega-denomination or write a creed that all are expected to sign. But it's getting easier to recognize once again our

common features as followers of Jesus Christ. While we may follow the one we call Teacher and Lord in different ways, with different language and emphases, depending on our age, location, and social world, we're all under a single tent. Together we constitute the same body of Christ.[17]

The idea is to boil Christianity down to a few "common features" and, for the sake of unity, to focus on a commonality so that all can get along. Diversity is encouraged and cherished. Differences are opportunities to work through the details of contextualized and contingent theologies with patience and, implicitly, without the objectivity required to make claims on validity. This is Clayton's "progressivism," which is not necessarily melioristic—a word that pertains to a belief in an overarching "grand" narrative of inevitable and wonderful progress—but it certainly reflects a liberal position instead of a conservative one, even though he states that the rigid opposition between the two sides is beginning to abate.

Emergents are typically known for their affinity for "postmodernism," albeit a postmodernism that sounds a whole lot like liberalism. What fascinates me about the involvement of emergents with the kind of approach represented in Clayton's work is that there seems to be some understanding of postmodern thought as the great "both/and" of our current philosophical milieu. I suppose the thinking goes something like this: If all truth claims are contingent, as postmodernism teaches us, then the difficulty of discerning truth should lead us to value all approaches to truth with equal legitimacy, thus invalidating all attempts at serious (unharmonious?) theological discourse. The problem that I have with this in regards to its claims of being "postmodern" is that the oft-quoted philosophers in these descriptions don't seem to be making this point at all. Rather, it is the same point that has already been made in a myriad of ways by liberal theologians throughout the twentieth century who were also responding to the problems associated with modern epistemology (I suppose you could say that if postmodernism is understood as liberalism's standard responses to the problems posed by the Enlightenment's claims to objectivity and universality, then this brand of progressive theology can be understood as "postmodern").

But more radical postmodern philosophers and theologians, on the other hand, offer a much more substantial critique of the left. Take Mark C. Taylor, for example. Taylor argues that support of any one position does nothing but increase its opposition. In other words, liberalism only inspires a firmer commitment from conservatism, and vice versa. So in response to liberal forms of tolerance, which are reflected in some of the most popular voices within emergent Christianity, Taylor suggests that "connectivity does not inevitably lead to greater unity; to the contrary, the more interconnected the world becomes, the more evident the differences among peoples and cultures appear to be."[18] Forms of liberalism that support the placid acceptance of others nullify the differences between peoples in ways that are dismissive. Taylor continues, "Individuals are nodes in synchronic and diachronic webs of relation."[19] Unlike conservatism, which often seeks to draw diachronic lines of "either/or" between ideological systems and their adherents, and liberalism, which is known for its "both/and" demands for equality to such an extreme that differences are essentially nullified and forgotten, Taylor urges a relational "neither/nor" that affirms and undermines at the same time.

Slovenian philosopher and social critic Slavoj Žižek critiques liberal individualism as well, preferring the Hegelian idea of the "break." He believes that the most popular tenets of liberalism are far too comforting and soft, and he argues instead for a return to radical action that is powerful enough to institute change.[20] For Žižek, liberalism is simply too self-appeasing and tame to actually effect change; it predominantly serves to placate our desires for justice rather than help us accomplish anything that might be construed as different.

If emergence Christianity is to radically enact or incarnate transformative change—as it purportedly desires to do—then it will have to face its overwhelming similarities to classical liberalism and move beyond them.

Escaping the Big Tent

The Internet makes everything from pornography to postmodernism accessible to any and to everyone. Blogs, wikis, Twitter, Facebook, and the like have significantly challenged hierarchical economies of thought, publicity, and the "celebrity." Young kids hit it big on YouTube, becoming household names and oft-quoted catchphrases. Movie stars make friends with their fellow Internet-addicted fans. Bloggers gain bigger followings than long-established newspapers, providing commentary on every event from fashion to fascism and pop culture to politics—as if such things were truly so separate.

Postmodernism, like TOMS Shoes or the iPad, is unfortunately hip. This means that some who deeply desire to be hip like to throw the "p-word" around. It has become the only socially acceptable way to talk about thinking, culture, and even the church. Throw in a digital dash of virtual reality, and one finds an overwhelming amount of postmodern hype plastered all over the Internet. In emergent circles, such hype almost always ends up sounding like classical liberalism and the promotion of "tolerance," all done with a faddish nod toward the epistemological humility often associated with Derrida's deconstruction.

Oddly enough, the road to popularity in emergent Christianity is lined with flashy billboards with giant smiling faces and speech balloons loaded with postmodern jargon. It is worrisome that the combination of postmodernism and the Internet has been "commodified" through global capitalism into one more way to make a name for oneself. The Internet makes the world smaller; it closes the gap between those who are "famous" and those who are not. Public figures interact on a daily basis with average Janes and Joes. Becoming well known is part and parcel to the American dream, and it is getting easier by the minute.

What I find most appealing about Taylor's approach to postmodernism is that it results in the ubiquity of art that is deeply rooted in imagination and creativity. So it seems tragic to me to hop on board the bandwagon in order to make a name for oneself, *particularly at the cost of exploring and creating in one's own context.* I am making an open call to those within emergence Christianity who seek to become blogging celebrities and authors: Stop trying to gain recognition for your creations and just be content to create. Stop selling your religion for traffic and hits. Live art. Love *the* impossible. Don't substitute the gleam in the Pan's eye for subtle forms of consumeristic capitalism that are enamored with a big tent. Imagine what's beyond Neverland.

When I step back and think about it, I can't help but wonder how we are in the midst of a "return to 'big tent' Christianity," like Clayton suggests. It seems to me that there is no tent, and perhaps there shouldn't be. All the talk of the big top is a strange insistence to return to something that never was and could never possibly *be.* Neverland has never been seen, and when what was seen was called Neverland, the trace excused itself out the back door unnoticed, and the Pan immediately began to imagine again.

But if we want to speak of Christianity, there is a table. It's a table established by the Incarnated God, who seemed to think that becoming something as simple as a human being was not enough. This God became present in bread and wine, remembered as broken and poured out. Like the crucifixion, the continuous breaking of bread as the body and spilling of wine as blood is the institution that undoes institutions, serving as a perpetual reminder that we can never access Neverland, and necessarily so. God undoes God's own Godness in the Incarnation, and the Incarnation is undone in the crucifixion and, I would suggest, in the breaking of bread. In further reversals, the crucified God is resurrected, and the bread and wine provide life for the church. Rather than a big tent under which we can all gather in the name of congeniality, there is a Table we gather around in shock and in horror as the notion of God is provocatively put to death and consumed. Around this Table, surrounded by God knows who, we realize that not only is there no tent, but there is no Christianity.[21]

What is most appalling to me is that I have participated in what I hope to undo. I have grounded the Pan in order to try to make a point. I, like Paul, am certainly "foremost" amongst the sinners I might condemn (1 Tim. 1:15). So I return to the words of Kierkegaard with which I began, in the most (con)trite hopes that such words might be true and might represent some part of my own salvation: "*Understand that to write a book and revoke it is something else than not writing it at all; that to write a book that does not claim importance for anybody is something else than leaving it unwritten.*"

Notes

[1] Søren Kierkegaard, *Concluding Unscientific Postscript to the Philosophical Crumbs*, ed. Alastair Hannay (Cambridge: Cambridge University, 2009), Kindle Electronic Edition: "Appendix Understanding with the reader," Location 12856–12863.

[2] See Dave Tomlinson, *The Post-Evangelical* (Grand Rapids, Mich.: Zondervan, 2003).

[3] See Tony Jones, *The New Christians: Dispatches from the Emergent Frontier* (San Francisco: Jossey Bass, 2008), 8, 20–21.

[4] Eddie Gibbs and Ryan K. Bolger, *Emerging Churches: Creating Christian Community in Postmodern Cultures* (Grand Rapids, Mich.: Baker Academic, 2005), 34–39; Tony Campolo and Brian McLaren, *Adventures in Missing the Point* (Grand Rapids, Mich.: Zondervan, 2003), 275–82. Although there are attempts by some to move totally beyond such negative definitions, it seems difficult–if not impossible–to escape. For example, Kester Brewin, who is cited by Gibbs and Bolger as one who hopes to rely on positive rather than negative definitions, has recently written about his fears of the emerging church reverting to corrupt institutions. In doing so, he clearly defines himself by what aspects of institutional churches he is strongly opposed to and offers a few helpful ideological suggestions to resolve those issues. My only concern about such things is that it may be precisely in the moments that we have negatively and certainly closed off certain possibilities that the Postmodern Pan begins to imagine about just those things that are now "off limits." For more of Brewin's recent thoughts, see his blog at http://kesterbrewin.com, particularly his series of posts at the end of June 2010.

[5] Peter Rollins, *How (Not) to Speak of God* (Brewster, Mass.: Paraclete, 2006), 39.

[6] I should be careful to clarify here. I say "some" for two reasons: First, not all who self-identify as "emergents" would agree with this general ethos–some who would disagree wouldn't be doing so with complete honesty; others would. Second, some who would truly fit the bill would never label themselves as "emergent." In fact, some who are quintessentially "emergent" (by most definitions) have never heard the term and wouldn't much care to.

[7] See Yvonne Sherwood, *Derrida's Bible: Reading a Page of Scripture with a Little Help from Derrida* (New York: Palgrave Macmillan, 2004), 9.

[8] See John D. Caputo, *On Religion* (London: Routledge, 2001).

[9] Mark C. Taylor, *After God* (Chicago: University of Chicago, 2007), 154. Taylor appropriates Hegel's understanding of Trinity to develop an interrelation between conceptions of God, the self, and the world. He writes, "The Trinity, in other words, not only represents the inner life of God but also discloses the truth about the self and world. When rationally comprehended, the Trinity reveals that God, self, and world are three-in-one and one-in-three–each becomes itself in and through the other, and none can be itself apart from the others."

[10] Jacques Derrida, "Structure, Sign and Play in the Discourse of the Human Sciences," in *Critical Theory Since 1965*, eds. Hazard Adams and Leroy Searle (Tallahassee: University Presses of Florida, 1986), 85.

[11] Jacques Derrida, "*Différance,*" in *Critical Theory Since 1965*, 133. Emphasis on "exceeded" mine.

[12] I should note that I do not intend to associate emergent Christianity with liberalism in order to demonize it as some of its more conservative detractors do regularly. Instead, I hope to problematize its claims to "being postmodern" and to point out the weaknesses of Enlightenment-based liberalism, which are just as "modern" as those of Enlightenment-based conservatism, and the necessity of moving past both conservativism and liberalism.

[13] See especially Taylor, *After God*, 33–42, 130–85.

[14] Jones, *New Christians*, 7.

[15] Jones, *New Christians*, 8.

[16] Jones has been especially vocal on this point. See Tony Jones, "How I Went from There to Here: Same Sex Marriage Blogalogue," The New Christians Blog, posted November 19, 2008, http://blog.beliefnet.com/tonyjones/2008/11/same-sex-marriage-blogalogue-h.html (accessed August 11, 2010); Tony Jones, "An Honest Question About Homosexuality," The New Christians Blog, posted on August 4, 2009, http://blog.beliefnet.com/tonyjones/2009/08/an-honest-question-about-gays.html (accessed August 11, 2010); Tony Jones, "What I've

Learned About Gays and the Church," The New Christians Blog, posted on August 13, 2009, http://blog.beliefnet.com/tonyjones/2009/08/what-ive-learned-about-gays-an.html (accessed on August 11, 2010); Tony Jones, "Just Another Means of Division," Patheos Blog, posted July 7, 2009, http://www.patheos.com/Resources/Additional-Resources/Just-Another-Means-of -Division.html?b=0 (accessed on August 11, 2010); Tony Jones, "The Complexity of Gender," The New Christians Blog, posted on August 20, 2009, http://blog.beliefnet.com/tonyjones/ 2009/08/the-complexity-of-gender.html (accessed on August 11, 2010); Tony Jones, "More on the Complexity of Gender," The New Christians Blog, posted on August 21, 2009, http://blog .beliefnet.com/tonyjones/2009/08/more-on-the-complexity-of-gend.html (accessed on August 11, 2010).

[17] Philip Clayton, *Transforming Christian Theology: For Church and Society* (Minneapolis: Fortress, 2010), 65.

[18] Taylor, *After God*, 231.

[19] Ibid., 239.

[20] Slavoj Žižek, *In Defense of Lost Causes* (London: Verso, 2008), 6–7.

[21] What I mean by this is something similar to the more theoretical aspects of works by scholars such as Ananda Abeysekara or Michael L. Satlow who, studying Sri Lankan Buddhism and the history of Judaism respectively, suggest that faith traditions have no unified history or essentialist definition. See Ananda Abeysekara, *The Colors of the Robe* (Columbia: University of South Carolina Press, 2002) or Michael L. Satlow, *Creating Judaism: History, Tradition, Practice* (New York: Columbia University Press, 2006).

9

Peekaboo Jesus

Looking for an Emergent Savior in a Post-Christendom Culture

Ross Lockhart

As I went through the city and looked carefully at the objects of your worship, I found among them an altar with the inscription, "To an unknown god." What therefore you worship as unknown, this I proclaim to you.
—ACTS 17:23

The shopping mall food court buzzed with the usual Monday-afternoon mix of chaos and energy. As a sea of retail-enticed humanity flowed all around me, I sat with my elbows on a small square table, hands over my face in yet another invigorating game of peekaboo with my two young children. All good things must come to an end, of course, and after several rounds of "hands open, hands closed" the children became restless and started squirming in their seats. It was clearly time for a snack. It didn't take long for Emily and Jack to settle down, this time distracted by an intoxicating mix of sippy cups and goldfish crackers that immobilizes toddlers for minutes at a time.

With this brief reprieve from "Daddy duty," I relaxed in my preformed plastic chair and eavesdropped on the conversation beside me. Two young moms, having distracted their own kids with snacks, compared notes on all the activities they had signed their children up for during the autumn. Their conversation quickly escalated into a game of "one-upMOMship," where dance lessons trumped piano lessons and gymnastics vied for importance over hockey. Just when the competing schedules seemed to stall, one mother played the trump card in this bizarre comparing of notes–swimming lessons. The other mother, her face contorted in a mixture of defeat and envy, asked with astonishment, "How did you possibly find time for swimming lessons?" "It was easy," gloated the triumphant mom in response, "we go down to the pool on Sunday mornings and all three kids have their lessons while my husband and I relax with a coffee and the newspaper. We just couldn't think of anything more important to do as a family on a Sunday morning." The other mom looked impressed. "Besides," continued the young woman, leaning in close as if to share a secret, "*what they learn at the pool will save their life.*"

A few years earlier I might have responded in shock to such a statement by tumbling off my hard plastic chair, spilling goldfish crackers and apple juice in a tremendous crash of public embarrassment. Not anymore. Of course, once upon a time we may have had the knee-jerk response of saying to that young mother, "Nothing to do on a Sunday morning? You *should* be in church and your children in Sunday school!" But that was back in Christendom–those glory days that as a Gen X pastor you always hear about in your "teacup" pastoral visits with elderly church members. "Reverend, I remember when there were a thousand children in the Sunday school and we had to set up special classrooms in the janitor's closet and the bathroom stall just to fit everyone in." The funny thing, however, is that those of us in leadership of this next generation don't remember those days. We recall Sunday school as sitting with a few other kids in a mold-infested, crumbling, 1950s-era Christian Education wing with a faded "blue-eye and blond-hair Christ" poster in the corner, aimlessly doodling on "connect the dot" Jesus coloring sheets to keep us busy. Christendom is not a part of *our* memory and that may be a huge advantage in the years ahead. Instead of trying to "get back" to the glory days, we look forward in hope, trusting that just as the Almighty went ahead of the people like a pillar of cloud by day and a pillar of fire by night, so too our Triune God is moving forward–the holy ground ahead of us saturated with prevenient grace.

Those mothers in the food court simply remind us that we now live and minister in a world in which Jesus is no longer as easily recognized as in the days when the culture conveyed the gospel (or a distorted version of it). It's like we are playing a game of peekaboo Jesus in the communities where we now live, work, and play. Certainly, as a thirty-something minister in Canada's largest Protestant denomination, I've learned over the years to accept and adapt to ministry in our post-Christendom context. While our country may snuggle geographically close to the United States, the role of religion in the public arena is far more European here than American. For example, there is not nearly as strong a link between the religious right and our political system. While the American president is expected to close a speech with "God bless America," the media and members of any political party would soundly scold the Canadian prime minister for invoking the Divine. Church-going has been in a steady decline since the 1960s, and now less than 20 percent of the population regularly attends worship. Where I live and minister, in West Vancouver, British Columbia, church attendance is estimated at only 2 to 5 percent of the population. As the old joke goes, the hardest thing about preaching "heaven" in Vancouver is that most people think they're already there. It's like Jesus is hiding behind one of those gorgeous West Coast Douglas fir trees, up the mountainside behind my home, playing a curious game of peekaboo with the world he came to save.

A Generation Raised without Religion

Not far from my home, through those beautiful trees in West Vancouver, lives Douglas Coupland, the famous cultural guru and author of the paradigm-shifting work *Generation X.* In his novel *Life After God*, written just a few years after *Generation X*, he makes the bold claim that those of us in our thirties and forties today in North America are "the first generation raised without religion."[1] Nowhere is that more true in general than here in Canada; nowhere is that more true in particular than in the West Coast city of Vancouver. When I compare my ministry today to other pulpits I've filled in places like Northern Ireland (where the troubles there put a unique European freeze on secularization) or rural pockets of eastern Canada (where Christian memory still lingers), here on the West Coast I am fascinated by what is truly a "post-Christendom" context. Vancouver and its twin city Seattle, just south of the border, reflect a culture and mindset that is sure to spread all across the continent in the years to come. As churches are sold and turned into condominiums, bulldozed for shopping malls (our new cathedrals) or, my personal favorite, when Mount Zion United Church was sold and converted into "Church Key Brewery" (with the slogan "Have you been to church lately?"), there is a growing sense of defeat and despair among the faithful. If Jesus is no longer visible and insists on playing this game of peekaboo with us, are we in the final inning of a hard-fought but ultimately futile gospel game?

Teaching an Old Dogma New Tricks

Hardly. I am discovering some encouraging signs of hope in this post-Christendom ministry. In many ways walking through the streets of my parish I feel a little like Paul strolling through the streets of Athens long ago. It is probably helpful for us to remember a time in the life of the church when Jesus also played a game of peekaboo with the culture. Long before cathedrals, schools, or hockey rinks bore the name of "St. Paul," the newly converted Saul of Tarsus wandered wide eyed in the idol-congested streets of Athens in Acts 17. It was hard for the struggling apostle to see signs of Jesus in that culture of sophistication and spiritual syncretism. Saul turned Paul, through an eye-shattering epiphany and the gentle touch of affirming Ananias, ran into a believer's brick wall. Paul's usual technique of setting up shop and sharing the gospel through a local synagogue breaks down in the city of Athens. He looks around for touchstones of the Savior and becomes frustrated with playing a game of peekaboo Jesus. As Paul considers his options, he looks at the culture around him and discards the lens of judgment and suspicion, replacing it with a viewpoint of grace and opportunity. For Paul, it's time to teach some *old dogmas new tricks.* Paul preaches evangelistically to the philosophers of the city by quoting "pop-culture" Greek poets and appealing to them differently than if he were speaking to a Jewish audience. Paul accepts the peekaboo Jesus reality and tries successfully to pry one hand off their eyes in order to see the unknown God in their midst.

Paul's ability to adapt both his evangelistic preaching style and method is a comfort and a challenge for those of us standing in our own contemporary Areopagus-like pulpits before a less-than-homogeneous congregation who are trying to figure out what they believe and what difference their lives are making in the world. For we too live in an age of overwhelming personal choice and freedom when it comes to what to believe and which values we allow to influence our moral decision making. The unknown God is everywhere around us. From the empty pew to the bar stool to the bus bench to the cold, hard plastic seat in the food court, we hear sincere and spiritually hollow statements, "We just couldn't think of anything more important to do on a Sunday morning." While another generation might chastise folks for not having their children in church school on a Sunday morning, we know that there are other ways of prying one hand off their eyes to end the game of peekaboo with Jesus. Just as Paul did not blast the Athenians for worshiping so many gods and instead found a playful and clever way to connect with people through the culture, so too God calls us to be more imaginative and flexible in proclaiming the gospel in this new ministry setting. I have no doubt that the young mom was totally sincere when she whispered to her friend in confessional tones, "What they learn at the pool will save their life." I began to wonder, however, if I invited her to one of our worship services on a Sunday, whether our members would view children's participation in church with the same urgency and passion as the life-saving lessons offered at the pool. Do we believe any longer that worship, preaching, and Christian education can literally save or transform one's life and mend this broken world?

Apostles, Atheists, and Apathy

Just at the moment when we should be standing up and pointing with excitement toward the unknown God, we have hit a low ebb in the life and work of most mainline denominations. When we stand to speak we are so often overwhelmed by discouragement and disillusionment in pulpit and pew that the best we have to offer is tongue-tied apostles suffering from liturgical laryngitis outside of the safety of our stained-glass sanctuaries. It would be like Paul standing up at the Areopagus and, just at the moment when people lean in with a genuine curiosity to hear "this new teaching," the apostle from Tarsus freezes with stage fright.

Some of our church leaders have privately confessed that operating for so long out of a "hermeneutics of suspicion" has left them feeling hollow and with little grace left to offer. Others have whispered that the dramatic change in both church and community culture has left them overwhelmed. As one retiring minister declared with resignation in his voice, "I was trained to be a caretaker of an institution, not an apostle for a movement. I don't know how to do ministry anymore." Still others have shared their shock at the growing presence of militant atheism in the media and feel ill equipped to speak faith in a "secular world." Of course, when Paul does present his gospel story in Acts 17 there is a mixed reaction from the crowd. Some scoffed at what he had to say, yet others were keen to hear him speak more about this unknown God in Jesus Christ. We too have our scoffers in the post-Christendom West with such vocal and virulent atheists as Richard Dawkins, Sam Harris, and Philip Pullman. Instead of first-century Greeks at the Areopagus, these angry atheists are attracting an unusual amount of media attention these days. At least the Greek scoffers seemed a little more polite! Today's militant atheists do not appear to be winning over the masses, however, with their straw man theology of God and their need to speak only about what they are against instead of what they are for. I find that the majority of young adults I share conversations with at the coffee shop, treadmill, or seawall are the furthest thing from angry with Christ. Our biggest obstacle today is apathy, not anger. Today's young adults, raised without religion, are surprisingly open to a story they have never heard before, just like the Athenians listening to Paul in the Areopagus, eager to hear more about Jesus.

So if our mischievous Messiah insists on returning to this peekaboo Jesus game, what does that mean for the practice of ministry in his church? How do we connect with this new generation of the children of God when the structures and style of our congregational life seem so foreign and inaccessible to the culture around us? After all, as Rob Bell concludes in *Velvet Elvis*, "Jesus is more compelling than ever. More inviting, more true, more mysterious than ever. The problem isn't with Jesus; the problem is what comes with Jesus."[2]

These emergent and missionally minded questions began to stir across the United Church of Canada a few years ago. After years of discussion, debate, and dithering, the General Council, made up of elected lay and clergy representatives, dipped deep into our denomination's "rainy day fund" and gave birth to the "Emerging Spirit campaign." Like a *Mission Impossible* agent, I was "activated" to be part of the "Canadian Emerging Church team." Summoned to "HQ," a nondescript high-rise office tower in Toronto that hides our national office (perhaps it's part of the peekaboo Jesus approach?), a sample of "emergent leaders" in the denomination shared thoughts, experiences, and hopes for mission.

An Emerging Spirit for an Emergent Church?

Emerging Spirit, conceived as a program of the United Church of Canada, was designed to nurture relationships with Canadians between the ages of thirty and forty-five who were not actively involved in a faith community. The following mandate was established:

1. Raise awareness and recognition of the values and beliefs of the United Church of Canada among thirty- to forty-five-year-olds.
2. Create a willingness among non–church goers to discover a United Church congregation.
3. Renew a sense of positive identity and enthusiasm for mission among United Church congregations.
4. Equip United Church congregations for ministry in the new Canadian context.[3]

The Emerging Spirit campaign, launched in November 2006, was divided into three significant areas of work. The first part of the program was developed in light of marketing research done by Environics and TerraNova Marketing Strategies, and in partnership with Smith Roberts and Co. Creative Communications, and focused on provocative advertisements for publication in major Canadian magazines that challenged Canadians to reflect on spiritual and moral issues in society. These advertisements in turn directed people to the second part of the campaign: http://www.wondercafe .ca. The new website, set up for Emerging Spirit, was designed as an interactive forum for young Canadians to discuss moral and spiritual issues in a safe and nonjudgmental environment. The website included profiles of United Church congregations and the ability for online users to locate a congregation near them. The third and final part of the campaign involved emergent pastors traveling the country, equipping congregations and their leaders to engage in missional conversations and actions within their own context. It was here, as a speaker at these weekend events that brought clergy and lay leaders together, that I encountered the hopes, dreams, and too often the despair present in so many of our congregations. People of good faith came frustrated with their congregation's inability to connect with young adults and felt stymied in regard to how they might transform their congregational culture and structures to be more accommodating and truly hospitable.

Many of the congregations I resourced remained trapped in the postwar 1950s model of "membership churches" that existed primarily for those in the pews rather than those outside the walls of the church. It reminded me of Michael Foss's delightful imagery in *Power Surge*, where he complains that too many mainline Protestant churches approach their ministry like belonging to a health club:

> One becomes a member of a health club by paying dues (in a church, the monthly or weekly offering). Having paid their dues, the members expect the services of the club to be at their disposal. Exercise equipment, weight room, aerobics classes, an indoor track, swimming pool–all there for them, with a trained staff to see that they benefit by them. Members may bring a guest on occasion, but only those who pay their dues have a right to the use of the facilities and the attention of the staff. There is no need to belabor the point. Many of the people who sit in the pews on Sunday have come to think of church membership in ways analogous to how the fitness crowd views membership in a health club.[4]

This perception of the church as a private club lingers outside the walls of the church as well. Recently, my wife, Laura, officiated at a funeral in our church for a young woman who died in a tragic accident. The church was full of young adults with little or no church connection. The next day Laura received an e-mail from a young mother who said how meaningful she found the service to be. She wanted to know if it was all right if she came to church on Sunday with her husband and children. "Am I allowed to just show up on a Sunday?" came the sincere question from a shaken woman, "or is it like a private club where you need to be sponsored in?" With impressions like that out in the community, it's no wonder mainline churches are struggling with Sunday attendance.

One of the major discoveries from the Emerging Spirit program, however, is that low Sunday church attendance should not be taken as a sign that faith is no longer important to people. Reginald Bibby, Canada's leading sociologist of religion, reported that at a time when only 20 percent of Canadians say they attend religious services just about every week, some 80 percent of Canadian adults and teenagers assert positive belief in God. Furthermore, this belief in God has remained virtually the same since 1975, despite the fact that attendance at religious services dropped between 1975 and 2000 from about 30 percent of the population to about 20 percent.[5] Nor were young Canadians simply abandoning God for mammon. Emerging Spirit research revealed that young Canadians between the ages of thirty and forty-five who were not involved in church still placed the greatest value on relationships rather than financial success. When asked by a national polling agency what is most important in one's life, three-quarters responded by saying children, family, and friends rather than work or financial situation. Whether online or face-to-face, people were seeking meaningful relationships. Yet in a sad stroke of irony, Leonard Sweet argues that in the last century churches have been moving away from this kind of relational space:

> Churches increasingly became not relational space but propositional place. Instead of going there to connect with God and with others in meaningful relationship, people started going to church to be convinced of transcendent truth, or, if they already numbered among the convinced, to have their beliefs and religious convictions confirmed from the pulpit. The church lost credibility as a place for sacred relationship when it chose to specialize in formulating and advancing a better spiritual argument. The result is that people who came to the meeting house got connected with ideas and formulas more than they did with God and with other people.[6]

While I agree with Sweet's perspective, and deeply believe that a mark of the emergent church is that people today are hungry to "experience God" and not just "hear about God," this is where the Emerging Spirit campaign hit a wee speed bump. The Emerging Spirit campaign *rightly* placed a strong emphasis upon hospitality and inclusivity. A great deal of the campaign was focused on creating a relational, not propositional, space—whether online or in the pew. We know that a hallmark of the emergent church in many different places is its emphasis on relationships rather than regulations. And yet, the challenge came in deciding what the next step would be. Like Paul standing at the Areopagus, somebody has to say something; somebody has to make the connection to the unknown God, our peekaboo Jesus. It would be like going all out to welcome guests at a dinner party, setting the dinner table with fine china and making the guests feel at home by offering them predinner cocktails, all the while knowing the host or hostess was locked upstairs in the en suite bathroom, not able to be "revealed." A little awkward, don't you agree? If the goal is to build a relational space instead of a propositional place, then surely we need to move from hospitality into conversation with our host or hostess.

The "J" Word(s)

My experience of the Emerging Spirit campaign is that most people shied away from engaging Jesus and opted instead for our other, safer "J Word"–Justice. Like most liberal Protestant mainline denominations, the United Church of Canada has wrestled with our J words over the years. Our church was born in 1925 out of a mix of denominations that were steeped in the social gospel movement.[7] Names like J. S. Woodsworth, Nellie McClung, or Salem Bland were "the north of the 49th parallel" equivalent of social gospel giants like Walter Rauschenbusch and Washington Gladden. As a result, there has always been a wonderfully strong social justice streak in our denomination. When our church was formed, however, the national committee responsible for social justice was twinned with an unlikely ally—Evangelism. The Board of Evangelism and Social Service was a force to be reckoned with, influencing government social policy and essentially operating out of a dual mandate to know Christ and make him known through justice. Somewhere over the decades, the evangelism part faded away, and we are left today with what often appears to be an unbalanced approach to mission in these emergent times. Leonard Sweet is right in that we have become a propositional place rather than a relational space, but the belief system we are too often selling to drowsy octogenarians in the pews is a vague notion of justice that is not rooted in the revelation of God.

Now, speaking as one who was raised in a "dyed-in-the-wool United Church family" where our socialist-leaning, gay-friendly, antinuclear marching beliefs, and so on, were taken for granted, I realize that I am skating on thin ice here. And yet, I worry that our proud heritage of social justice is in danger of becoming a millstone tied around our necks in these emergent times unless we rediscover a balance of evangelism *and* social justice. With a whimper rather than a bang, the practice of the Emerging Spirit campaign for many steered safely toward arm's-length discussion rather than commitment to discipleship and *generic justice* rather than *generative faith* in Jesus. It appeared that too often providing hospitality came at the expense of proclamation of the gospel, community without the confession of sin, and relationships without need of resurrection. I completely understand why many in the emergent church argue for "conversation rather than conversion," but my extreme post-Christendom context conversion is happening all the time.[8] A culture that strives every minute for you to convert from Pepsi to Coke, Gap to Calvin Klein, and Cialis to Viagra is anything but benign. As Bryan Stone reminds us, we live in a "culture of conversion" where in "every direction we turn, we are offered the promise of 'makeover,' whether of body, face, wardrobe, career, marriage, home, personality, or soul."[9] Driven primarily by the powerful, quasi-religious influence of consumerism and empire, "places of belonging" today—outside the church—exercise considerable control and influence over the population that serves as a formidable challenge to the gospel.[10] As Stone concludes:

> To be converted is not something strange or out of the ordinary in our world. It is roughly equivalent to the air we breathe. In fact, part of what makes the call to Christian conversion strike us as so radical and invasive today is the level to which we have become acclimated to our ongoing conversion and formation by a staggering range of powers that contradict Christian faith and community and serve ends other than the shalom of God's reign.[11]

If the culture in a post-Christendom context does not convey the gospel message (and why should we expect it to?), then the Holy Spirit surely has a special role for ambassadors of Christ to play in the game of peekaboo Jesus. Don't get me wrong: How we live (justice) is essential, but so too is being able to articulate our faith in the One who gives us life (evangelism).[12] Peter Rollins, a Christian philosopher from the Ikon collective in Belfast, Northern Ireland, highlights the unique gift that the emergent church offers our understanding of evangelism:

> We need not look far to find that our religious communities influenced as they are by the movement known as modernity, have tended to emphasize the idea of "being" and "destination": one *becomes* a Christian, *joins* a church and *is* saved. From this idea of destination flows our understanding of evangelism as a means of sharing our faith and encouraging others to embrace it for themselves. For those involved in the emerging conversation, this view distorts the deeper meaning of evangelism, for once we acknowledge that we are *becoming* Christian, *becoming* Church and *being* saved, then the other can be seen as a possible instrument of our further conversion. Even a brief reflection upon the darkness in our own lives bears testimony to the fact that we need to be evangelized as much, if not more, than those around us.[13]

The stereotypical "evangelistic" language of "When were you saved?" or "Have you been washed in the blood of the lamb?" are as foreign to us in the emergent church today as a Beta tape player is to a new iPad. Instead, the evangelism I am longing to integrate with social justice is a deep and sincere articulation of faith that believes that in the process of sharing not only will the hearer be changed by grace, but so too the speaker. I am longing for the Spirit to move us to a place where evangelism and justice can mutually inform one another, where speaking about Jesus goes hand in hand with living for Jesus. Perhaps this is where the emergent church can offer old, mainline denominations the greatest hope.

Like Paul in Athens, we too engage our peekaboo Jesus in this confused world, with a passion for sharing our faith and seeing justice take root. What might we strive to do in order to offer an emergent-like message similar to the one Paul delivered in Athens? While there are several responses to this question, I wish to explore the ways that preaching can still play a transformative role in a post-Christendom context—a role that will help listeners enter into conversation with the host or hostess who has been removed from the conversation far too often. Over the last several years of playing my own little peekaboo Jesus game I have noticed three critical areas for proclamation.

Biblical Preaching

David Bartlett, my former teacher, argues that "Right preaching is the interpretation of Scripture. There is much excellent Christian speech that is not preaching [because] unless it is an interpretation of the text or texts that the congregation has just heard read aloud, it is not preaching."[14] And yet, while scripture is central to proclamation, the Bible, like peekaboo Jesus, remains removed and inaccessible to most. When I ask newcomers to describe the Bible to me, they say it is "clumsy," "foreign," "awkward," "frightening," "overwhelming," and "cryptic." It would appear that while homiletical approaches of the last century placed a greater emphasis upon preaching that engaged the biblical text and provided cultural background and context through historical criticism, our church members remain uncomfortable handling the sacred texts themselves. As Ken, a young high school principal, recently said, "The Bible has always felt clumsy to me. That's why you have to teach me Sunday morning when you preach. It's through your sermons that I learn more about the Bible and who God is."

When I reflected on my research with young adults and their desire for (and struggle with) scripture, it became clear that they wrestled not only with a lack of knowledge of the stories of faith but also with a desire to know that the message was indeed good news for *their* lives. Sarah, a young executive with an international courier company, summarized this tension in the following way:

> I struggle with the Bible itself when I read it on my own because there are parts of it that seem contradictory and brutal. I don't want to pick and choose what to believe so I find that when I read the Bible on my own without knowledge of the context it is frustrating. Going to church and especially hearing a meaningful sermon helps me put all the pieces together.[15]

Dan, a young high school teacher, echoed Sarah's call for help, saying:

> Teach the faith. We are on a personal journey, but how can people decide if they don't understand the basic tenets of the faith? If you stop teaching the faith, then I can find no shortage of other "gurus" who will teach me a way of life that does not lead to participation in a church. (Dan Douglas, personal communication)

With church attendance in decline across Canada, the young adults who are present in our pews on a Sunday morning taught me that they are cautiously searching for the bread of life that will not leave them hungry and the streams of living water that will not lead to parched lips. It is the life-saving gospel of Jesus Christ found in scripture that can fulfill humanity's desires, curb sinful inclinations, redeem a lost and lonely generation, and establish a relationship with the risen One that can and will transform their lives.

When we reflect on the need for emergent preaching to be biblical, we draw on the best of the historical-critical method and confirm that preachers need to educate their congregations on the context and cultural influences that shaped the biblical story, but that is not all. Even more important, biblical preaching takes the listener into the biblical story for a purpose—to introduce them to the life-changing presence of Jesus Christ and enable the listener to experience the grace of the cross in light of the judgment in this world. Biblical preaching is essential in this post-Christendom world as a way to point toward the unknown God in our midst—and by our preaching we pray that Martin Luther was right when he claimed that preaching is an encounter where Christ is absorbed—that is to say, embodied—in the congregation.[16]

Relevant Preaching

While Paul made great connections with the culture in Athens quoting poets in his game of peekaboo Jesus with the Greeks, our attempt to be relevant today with the gospel often draws scorn and anger from church leaders. Like a flyswatter in a moist hand on a hot, humid August day, I've encountered countless pastors over the years who are ready to strike the fly in the ointment called "relevancy." And yet, I believe our preaching needs to connect with our listeners on cognitive and emotive levels. Proclaiming the gospel to newcomers and longtime members alike requires a curious mix of practicality and mystery. To put it differently, relevant preaching requires some application to our everyday, ordinary lives, but when it appears to be a cookie-cutter/one-size-fits-all approach to life, in which God is too easily accessible, the listener's finely tuned "postmodern ear" becomes suspicious.[17] The preacher must remain with the congregation as both the "teaching elder" and the "seeker" at the same time, with the understanding that these two roles are not mutually exclusive. Relevant preaching in a postmodern context does not claim to have all the answers, but instead connects with others on a journey that is continually unfolding, particularly by entering into the stories of scripture that can profoundly shape our lives. When preachers try to claim overarching certainty, or an absolute mastery of the narrative that doesn't leave room for a wide variety of experiences, they lose credibility with postmodern listeners and are no longer viewed as relevant. As John D. Caputo argues in his deconstructionist approach to postmodernism and the church:

> The spiritual journey on which we are embarked is, we say, a journey of *faith.* That means that those who insist they *know* the way have programmed their lives on automatic pilot. They are knowers (Gnostics) who have taken themselves out of the game. They are like vacationers eager for an adventure, to set forth into the unknown—but not without an air-conditioned Hummer with four-wheel drive, an experienced guide, and reservations at a five star hotel.[18]

Relevant preaching to the times we live in is especially important in our context when the church no longer enjoys the privilege of being at the center of society. For so many Canadians, the church, and its Christian message, has become irrelevant to pursuing a meaningful life. If, when the Holy Spirit calls people back into the church on a Sunday morning by personal tragedy, spiritual curiosity, or social duty (Christmas, Easter, baptisms, funerals, and so forth), will the church's supposed "irrelevant message" be confirmed or will the skillful preacher be able to shatter the widely held stereotype with a relevant message? As my friend Grant, who lives in Ontario, wrote in a recent e-mail:

> We attended church intermittently over the years and usually due to family events or public holidays. My image of the church was a place full of stuffy people and irrelevant teachings. What we discovered is that the warmth of the congregation and the personality of the minister combined with the relevance of the message makes all the difference in the world.

The challenge for preachers in a peekaboo Jesus culture is to convey a Christian message that is suitably applicable to their lives while leaving room for their ongoing soul struggles and new discoveries of faith. It is, in short, preaching that values the questions of faith as much as the answers that are discovered along the way. It contains a combination of practicality and mystery. Preachers who wish to be relevant in the postmodern world must necessarily wrestle with a homiletical ambiguity that values the way stories shape our lives but resists absolutizing them.

The United Church of Canada has, ironically, been the most progressive and relevant of all the Canadian churches regarding social issues, yet it has struggled to proclaim its theology in a way that is both understood and accepted by the mainstream society. A recent article in *The Globe and Mail*, our national newspaper, highlighted this concern perfectly. Regarding the city of London, Ontario's decision to ban bottled water, columnist John Barber wrote: "Fittingly, it was the United Church of Canada that got the process going two years ago when it boldly drove plastic water bottles out of its temples. Although such mainstream moralists have a difficult time with the big questions–for example, the existence of God–they can still tell black from white when they see it."[19] Even while in the forefront of social action, The United Church is still dismissed as an irrelevant mainstream moralist! As a result, our proclamation must balance the need to be prophetic and countercultural in its call for an alternative lifestyle grounded in the reign of God, with the need to express that call in terms that are understandable and compelling for the people of the day.

Authentic Preaching

Making sure our proclamations contain a deep sense of authenticity is both critical and challenging for Christian leaders since it requires the preacher's character and discipleship to influence the content and delivery of the message in our postmodern context. David Lose argues that preaching "that seeks to be both faithful to the Christian tradition and responsive to our pluralistic, postmodern context is best understood as the public practice of confessing faith in Jesus Christ."[20] Lose claims that confessional preaching means reclaiming a Christian practice that rests not on empirical proof but on a living confession of faith, leads not to certainty but to conviction, and lives not in the domain of knowledge and proof but rather in the realm of faithful assertion.[21] If Lose is correct, then the authenticity and character of the preacher are tied to the validity and passion of the proclamation in a postmodern context.

Michael Frost picks up on this theme of authenticity when he writes that church leaders must earn a right to be heard in the postmodern world:

> When we have no impressive buildings and no swollen budgets to sustain our work, often only then do we realize that the best we have to offer this post-Christendom world is the quality of our relationships, the power of our trustworthiness, and the wonder of our generosity . . . Is it too simplistic to say that we earn that right [to be heard] through our authentic lifestyles? In a culture yearning for authenticity—the real—the pressure is on us in the Christian community now more than ever to put our time and money where our mouth is and live what we preach.[22]

I recall a conversation with a newcomer to the church named Tanya, who is in her early thirties. During a small-group ministry exercise, I asked her what she felt the role of the sermon should be in worship. She replied,

> I choose church over Starbucks on a Sunday morning because of a need to be close to God. The reason I listen to the minister is because "I feel" that he/she has a relationship with God. Instead of being focused on speaking well or being knowledgeable *about* God or scripture, the minister is focused on letting God speak *through* him/her with real passion and excitement. God working through someone is never boring! (Tanya Cooper, personal communication)

I marvel at the emergent desire within my own congregation for passionate, biblical preaching that in the proclamation and living out of the gospel reflects an authenticity that this sin-sick and cynical world is longing to hear. That kind of proclamation of the unknown God will be heard in the food court or sports court, the classroom or locker room, the shopping mall or city hall.

The End of Peekaboo Jesus?

I recently spent the afternoon playing "hooky" from a preaching conference in Nashville, Tennessee, with my buddy and doctoral colleague Rhoda Montgomery of College Station, Texas. We decided to check out the Country Music Hall of Fame. With its soaring architecture and folksy greeters we felt right at home—it was like being welcomed into a big ol' church. As we worked our way through the museum we came to a special exhibit of the legendary country music star Brenda Lee, who is famous for such hits as "I'm Sorry" and "Rocking Around the Christmas Tree." It was fascinating looking at all the exhibits, old dresses and shoes, musical scores and album covers, pictures of her with other famous celebrities, and a handwritten note of appreciation from Elton John. Amazed by the collection of such a full and meaningful life, I turned to Rhoda and said, "Is Brenda Lee dead?" "I don't know, honey," replied Rhoda in her Texan drawl, "but she's either dead or buried alive under all this memorabilia." As we turned the corner and neared the end of the exhibit there was a crowd of senior citizen visitors gathered around a short, striking woman of a similar age. Seniors were jostling with one another for a picture with this mysterious stranger. Rhoda looked at me and we both exchanged a look of disbelief as we both asked the same question: "Is that the real Brenda Lee—alive after all?" Sure enough, as we approached, the living legend greeted us with a warm smile and embrace. "Hello, y'all," she beckoned, "come on over and get your picture with Brenda Lee." Rhoda and I stood there with goofy grins—utterly speechless. That doesn't happen to preachers very often.

Later, as we strolled down the street in silence, I thought about a story that Luke told at the end of his gospel about two followers of Jesus on a road with a signpost for Emmaus. I wondered whether those two disciples long ago who were playing their own game of peekaboo with Jesus shared that same feeling of astonishment. On that day the mysterious companion proclaimed a message that was biblical and relevant to their times, ultimately revealing his authentic identity in the breaking of the bread. Could it be that, even now, as we emerge from our stained-glass bunkers in the church (like a postmodern troglodyte from a prehistoric cave) to proclaim the unknown God, Jesus might meet us and put an end to his peekaboo ways? From the ordinary breaking of bread at a table long ago to the in-breaking of grace at an ordinary food court table of today, the world is soaked in Christ's revelation. Once thought dead, or at least buried alive under the church's memorabilia of dusty hymnbooks, diamond-encrusted cross earrings, and surplus WWJD bracelets in an old museum-like cathedral somewhere, could *we* witness the great emergence of the One who is life, grace, and joy eternal? Heaven only knows. But I can't wait to find out.

Notes

[1] Douglas Coupland, *Life After God* (New York: Pocket Books, 1994), 161.

[2] Rob Bell, *Velvet Elvis: Repainting the Christian Faith* (Grand Rapids, Mich.: Zondervan, 2005), 167.

[3] Lesley Harrison, ed. *Living the Welcome: The Journal* (Toronto: The United Church of Canada Publishing House, 2007), 7.

[4] Michael Foss, *Power Surge: Six Marks of Discipleship for a Changing Church* (Minneapolis: Fortress, 2000), 15.

[5] Reginald Bibby, *Restless Churches: How Canada's Churches Can Contribute to the Emerging Religious Renaissance* (Toronto: Novalis, 2004), 14–15.

[6] Leonard Sweet, *The Gospel According to Starbucks: Living with a Grande Passion* (Colorado Springs: WaterBrook Press, 2007), 132.

[7] The United Church of Canada consists of a union of Methodist, Presbyterian, and Congregationalist denominations that joined together in 1925.

[8] As my friend Rob Fennell has observed: Why is the commercial sector the only sphere of human society that is allowed to proselytize and convert? Which they plainly do, all the time.

[9] Bryan P. Stone, *Evangelism after Christendom: The Theology and Practice of Christian Witness* (Grand Rapids, Mich.: Brazos, 2007), 258.

[10] The World Alliance of Reformed Churches defines Empire as the convergence of economic, political, cultural, geographic, and military imperial interests, systems, and networks that seek to dominate political power and economic wealth. Empire crosses all boundaries, strips and reconstructs identities, subverts cultures, subordinates nation-states, and either marginalizes or co-opts religious communities.

[11] Stone, *Evangelism*, 258.

[12] I am defining evangelism as a congregationally sponsored process that helps people place their trust in Jesus and, by the Spirit's power, transforms them within community into disciples of Christ who participate in God's saving mission for the world.

[13] Peter Rollins, *How (Not) to Speak of God* (Brewster, Mass.: Paraclete, 2006), 5–6.

[14] David L. Bartlett, *Between the Bible and the Church: New Methods for Biblical Preaching* (Nashville: Abingdon, 1999), 11.

[15] Personal correspondence.

[16] Jana Childers, *Performing the Word: Preaching as Theatre* (Nashville: Abingdon, 1998), 30.

[17] While there are many ways to define "Relevant Preaching," I choose to define it in terms of a homiletic that helps bring the listener deeper into God's presence through linking God's story in scripture with an individual's and congregation's life story (all the while recognizing the culturally rooted contingencies and varied aspects of our stories). What I am describing here is a homiletic that values the power of engaging our stories—and the stories of scripture—while at the same time resisting metanarratives.

[18] John D. Caputo, *What Would Jesus Deconstruct? The Good News of Postmodernism for the Church* (Grand Rapids, Mich.: Baker Academic, 2007), 41.

[19] "Putting a Cap on Our Bottlemania," *The Globe and Mail*, Section A, Tuesday, August 19, 2008.

[20] David Lose, *Confessing Jesus Christ: Preaching in a Postmodern Word* (Grand Rapids, Mich.: Eerdmans, 2003), 3.

[21] Ibid.

[22] Michael Frost, *Exiles: Living Missionally in a Post-Christian Culture* (Peabody, Mass.: Hendrickson, 2006), 99.

10

Mobius Operandi

Ambiguity and the Challenge of Radical Discipleship

Brandon Gilvin

In seminary I learned that ambiguity could be a gift.

At the end of my second year, Viki Matson, director of field education, was asked to speak at our baccalaureate service. She talked about the tension of being a progressive person of faith: We are people who work for institutions with roots that stretch back thousands of years, and yet we often find ourselves feeling somewhat on the outside of that institution, feeling a bit on the outside for our not-quite-orthodox perspectives on social issues, theology, gender, and sexuality, and bringing to our vocations experiences that nuance our perspectives on doctrine, tradition, and even the aesthetics of worship.

Viki pulled out a strip of paper. On one side was written "I am inside the institution," and on the other, "I am outside the institution." She fashioned the piece of paper into a Möbius strip, a circle that turns in on itself, creating no clear outside and no clear inside. Both statements, Viki told us, were equally dominant. Our vocation is lived out from both vantage points.

This lesson is one of many that I have learned from Viki about the art of ministry, but is likely the one for which I am most grateful. Without understanding that the ambiguity of the life of faith lived out in the church

109

is not a problem to be solved, but a place where ministry could happen most creatively, I would have no way to minister in a world where we all stumble with ambiguity, where life is not black and white, where we all struggle with life, death, grief, and joy, and the shades of gray in between.

I bring the many gifts of a religious institution—the corpus of biblical studies and theology, an understanding of how systems can be helpful, and a cadre of colleagues and mentors, but I remain grounded in a hermeneutic of suspicion and an understanding of the damage that systems can do to individuals. It is in this space that I best minister. It is a gift to attempt to do holy work in such a space.

But what on earth does that even mean?

Although I am generally not one to quote biblical texts without introducing a reconstruction of the historical and literary contexts and multiple other caveats, I must admit that every time I consider this ambiguous space, Phil. 2:12 immediately comes to mind: "Beloved . . . work out your own salvation with fear and trembling."

What I love about this verse is that it evokes several things—for one, the importance of the individual as interpreter of the world she encounters and how grace enters into the world, as well as the unambiguous call to do so with humility. After all, one can only attempt to discern the fullness of God with full awareness of one's own limited subjectivity.

Second, this exhortation calls us not just to "work something out" as if we were patients on a counselor's couch, working out something in our own heads. Salvation has been—since the earliest days of the cult of YHWH—at the very least about the neighbor with whom you're crossing the Yam Suph. It's about doing something. It's about community.

It's about the whole world.

Sometimes we can build small communities of faith in our dorm rooms and organize for a campaign against violence in the Congo on campus, and sometimes we need the larger mechanisms of an organized community—a denomination, an ecumenical organization, or a relief and development fund like the one I work with—to provide the resources to jump-start that campaign.

But we must also remind our larger, organized communities that mechanisms, plans, and protocols are not God. That using them, following them, and utilizing them requires us to pick them up with a good dose of fear and trembling. Thus the call is to obedience but never acquiescence, to question but not to be obstinate.

The call is to live and work it out in curiosity, out of hope for the day when the wolf and lamb lie down together with no fear, but to take our own steps with fear and trembling.

In other words, the call is to live in ambiguity.

I believe image and story best express all of this, and best call us to action. Ultimately, I'm more of a "Luke-Acts" guy than a Paul or pseudo-Paul kinda guy, so rather than spill more ink pontificating on a verse or two, I'd rather tell you a couple of stories–both about communities who chose to follow Jesus. My hope is–every time I remember these stories–that I might remind myself of what it means to negotiate what it means to be part of–and outside–the institution.

> After this the Lord appointed seventy others and sent them on ahead of him in pairs to every town and place where he himself intended to go. He said to them, "The harvest is plentiful, but the laborers are few; therefore ask the Lord of the harvest to send out laborers into his harvest. Go on your way. See, I am sending you out like lambs into the midst of wolves. Carry no purse, no bag, no sandals; and greet no one on the road. Whatever house you enter, first say, 'Peace to this house!' And if anyone is there who shares in peace, your peace will rest on that person; but if not, it will return to you. Remain in the same house, eating and drinking whatever they provide, for the laborer deserves to be paid. Do not move about from house to house. Whenever you enter a town and its people welcome you, eat what is set before you; cure the sick who are there, and say to them, 'The kingdom of God has come near to you.' But whenever you enter a town and they do not welcome you, go out into its streets and say, 'Even the dust of your town that clings to our feet, we wipe off in protest against you. Yet know this: the kingdom of God has come near.'" (Lk. 10:1–11)

They were not ordinary blueberry pancakes
The smell of which awoke us
On a November morning
Just an hour outside of Atlanta
And it was not an ordinary farm
Where we found ourselves
worlds away from the sprawl,
the traffic and the noise of the city.
Because it was November
The air was crisp.
But because we were in Georgia
It was still Sunny
Warm
And dew glistened.
Had we been anywhere else
Surely there would have been frost
We were at the Jubilee Partners
An intentional Christian community
Where people lived together, made decisions entirely by consensus,
And worked together to make a real difference in the world.

Our little group of self-styled pilgrims
and peacemakers
had nestled in overnight on bunk beds, couches and sleeping bags
on our way to
Fort Benning, Georgia.
To mark a solemn occasion.
We would be marching with
friends from all over the country
To the gates of Fort Benning
Where we would recite
With the rhythm of a sacred liturgy
The names of men, women, and children
Murdered by security forces in El Salvador
Guatemala, Honduras, Nicaragua.
Security forces trained . . . on the other side of the gates
At what was now called the
Western Hemisphere Institute for Security Cooperation.
So as we stumbled out of our makeshift beds
Enticed by the smell of pancakes and coffee
We needed to be up and on our way
We had things to do.
We had to make our way to stand for Justice
To follow the path of Jesus the peacemaker
To say that violence done in our names,
paid for by our tax dollars,
victimizing people living in poverty
Cannot be ignored
Government sponsored violence . . . no matter whose government . . .
Must be confronted with a voice that announces
The kingdom of God.
And we would be that
Life changing
Life breathing
Voice
We were in a hurry . . . we needed to get on the road
There was Important stuff to do.
But down in the dining hall,
We were met by a man, tall and gangly
A twinkle in his eye, gray stringy hair
A white beard, dressed in flannel
And denim
Who welcomed us
And told us that before breakfast,
There would be a tour.

* * *

The morning sun welcomed us as we
strolled around the lush Georgia hills
and walked along the clay and gravel roads
As we walked by the enormous blueberry bushes
that had supplied the fruit for the pancakes
we could still smell,
this tall man told us, in his sorghum sweet southern drawl,
a bit about the community.
We make all of our decisions by consensus, not by majority rule
It seems to us the most just way of doin' things
We make sure that the entire community is behind something,
which is wonderful
But it's time consuming.
With a twinkle in his eye, he said,
It took us almost three years to decide whether or not we would get a milk cow.
The Jubilee Partners were involved in their local community,
They sent their kids to public school,
held jobs in the community, engaged
issues on local, national, and international levels,
but also made clear distinctions about what they would not do.
We decided, as a community,
that we wouldn't participate in the American Health insurance industry
So instead of insurance, we have a fund of $30,000 that we all contribute to,
    that is there if anyone has a serious medical concern.
We go on faith a lot.
The path we were taking
wound its way
to what looked like
a small village.
One of our projects here at Jubilee Partners is refugee resettlement.
We work with resettlement organizations from Atlanta and we help integrate
    refugees when they first arrive.
Pointing to the cabins,
he told us that families could live there
while they learned life skills,
while resettlement organizations helped coordinate jobs
and more permanent housing,
and while they attended English and basic Literacy classes.
Most of all,
we make sure that people
have a place to feel safe.
They come from places rife with conflict.

Many of them have seen family members
die in front of them.
We give them a sense of home,
temporary though it might be.
He waved, then pointed.
That family there is our only arrival right now.
Resettled from the Congo.
They were on their way
to the small schoolhouse
where we were now standing.
He welcomed them warmly,
and two young women who were
volunteering to babysit the children
of the Congolese family took them in their arms,
and the parents sat down, ready to do their conjugations.
And we moved on.
And we came to a hill, covered by trees,
and dotted with crosses.
Along with hosting refugees
and helping them integrate,
along with being a witness for radical Christian community,
the Jubilee Partners took seriously another powerful ministry,
echoing Jesus' words in Matthew:
When I was in Prison, you visited me.
They wrote and visited
men and women
sitting on
Georgia's death row.
They visited the nearby federal prison
whenever they could.
They said prayers over their pictures daily.
We passed by their photos
In the dining room
Polaroid instant photos mostly,
others taken in their cells.
When each prisoner was put to death,
if the family couldn't . . . or wouldn't . . .
take the body for burial,
they would be buried here on this plot,
and given a cross bearing each one's name.
We stood, feeling just how sacred this place,
how sacred this hill was.
How sacred this work was.
So what do you do? One of our group asked.

Well, our tour guide answered, *I live here.*
But are you a minister? A social worker? A saint? What do you DO here?
Well, I used to be an English Professor.
And then I met Jesus.
And now This, he said, gesturing to the blueberry fields, the school, the
    cow, and that silent hill full of crosses
This is what I do.

*   *   *

You have heard it said:

Go out into the world, don't take anything, find a place, stay in
one house, and share with everyone you meet the kingdom of
God. Beware, because you are being sent out among the wolves.

But I tell you,
sometimes when you are out there,
amongst the wolves,
you will find that the people
who take you in,
the people
who give you water,
who become your friends,
will be the ones
who share the kingdom
with you
sometimes it will look like
a lonely hill
dotted with crosses,
and sometimes
it will smell like blueberry pancakes.

*   *   *

For more information about the Jubilee Partners, check out their website
(http://www.jubileepartners.org) or, even better, give them a call and visit.

For more information about the School of the Americas and the yearly
demonstration held at Fort Benning, visit http://www.soaw.org.

To use a denominational structure to make real, sustainable change,
visit http://www.weekofcompassion.org.

11

Emerging from the Lectionary

Emily Bowen

I'm a rules follower. I get this trait from my mother. If there is something I'm supposed to do a certain way, chances are that's the way I'm going to do it. I'm the person who likes to have all the guidelines for a paper laid out before I begin writing. If the paper is supposed to be ten to twelve pages, I'm the person who turns in ten to twelve pages. Not more, not less. I'm the person who turns the paper in on the day it's due because, hey, that's the due date! I figure rules are in place for a reason. And that reason is not for them to be broken. Rules are in place to order our lives, to protect us, to protect others, to keep us from being jerks, to keep us on course . . . you get the picture. I try to do what's right, and for me, that falls right in line with what the "rules" tell me is right.

My respect for rules resulted in my being a good little mainliner. I went to church every Sunday because that's what you were supposed to do. Unlike a lot of other people my age, I continued my weekly attendance at church throughout college, even when I wasn't employed by a church. My steady involvement in church led me to seek continued work in the church and pursuit of a master's degree. It was during my time at seminary that I learned about a BIG rule that mainline pastors were encouraged to follow: the Revised Common Lectionary (RCL). My time in various classes and my participation in weekly chapel taught me the value of the RCL. I realized that the church I grew up in had been using the lectionary and I just didn't realize that's why we had the readings we did. Well, my new-found knowledge made me a staunch supporter of the RCL and I touted its virtues to anyone who asked about it. If I'm being totally honest, I even looked down a little on mainline churches that didn't use the lectionary, as if they were somehow meandering off into the land of proof-texting and succumbing to the temptation to focus only on their favorite verses, rather than tackling the whole Bible and all the difficult (and I mean the word "difficult" in a variety of ways, ranging from hard to hear to hard to find anything to preach about) texts within. Lectionary-guided worship and preaching seemed to me to be the "right" thing for mainline churches to do.

Background on the "Big" Rule

Developed in 1983 as an ecumenical revision of the Roman Catholic three-year lectionary that had been released in 1969 following the reforms of the Second Vatican Council, the RCL is built on a three-year cycle with four texts for each week. The four texts are as follows: a passage from Hebrew Scripture, the apocrypha, or Acts of the Apostles; a Psalm; a selection from an epistle or Revelation; and finally, a reading from a gospel. Each of the three years is assigned a gospel: year A–Matthew, year B–Mark, and year C–Luke. The gospel according to John is divided up among all three years, showing up primarily during Eastertide, but also during Advent, Christmastide, and Lent.

A great number of mainline churches follow the RCL. Rules follower that I am, I decided to go along with this big rule. It was easy to do, really, because there are so many things that I like about the lectionary. It flows quite nicely with the church year, building the texts effectively to prepare us during the seasons of Advent and Lent for the seasons of Christmas and Easter, respectively. There is a nice journey through a number of the great stories in Genesis and Exodus, 1 and 2 Kings, and 1 and 2 Samuel. Since there are four readings for each Sunday, it draws upon all parts of the Bible, not just one. Following the lectionary prevents preachers from just using their favorite scriptures, which helps curb the molding of the Bible (and God) into one's own image. And I really appreciate that all over the world, people are sitting in churches of different denominations, hearing the same texts being read and preached on. It further fosters the spirit of ecumenism many of us long and work for, and opens up the avenues of study and discussion that are so crucial to sermon preparation. I have a number of friends who are also ministers, and we are often preaching on the same texts and can therefore share and bounce ideas off of one another.

However, being in full-time ministry for over eight years has changed me. The more time I spend in ministry, the more I question the rules I've been following. So here I am, ten years removed from my first seminary introduction to the lectionary, still a good little mainliner, but actually thinking about jumping off of the RCL bandwagon and wandering off into the wilderness of preaching without it. Emergent church "spokesman" Brian McLaren's words of wisdom, while not written to address my marriage to the lectionary, could very well speak to the concerns that have been awakened in me:

> When people tell us to be quiet and accept the conventional answers we've been given in the past, many of us groan like the ancient Hebrews when they were forced to produce bricks without straw. We cry out to God, "Please set us free!" We cry out to preachers and theologians, "Let us go! Let us find some space to think, to worship God outside the bars and walls and fences in which we are constrained and imprisoned. We'll head out into the wilderness—risk hunger, thirst, exposure, death—but we can't sustain this constrained way of thinking, believing, and living much longer. We need to ask the questions that are simmering in our souls."[1]

So, however tentatively, into the wilderness I go.

Starting to Question

My conviction to make this move strengthened last summer as I worked on a sermon based on 2 Sam. 6. The lectionary assigned 2 Sam. 6:1–5, 12b–19 as the Hebrew Scripture for that particular Sunday. In this passage, David and his companions set out to bring the ark of the Lord to Jerusalem. Much dancing and playing and singing of music ensued. Once they arrived in Jerusalem, David offered burnt offerings and offerings of well-being before God, and then he blessed the people in God's name and the whole multitude of Israel joined in a feast. It's a nice story and all, but I just had to see what was being left out with that little comma (which I read as ellipses) between verses 5 and 12b. Here is what I found:

> When they came to the threshing-floor of Nacon, Uzzah reached out his hand to the ark of God and took hold of it, for the oxen shook it. The anger of the Lord was kindled against Uzzah; and God struck him there because he reached out his hand to the ark; and he died there beside the ark of God. David was angry because the Lord had burst forth with an outburst upon Uzzah; so that place is called Perez-uzzah to this day. David was afraid of the Lord that day; he said, "How can the ark of the Lord come into my care?" So David was unwilling to take the ark of the Lord into his care in the city of David; instead David took it to the house of Obed-edom the Gittite. The ark of the Lord remained in the house of Obed-edom the Gittite for three months; and the Lord blessed Obed-edom and all his household. It was told King David, "The Lord has blessed the household of Obed-edom and all that belongs to him, because of the ark of God." (2 Sam. 6:6–12a)

Well, there we have the motivation for David to continue transporting the ark of God to Jerusalem. Dancing and singing before the ark resumed and the four verses that close out chapter 6 are as follows:

> David returned to bless his household. But Michal the daughter of Saul came out to meet David, and said, "How the king of Israel honored himself today, uncovering himself today before the eyes of his servants' maids, as any vulgar fellow might shamelessly uncover himself!" David said to Michal, "It was before the Lord, who chose me in place of your father and all his household, to appoint me as prince over Israel, the people of the Lord, that I have danced before the Lord. I will make myself yet more contemptible than this, and I will be abased in my own eyes; but by the maids of whom you have spoken, by them I shall be held in honor." And Michal the daughter of Saul had no child to the day of her death. (2 Sam. 6:20–23)

While there are times when those elusive ellipses are there for the sake of time, to condense the reading so you don't have to sit through twenty minutes of scripture reading before the sermon, or to remove verses that don't seem pertinent to the particular story being told, that certainly doesn't seem to be the case in this selection from 2 Samuel. It seems to me that these verses were taken out of the reading because they're the verses that make us squirm! The lectionary gave us a nice, neat little story of David transporting the ark of the Lord to Jerusalem, dancing and celebrating in the presence of God and blessing the people in the name of God. But as you can clearly see, God's striking down of Uzzah was excised and the displeasure of Michal at seeing David dance before the Lord and subsequent barrenness of Michal were left out. As a preacher, I have to admit that I was initially glad those verses were left out of the lectionary. It gave me a solid excuse to avoid them like the plague! Who wants to touch those texts? I don't know about you, but I tend to want to avoid the texts that deal with God smiting people. They make me uncomfortable. And they really don't jibe with my understanding of God. And yet, there those texts are, right in the Bible, crying out for me to preach them (all because my curiosity got the better of me and I just had to see what the ellipses were leaving out). There is a certain feeling of safety and comfort that following the rules brings us, even while they bind us. McLaren offers words that cut a little too close, but nevertheless warrant sharing:

> You can't go on a quest if you're locked in a closet, cell, or concentration camp. And you won't go on a quest if your captivity is sufficiently comfortable. That's where we find ourselves: in a real-life version of the classic movie *The Truman Show*. We live in a comfortable captivity. Everywhere we turn we are surrounded

by padded chairs, nice broadcasts of music and teaching, pleasant lighting and polite neighbors, all designed and integrated to keep us content under the dome . . . The chains, locks, bars, and barbed wire that hold us are usually disguised so well that they have a homey feel to us. We see our guards not as guards at all, but as pleasant custodians in clerical robes or casual suits. They've been to graduate school where many of them mastered the techniques of friendly manipulation, always with a penetrating smile and a firm, heavy hand on the shoulder.[2]

Following the lectionary is safe. We don't have to think about which text to preach on, because the choice has already been narrowed down to four! But as I read McLaren's words, I am reminded of one of the driving forces behind the Reformation of the sixteenth century. There was a move to put the Bible in the hands of the people. Before this time, clergy were the intermediaries between the people and God. The laity, it was believed, did not have direct access to God. But the translation of the Bible into the vernacular was a step toward breaking down that barrier. No longer were people only hearing words from the Bible through their priests; they were able to read and discern for themselves. Today we can all pick up a Bible and read and discern for *ourselves*, but our practice in worship, our use of the lectionary, in some ways controls our reading and influences us to read the texts through certain lenses. These words prompt my reflection on the ways that the lectionary binds us without our realizing it, and my discoveries in that week's reading from last summer shed light on bars holding us in place.

The Dangers of Playing It Safe

The presentation of the text from 2 Sam. 6 gave me pause, but it wasn't just that week. It's something that had been brewing for a while. While at first glance it may seem that the RCL covers all the bases, after closer scrutiny, the cracks begin to show. A few months ago, I heard about a worshiping community that saw through these cracks and decided to use all the texts that were left out of the lectionary as their texts for worship, and I was intrigued. Ever since then, I've been thinking about going through my Bible and highlighting all the texts that appear in the lectionary, taking note of texts that are used more than once, and seeing for myself what is privileged and what is left out. I am interested in discovering the biases of the lectionary, and a quick perusal reveals that quite a bit goes by the wayside. For example, Isaiah makes up more than one-third of the Hebrew Scripture readings. Only Genesis and Exodus of the Pentateuch get any serious attention. Many of the stories we heard growing up in the church have been left out, like the walls of Jericho tumbling down, Jonah in the belly of the big fish, and Daniel in the lion's den. And if these and other texts aren't in the lectionary, how will they ever get addressed in churches that strictly go by the lectionary, even utilizing lectionary-based Sunday-school curriculum? Additionally, the structure of the lectionary tends to favor the gospel reading over the others. Just think of the worship services you've been to and how the scripture readings often build to the gospel (the only reading for which we stand). And what about the Sundays in which the first reading is from Acts rather than from Hebrew Scripture? That unfairly advantages the New Testament when our Bible is clearly made up of both Hebrew Scripture and Christian Scripture.

Here is where the most insidious drawback of the lectionary comes into play. In the early days of my ministry, I began looking at the four lectionary texts side by side for the purpose of worship planning, and this exercise revealed something alarming. Often it appeared as though the Hebrew Scripture and the gospel reading were matched in some way, as though they are analogous, thereby tempting the readers to draw parallels where none may exist, resulting in a Christianization of Hebrew Scripture. Yet Hebrew Scripture is so much more than a prelude to the New Testament. These texts have a life of their own, apart from the New Testament, and it is important to honor that in our reading and understanding. Also, it is the Hebrew Scriptures that inform the New Testament, not the other way around. The Bible is not meant to be read backward.[3]

And yet, the ease with which Christianity has practiced the supersession of Judaism is remarkable and frightening to behold, in large part because many do not even realize that it's happening. And here it happens in abundance throughout the lectionary. Hebrew Scriptures are chosen for their connection to the gospel reading for the week. Such a pairing plays into a hermeneutic of promise and fulfillment and relegates the Hebrew Scriptures to being nothing more than a prelude to the New Testament. Such a move is irresponsible. This is seen most strongly in the lectionary readings for the season of Advent. The Hebrew Scriptures are all lined up during the four weeks of Advent in each year of the RCL cycle in order to set the stage for the birth of Jesus. I have too often heard these texts treated as prophecies in the "Nostradamus" sense rather than as prophetic in the "interpreting God's will" sense.

The Hebrew Bible is replete with the stories that have formed our faith and have inspired us on our journeys, and yet it is often passed over in favor of the New Testament. I wonder, if we took a poll, what percentage of sermons are preached on the gospel text over the other texts in the lectionary? During the time I wrote this essay, the story of the aftermath of David sending Uriah off to war so he could have his way with Uriah's wife, Bathsheba, appeared in the lectionary. In this story, God sends Nathan to David to shed light on the evil that David has done. David acknowledges his sin, and Nathan tells him, "Now the Lord has put away your sin; you shall not die. Nevertheless, because by this deed you have utterly scorned the Lord, the child that is born to you shall die" (2 Sam. 12:13–14). And this is what comes to be. The gospel reading for this very same week in the lectionary cycle comes out of Luke and in it, Jesus eats at the home of a Pharisee. While there, a woman of ill repute comes to Jesus with an alabaster jar of ointment. She falls at Jesus' feet and, while weeping, washes his feet with her tears and wipes them with her hair. She then proceeds to kiss and anoint his feet with the ointment. The Pharisee thinks that perhaps Jesus does not know the reputation of this woman, but Jesus speaks up and shares a story with the Pharisee to illustrate the appropriateness of the woman's actions: "'Therefore, I tell you, her sins, which were many, have been forgiven; hence she has shown great love. But the one to whom little is forgiven, loves little.' Then he said to her, 'Your sins are forgiven'" (Lk. 7:47–48). What are we to do with these texts? There is a great deal going on in both of them, so how are we to decide which one to preach on?

While researching these lections, I ran across the story of a minister who decided to preach on the gospel text. Of course, the Hebrew Scripture was still read in the service, part of all that built to the gospel reading, so both passages were part of the service, hanging in the air throughout the morning. After worship, a member of the congregation was overheard voicing his own reflection on the scripture readings for the morning: "The God of the Old Testament kills babies," he said; "Jesus forgives those who weep."[4] Understandings such as this are too prevalent in the church, to say the least. I can't tell you how many times I've heard people describe the "God of the Old Testament" as vengeful and full of wrath, but then proclaim that the "God of the New Testament" is a God of love. Last time I checked, they were the same God. The lectionary has done a disservice in utilizing a structure that perpetuates this myth of wrathful God versus loving God.

Admitting Defeat

I tried so hard to make the lectionary work, to put it to its best use. At one time, I thought that it would be an interesting discipline to utilize the lectionary by preaching every single lectionary text over a twelve-year period. Tackle the Hebrew Scriptures and Acts the first three years, then the Psalms, then the Epistles and Revelation, then the gospels. But still, important things would be left out. Things that we need to talk about in church. Like the stories in Judges about what it was like when there was no king in Israel and the people did what was right in their own eyes; a time when Jepthah sacrificed his child in a misguided promise to God; a time when a Levite allowed his concubine to be gang raped and then feigned outrage over her death in order to start a war. Like why John's gospel has such harsh language against the Jews. Like how some of the most difficult texts are telling us as much about humanity if not more than they are telling us about God. Because let's face it, as much as we would like it to be, church isn't only a place we come to in order to feel better about life. Don't get me wrong, it is OK for us to feel good about life and God and the work we are called to do in this world, but that's not what church is *all* about. It's like the saying goes: The gospel afflicts the comfortable and comforts the afflicted. At times we squirm in our seats because of the things described in the Bible. At times we want to close our ears to what Jesus calls us to do. At times we are not ready to hear what God is saying to us. And yet still the Word is near, waiting to be released from this book, waiting to be explored in the context of our worship, and it is not to be shied away from. Sometimes the things we avoid talking about in church are the things we need to talk about the most. All of the words on these pages speak to us. All of these stories and songs and exhortations and letters tell of the hopes and fears of a people who yearned for God as we yearn for God. If we are really to take the Bible seriously, we need to take a more complete look at it.

Rules follower though I've been, I haven't really been that way when it comes to the way I see and understand God. I've always been interested in pushing the boundaries of our understandings of God, of nudging people to think of God as more than any label or attribute they've given to God. God in the box has never been for me. So why is it I've succumbed to the lectionary so completely? Why has this been the rule I've adhered to so often?

I've determined that it's time to break that big rule.

But We've Always Done It This Way!

We've heard it said for decades now that attendance in mainline churches is diminishing. When we look out into our sanctuaries we often see that those occupying the pews are getting older, and there is not a huge influx of new people to sustain the membership. It's been hard to be a pastor in a mainline church, an institution that is so caught up in following the rules, in doing things the way they've always been done. For a long time, that's what made the mainline church a good match for me. But such a mentality does not bode well for the future of the church. If you always do what you've always done, you'll always get what you've always gotten. And for the mainline church, *that* doesn't even seem to be the case anymore. It may have worked up through the 1960s or 1970s, but since then, our tried-and-true methods of bringing people in through our doors have failed us.

As Brian McLaren writes in *A New Kind of Christianity,*

> I believe that in every new generation the Christian faith, like every faith, must in a sense be born again . . . I believe that, as with Sarah and Elizabeth, just when you think the old girl is over the hill, she might take a pregnancy test and surprise us all.[5]

What if learning to break the rules gives us the shot of hope, the spark of vision that we so desperately need? The moves being made in the emergent church have been a source of inspiration for me, motivating me to break the rules.

Instead of pretending that the culture doesn't exist, the emergent church takes cues from the culture. But it doesn't do it in a put-a-Starbucks-in-your-gathering-area kind of way. Instead, it is taking cues from (if not to say it is an outgrowth of) the general empowerment that the everyday regular Jane or Joe feels to offer their perspectives to the world. The emergent church is a new kind of reformation, one that, like the Reformation before, seeks to put faith in the hands of the people. More than that, *it seeks to put the ways in which faith is lived out and embodied in the hands of the people.* Liturgy is becoming the work of the people in a way it never has before because the people are actually a bigger part of working out the liturgy.

One of the beauties of our faith (and of the manifestation of the church) is that it does not have to remain stagnant and unchanging. Like jazz, there is a lot of room for free-flow movement and improvisation that is built upon years of tradition. While there are signs of this in the mainline church, especially regarding preaching as a communal proclamation,[6] the emergent church is offering a "both/and" by drawing upon the richness of ancient symbol and ritual, all while encouraging the exchange of ideas and new ways of looking at church. What if we take a page from this model and actually read the Bible together to share our ideas, reflections, frustrations, and roadblocks that rise to the surface in our communal study of the text? What if we stopped looking to some elusive body "out there" to dictate to us the ways we are called to do and be church and start looking to ourselves to discern that call?

And Finally, the Alternative

Is it possible that we need to heed the words of the prophet Amos, who reminds us that all of our rules following is useless if we've forgotten what it is all for (cf. Am. 5:21–24)? Professor, speaker, and all-around emergent Renaissance man Barry Taylor put in brilliantly when he wrote, "I believe our commitment to the religion of Christianity has led us into a cul-de-sac of ineffectuality and redundancy."[7] He later goes on to write:

> For Christian faith to remain viable, we are going to have to let go of the attractional model—inviting people to come to us—and instead go to where they live, and to there live out our faith. A Chinese proverb says we should "Go to the people. Live among them, learn from them. Love them, start with what they know, build on what they have."[8]

It's not about us—the clergy—bestowing all the great knowledge we learned in our esteemed seminaries upon the people we serve. It's about engaging those people, asking them questions, hearing their concerns, meeting them where they are, and then accompanying them on the journey.

Yes, of course we put all of that great knowledge to use in our work, but we no longer allow it to remain supreme, to seduce us into thinking we have all the answers and the poor people out there will just run in circles without us. Like Taylor says, the mainline church is doing a pretty good job at residing in that cul-de-sac. It's time to venture out and break the monotony. Perhaps we could take the text to the people—all the text, and not just our prized verses—in order to help people find themselves in the text. And maybe, just maybe, in taking on the whole Bible, we'll find that people are more drawn to the riches within the book: the humor and the heartbreak, the darkness and the paradox, the stories and the parables. As it is, there is well-deserved suspicion from those on the outside of our walls at the picking and choosing of favorite texts or the endless cycle of selected lectionary readings that happens in so many of our churches. The answers we've tried to offer to people in their life struggles are not as easy as we often make them out to be when we quote a biblical passage here and a biblical passage there. Engaging the texts of the Bible can often be as much a struggle as what we face every day. Maybe our practice of reading the Bible in church and with people of faith should reflect that.

The relationship between educated clergy and spiritually hungry laity can lead to some fruitful learning for both parties as we endeavor to learn from one another. Clergy shed light on the text through the study of context, historical placement, language, and so on, while the laity brings individual experience and fresh perspective, opening up the text in new ways.

So as my reflections on breaking the rules come to a close, I realize that I haven't really offered any concrete solutions or alternatives to using the RCL. But that's really the point, isn't it? I mean, if I gave you all the answers, how would you find the motivation to enter into conversation with your community of faith and discover those answers for yourselves? The answers I would give wouldn't turn out to be answers at all. Besides, the alternatives congregants and I come up with in our community of faith may not work for your community. The ways we read and reflect on the Bible won't look the same as the ways you do. That's the beauty of the emergent church. It's how the act of being and doing church emerges in your context, emerging from the giftedness and passions and yearnings in your own community. The cookie-cutter approach doesn't work. It isn't true to who we are as diverse communities of faith who join together to make up the one body of Christ.

What might it mean to be a rule-breaker? I would suggest that you take the road less traveled. Venture out into the wilderness of the Bible in your own way. Don't follow the road map that someone else who doesn't know your community laid out for you twenty-eight years ago. Listen to the people around you. Tune in to their questions, their needs, and their yearnings. Take their concerns seriously. Listen to how the text speaks its words of transformation in your community. Recognize the many ways to experience and muddle through this complicated, contradictory, jumbled, beautiful book of our faith. I'm excited to see what we come up with and what we all discover.

Notes

[1] Brian McLaren, *A New Kind of Christianity: Ten Questions That Are Transforming the Faith* (New York: Harper One, 2010), 22.

[2] McLaren, *A New Kind of Christianity*, 31.

[3] For two lectionary-based commentaries that take these concerns seriously, see especially Ronald Allen and Clark Williamson's *Preaching the Gospels Without Blaming the Jews* (Louisville: Westminster John Knox, 2004) and *Preaching the Letters Without Dismissing the Law* (Louisville: Westminster John Knox, 2006).

[4] Walter Sundberg, "Limitations of the Lectionary," in *Word & World*, accessed online at http://www2.luthersem.edu/Word&World/Archives/10–1_Catechism/10–1_Sundberg.pdf.

[5] McLaren, *A New Kind of Christianity*, xiii.

[6] See especially Lucy Atkinson Rose, *Sharing the Word: Preaching in the Roundtable Church* (Louisville: Westminster John Knox, 1997); John McClure, *The Roundtable Pulpit: Where Leadership and Preaching Meet* (Nashville: Abingdon, 1995); Charles Cosgrove and Dow Edgerton, *In Other Words: Incarnational Translation for Preaching* (Grand Rapids, Mich.: Eerdmans, 2007); and O. Wesley Allen, *The Homiletic of All Believers: A Conversational Approach to Proclamation and Preaching* (Louisville: Westminster John Knox, 2005).

[7] Barry Taylor, "Converting Christianity: The End and Beginning of Faith," in *An Emergent Manifesto of Hope*, eds. Doug Pagitt and Tony Jones (Grand Rapids, Mich.: Baker, 2007), 169.

[8] Barry Taylor, "Converting Christianity," 170.

12

Improvising with Tradition

A Case (Self) Study

Timothy Snyder

Jazz is not just, "Well, man, this is what I feel like playing." It's a very structured thing that comes down from a tradition and requires a lot of thought and study.

—WYNTON MARSALIS[1]

A Confession

I have a confession to make: I am a Lutheran poster child. I am not sure how this happened. It seems so surreal now, but growing up in the Lutheran Church, I was the kid who was always in the youth director's office, always at some youth retreat, and the one serving on youth boards and in youth leadership roles. I find it funny now that when I was sixteen I was flying around the country to participate in meetings of the board of directors of the Evangelical Lutheran Church in America (ELCA).

But that is not the point of my confession. The point of my confession is that for all of the opportunity, affirmation, and growth I have found in my own Lutheran tradition, a certain dark side filled with unhelpful expectations, painful shortcomings, numerous disappointments, and even outright betrayal are all a part of the story I am about to share. My confession is this:

Although I will make the argument that unless "you apprentice yourself to a tradition, you will never innovate," I also understand that there is a cost involved. Yet it also seems to me that it is precisely in the cost–in the most unlikely of places–that God is showing up and is doing something quite creative and exciting in the mainline church today. Let me explain what I mean.

"I Dream of a Church Where . . ."

I remember the conversation like it was yesterday. Only weeks before I had moved into the dorm at Texas Lutheran University and I had met Jeff. We were roommates our freshman year of college and were both music education majors. We had the exact same class schedule (which increased the probability of us actually making those 8:00 a.m. classes quite significantly!). Jeff grew up in Texas; I moved around often as a kid. Jeff was a tall and hearty guy who wore his cowboy boots and hat with a certain kind of distinguished pride; I was skinny and average in height with nothing distinguishing about my wardrobe. We were driving home one day in Jeff's Ford F-150 pickup truck when the conversation happened.

"Hey, Jeff," I said. "Have you been to any campus ministry events?"

"No," Jeff replied in his short, abrupt, and frank sort of manner.

"What do you think about campus ministry?" I asked.

"Not much," he replied.

"Yeah? Me too. What are we going to do about that?" (I asked this question with a degree of gravity that surprised me even as I said it out loud.)

Jeff didn't answer–there was just this heavy silence. It was one of those nonassuming conversations that neither of us could let go of. One night as Jeff came home late from a party (Jeff always knew where parties were; I never did figure that out), I told him that I discovered that the chapel was left unlocked. By then the two of us had taken part in many late-night conversations about our own faith lives and about many of our friends– friends we would have the deepest conversations with over a last-call pint but who would never show up for daily chapel. That night we continued the conversation we began weeks before and created what we would later come to call "Intermission."

In those early days our ambitions were simply to create the kind of space where we could express our faith and doubts about what it means for us to be young adults with various kinds of spiritual convictions. As our small circle of friends grew, we ended up facilitating creative worship with prayer stations, labyrinths, and the arts because we desperately wanted to avoid becoming "worship leaders." Every week we sought to create a brand-new space using patterns we discovered to be helpful frameworks for our lives. Some of those patterns were themes from scriptures, others were ancient spiritual practices, and still others were inspired by music and film.[2]

Two years after the initial conversation in Jeff's pickup truck, we found ourselves on a journey that continues to shape us in profound ways. Jeff and I both exchanged our music degrees for liberal arts degrees in theology as we found ourselves discerning calls to ministry. Around that time I was invited to participate in a more formal conversation among emerging leaders in the ELCA. Then, in an old neighborhood grocery store that had been converted into a coffeehouse outreach to young adults, a few dozen leaders went around and, by way of introduction, shared for a few minutes about the creative things God was doing in their cities. That was the first time I realized that "Intermission" was part of a much wider movement. It was only then that I realized the full gravity of my question to Jeff.

During those early days of conversation, I was invited to take the seedling of what we were learning about ministry with my generation and plant it in the wider community beyond our campus setting. I soon found myself sitting down with four others at a midnight meeting at IHOP. Over pancakes and the dangerous bottomless pot of coffee we stumbled our way into a sort of communal prayer–part lament and part visioning. Late into that night we went around the table finishing the sentence: "I dream of a church where . . ." That night a new experiment was born. We called it the Netzer Co-Op. "Netzer" comes from a Hebrew word for "sprig or shoot," as in the image of new life that springs forth from Jesse's old tree stump in Isaiah 11. From the very beginning we knew we were creating a fresh way of doing church and so we embraced the alternative, shared-ownership ethos of cooperatives. It later took on a more pronounced theological significance as we embraced the priesthood of all believers vibe of our Lutheran tradition and frequently spoke about what it means to cooperate with the God who is alive and active in our world.

In the sections that follow, I share the story of the Netzer Co-Op through the telling of several improvisational episodes that became defining moments for our community's life together.

Shindig Liturgy

When we gave birth to the Netzer Co-Op, two of us initially took the lead as facilitators and organizers. My cofounder (Brianna) and I were both lifelong Lutherans who deeply loved the depth of the liturgical calendar, the emphasis in Lutheran preaching on law and gospel, and the centrality of the sacraments, especially Holy Communion. Not knowing how to start a church, we began by gathering friends for a monthly worship service that looked very similar to Intermission. It included an organic order of worship, prayer stations, and ancient faith practices such as Lectio Divina and the Ignatious Examine. But we also made two commitments in those days: First, we committed ourselves to conversational approaches to preaching, because we knew we needed to hear from those who had gathered together. Second, we used music that was either written by us or by our friends. The intention here was to seriously value the expressions of the people who were gathering together for worship.

Early on, in the middle of one of those conversational preaching moments, a young couple arrived. We were just happy they showed up, so we quickly made room for them in our circle of sofas. Afterward, the young girl told us that despite growing up in the Lutheran Church, it was by seeing our circle literally open to make room for her that she felt like her voice was valued in worship for the very first time. It was a moment that solidified our commitment to preaching as conversation.

A few years later, we realized the significance of our music and the way it performatively shapes us. As we experimented with our worship we grew to love the music of Aaron Strumpel, an artist-missionary I had worked with for several years. We hosted house concerts for Aaron and other musicians and often these events would close in deep times of worship. One of Aaron's songs became a sort of theme song for our little community:

> Give me your hand and we'll walk
> Walk down together
> Lift up your hands and we'll sing
> Sing here together
> How good it is to know You God
> How lovely is . . . Your Bride
> How blessed we are . . . to have . . . each other
> You hold us all close . . . by your side
> Come with me now and we'll dance
> Dance here together
> Lift up your heart and we'll dream
> Dream here together
> (with increasing number of voices, volume, and intensity)
> There's no one too poor, too dirty, too broken,
> too naked, too stupid, too drunken
> To be . . . thrown outside His Love.[3]

One Sunday when Brianna and I were both out of town at a conference, our music leader met a homeless man outside the church and welcomed him in. We had a pretty relaxed atmosphere in worship and so it only made sense that this man ought to join us if he was so inclined. Welcoming him to participate was one thing, but participants weren't quite sure what to do when the man drank the whole chalice full of communion wine before the service even started. It was a night full of awkward moments, chaos, and humor as the community was confronted with what it might mean to include a homeless man in the same way they would welcome anyone else into our fellowship. Fortunately for us, that was not the night someone from the bishop's office showed up unannounced! All of a sudden we encountered very difficult, complex questions related to hospitality, and it challenged us in ways we never expected.

Pumpkin Pancakes and the Rhythm of Life

Only a few months after we began the worshiping community at the co-op, our core team went to a weekend conference put on by several leaders of emerging churches in Austin, Texas. Although the speakers were phenomenal, it was a bit strange for us to be talking about being a different kind of church inside a multi-million-dollar auditorium. Our first evening there we found ourselves at a local twenty-four-hour pancake diner. Over pumpkin pancakes and some more coffee we began to debrief what we had heard during the day. The conversation quickly spilled over into unsurfaced tensions regarding our community life together at the co-op. For months we had been consistently worshiping together, but many in the community were getting anxious to integrate what we were exploring in worship with their daily lives. There was a growing skepticism that being primarily a worshiping community would allow us to become the kind of church we were dreaming of. At the height of what rapidly escalated into a full-blown argument, one of our most unassuming—but brilliant—core team members suggested that we skip the conference the next day, pool our money to buy sack lunches, and simply give the lunches away to the very prominent homeless population in Austin. In my own self-righteousness I opted not to join them, and the next day I returned to the conference.

I wish I had joined them, however. That weekend would change the very rhythm of our community life, and soon these initial experiences gave way to our "Likewise Experiments." Based on the story of the Good Samaritan, we hosted events and conversations that called on ourselves and our peers—all from quite well off, white, middle-class backgrounds—to build relationships with our new homeless friends in Austin. Before the Likewise Experiments, we were an insular group of friends who liked to get together for creative worship. But afterward, we began to understand that the spiritual life is both an inward and outward journey. With an entirely new way of orienting our community life, we began to take more risks and bolder steps into becoming the community we had dreamed of months before. I am still not sure what it is about late-night conversations, pancakes, and dingy diners that always provided important turning points, but I suspect it had everything to do with our willingness to improvise.

Soccer-Mom Minivans and Matching T-Shirts

For months I had wanted to have lunch with Ashley, who had participated in some of the events at the co-op. I had known Ashley since high school (we were Lutheran poster children together) and now we were both attending a Lutheran college. Ashley was a business major and I knew we badly needed her gifts of organization and administration in the community.

It was an area we were severely deficient in at the time. We met in the student center for a quick bite to eat in between classes. It was the end of the semester and we both had a million other things on our minds.

As is true at most college campuses, Texas Lutheran University had a meal plan system that provided a certain amount of money to be credited to your student account to purchase meals. If you didn't use your credit by the end of the semester you would lose it. So as we got our lunches we were joined by several students buying cases of Gatorade, energy bars, and anything else nonperishable they could get their hands on in order to use up the remainder of their credit. That's when Ashley asked the cashier how much the premade sub sandwiches cost. I didn't understand why she was asking at first, but then she leaned in and reminded me of the Likewise Experiment we had planned for the upcoming weekend. "What if we convinced everyone to use their remaining credits to buy sandwiches for our homeless friends instead of all this other crap?" It was a brilliant idea and a great example of exactly why we needed Ashley on our leadership team. By the end of the week, students had donated thousands of dollars in unused credits and we had over four hundred sandwiches to deliver. It was a beautiful subversion of the status quo in exchange for kingdom economics and it was covered in both the local and student newspapers. The whole thing had taken us by surprise.

After spending hours volunteering alongside dining services staff to make the sandwiches, as well as plotting out our distribution routes, we were finally ready for our jubilee-esque experiment. After dividing up the routes, we planned on meeting back up at the Austin Resource Center for the Homeless (ARCH), a popular hangout spot for the homeless community.

When we arrived at the ARCH after our route, I saw Ashley in what appeared to be an intense conversation with one of the regulars. The sandwiches had long been gone when this conversation began. Ashley had been sharing the story of where the sandwiches came from with one of the guests at the ARCH when a rather intense man confronted her with a stunning question: "What are y'all still doing here? Aren't you going to pull up in your soccer-mom minivans and matching T-shirts and leave again as quickly as you came?" If that was our plan before, which it was not, at that moment our plans would have changed. "No," Ashley replied, "we were going to just hang out here for a while if that's OK." "Good!" the intense man barked as he pointed up the hill to several police cruisers, "because do you see those cops? As soon as you leave they will disperse us. They don't like this many of us to be together at one time for too long." We stayed the rest of the afternoon.

Our Likewise Experiments were not really about sandwiches or about the health kits we later handed out, although those were important services. The experiments were actually about us learning to build relationships of dignity, mutuality, and love. But the truth is that they were never really

mutual because we learned far more from our homeless friends than anything we ever gave them.

The relationships that we built after that Saturday in November continued to grow. Later on, our community learned of a Christian camp of
homeless people living on the edge of town and attempting to become sober
together. I vividly remember the first time we visited their camp. After
crossing what seemed to be the bridge to Terabithia, a world completely
foreign to our own comfort zone, built from scraps of wood that had been
collected from construction sites, we were welcomed to sit by the campfire.
As we sat there on that spring morning we were strangely warmed by the
coziness of the rustic camp.

About a year later, we moved our little community from Seguin, Texas,
an hour from Austin, to the downtown area. Part of the reason for moving
was that if we were going to be serious about being in lasting relationships
with our homeless friends, we had to plant our community in a place accessible to them. Once we had moved to Austin, we listened to our friends on
the streets and learned which social-service organizations had good repu-
tations and which were doing more harm than good. We partnered with
Mobile Loaves and Fishes, a national organization with its headquarters in
Austin, mostly because it seemed like everyone we met on the street had
Alan Graham's cell phone number (he is the CEO of the organization). Alan
helped us get even more serious about our commitments to the homeless in
Austin by leading us on a street retreat—a forty-eight-hour spiritual retreat
spent in solidarity with our friends. Not everyone in our community was
ready for this retreat, but it was a far cry from soccer-mom minivans and
matching T-shirts.

Elders and Curators

Two years into our journey at the co-op, we were invited to our first
Synod Assembly. At the bishop's request, two of us from the community
attended the event as voting delegates. At one of many social receptions,
Jill (one of the representatives from the co-op) introduced herself as an
elder from the Netzer Co-Op. Because this is not a typical title or role in
the Lutheran Church, the nice lady asked, "Elder? What is that? Do you
get some kind of fancy robe for that?" Jill quickly played along: "Oh, yeah,
and you should see the neat pointy hats and decorative chairs we get too!
They're fabulous."

Truth be told, the co-op actually had a pretty reckless beginning. Perhaps you knew this already, but there are lots of things that twenty-year-olds
will do for ten thousand dollars. It was this spirit of unreserved ambition that
led us to finally do something about the dreams we first shared at IHOP.
But in a moment of rare intuitive wisdom, we asked several of our mentors to walk alongside us in our experiment. As elders in our community,
we asked them to mentor our leaders, serve the community as spiritual

directors, and weigh in on our decision-making processes. By drawing upon the wisdom of one of our elders, we crafted language that helped us distinguish their role from that of a conventional governing board. This elder spoke of a friend who had been part of two very different marriages: The first spouse was an accountant by trade. In this marriage, everything was about accountability and the bottom line, including relationships. In the second marriage, however, the spouse was an editor. The latter marriage was about crafting the best story—it was about edit-ability. This parable of sorts became quite helpful in casting our vision for how elders would shape the co-op community.

When we began the co-op, we wanted to create a hospitable place for those who had negative experiences of church. We also knew that language had a profound impact on the imagination of our community, especially our leadership. For these two reasons we were constantly creating unique ways of talking about what we were up to. At the recommendation of one of our elders, who was an artist by trade, we decided to call our ministers "curators."[4] We knew we needed a new imagination about what leadership looked like in a community like the co-op. There were no ordained pastors, no one even had a college degree when we started, and we were all peers. To say we were all skeptical of religious authority would have been an understatement! We organized our leadership by our emphases on both the inward journey and the outward journey, with a curator for each. The role of the curator was to guide, suggest, give context, tell the story, make the history available, and give attention to the whole trajectory of the journey. As Jonny Baker of Grace (London) once told me, "When you experience good curation it makes all the difference, but no one knows any famous curators. Their work is felt, but they are completely behind the scenes."

During my three years at the co-op, we never had anything other than peer-based lay leadership. I suspect that will always be part of our identity. Though it was out of the necessity of our context that we created this model of leadership, it was also situated well within a long history of alternative laity-led Christian communities (e.g., the Christian-based communities of Latin America, the underground prayer groups in Nazi Germany, the earliest monastic communities, and so on). Such a concrete expression of the Lutheran theology of a priesthood of all believers rooted our identity in a tradition in ways far beyond denominational loyalty.

212 South Camp Street

If there was one book that had the most impact on our little community, it was Shane Claiborne's *The Irresistible Revolution.*[5] The parallels of an idealistic community of college students engaged with the urban poor was certainly aspirational for us. But what was even more inspiring was Shane's invitation to find out what the kingdom of God looked like right where we were.

Several members of our core team wanted to create a Christian community house from the earliest days of the co-op, and for some it was the sole reason they got involved. Three of us moved into 212 South Camp Street with high hopes of creating a rule of life rooted in communal prayer, shared work, and serving our neighbors. It was a noble beginning with good intentions and good effort. We chose the house because it was located right behind the coffee shop where two of us worked (and in which our worship space was housed).

During that summer we learned a lot about the commitment and discipline it took to sustain that kind of intense community. It was very hard to do. As we all began another semester of college, continued our involvement in the wider co-op community, and kept up with our own busy work schedules, our energy for the community house dwindled. We hosted worship gatherings, house concerts, and community meetings at the house. Living together while building relationships with the camp of homeless friends in Austin helped give context to our struggle for sustaining the kind of community we had hoped for.

But in the end, it simply did not work (being the church isn't always pretty). Although 212 South Camp Street shaped the lives of those who lived there, as well as those in the wider co-op community, ultimately it was a failed experiment that probably ended up doing more damage to the relationships inside the house than it did for any kind of formative discipleship. Failing, however, challenged us to seek repentance and each other's forgiveness, which meant we were doing church in the most transformative of ways.

Jesus at a Pub

Just a block away from the congregation that hosted the co-op when we first moved to Austin is a favorite community hangout: the Spiderhouse Cafe. The Spiderhouse is an Austin icon filled with creative hipster types, college students, and a few businessmen and women thrown in for good measure. Along the wall in the back room are hundreds of notes written in Sharpie on the wall. Although written in black, most had quite colorful language. By the window, halfway up the wall, by my favorite booth, was this note: "I love you all. I can't say the same for God–JBF." I wish I knew who JBF was because it sounds like he or she has quite the story to tell. The comment was symbolic of a very typical attitude and sentiment about faith, Christianity, and God in Austin. It was that sensibility that drove us to create "Jesus at a Pub," a casual space to talk about spiritual questions and yearnings over a pint of beer or a cup of coffee. We started these monthly conversations at the Spiderhouse.

What we discovered at Jesus at a Pub was that many of our friends, as well as friends of friends, needed a safe space to ask questions that have no good answers, to deconstruct their past experiences of church, and to voice the fragility of whatever faith they did have. Our conversations grew, and often patrons already there would overhear the kinds of conversations we were having and join in (sometimes constructively, sometimes not). These conversations became the place where our understandings of scripture and our theological commitments were genuinely tested against the experiences of others. But the point was never to do anything other than provide a safe space for these conversations to take place. It was not about conversion or getting anybody to worship or anything else. Because the co-op intentionally resists the temptation to try to make these conversations anything other than what they are, they continue to grow in both breadth and depth.

On Jazz and Tradition

For several years as a child I lived just outside of New Orleans, where there aren't many Lutherans. Garrison Keillor's mythical, but iconic, representation of Lake Wobegon Lutherans with their mild manners and modest piety never would have matched the spirit of Lutherans in New Orleans. "The Big Easy," as it is called, lives up to its name. It is a place where the people are loud and friendly, where southern hospitality is a way of life, where the beignets and coffee with chicory are flowing all day and night, where the brass bands lead funeral parades in both dirge and jubilant marches, where Mardi Gras is cause for letting kids out of school, and where the food is kicked up more than a few notches with bold flavors and spices—and of course it is also the birthplace of jazz.

All the best jazz musicians know that creativity is found at the intersection of the given—also called "tradition"—and the unpredictable. During college I took a course on jazz improvisation. I remember the awful feeling in my stomach the first day we all had to give it a go. Not to brag, but I had played trombone for seven years and had played some of the most challenging music written for ensembles. I was an all-state musician going to college on a performing-arts scholarship and majoring in music, and yet at that moment none of that seemed to matter. I knew the given quite well: the scales, the literature, the history, and the theory. But it was the unpredictable that created the nervousness in my stomach. When it was finally my turn to play that day in class, I took one last glance at the key the piece was in, took a deep breath, and started in.

It was terrible.

When everyone had finished their turn, our professor looked down and then back up. "Remember," he told us, "there are no wrong notes in jazz. Only poor choices."

Wynton Marsalis, the only trumpet player to have received a Grammy Award in both jazz and classical music in the same year, says, "Jazz is not just, 'Well, man, this is what I feel like playing.' It's a very structured thing that comes down from a tradition and requires a lot of thought and study."

Jazz has a complex history and it is difficult to define with precision. Jazz emerged from the blending of New Orleans ragtime piano, brass bands, African folk music, and the blues, which was coupled with a social context of lament, praise, and yearning. As jazz developed, it grew into a family of musical styles including swing, Latin, Afro-Cuban, bebop, fusion, and rock. Jazz has utilized soloists, duos, trios, quartets, combos, big bands, and even symphonies. Along with this diversity of ensembles came a diversity of instrumentation and a complex range of musicianship from self-taught players to virtuosos trained at the leading conservatories. So what holds it together? Jazz improvises.

Improvisation is a storyteller. It is the way jazz tells its heritage, its struggles, and its future. Through improvisation, both the medium and the message in jazz are one and the same. It is both composing and performing simultaneously. All the best jazz musicians know that any performance has to be contextual. It happens in a particular place, at a particular time, and before a particular people. Jazz, as it turns out, is a tradition of improvisation.

The same thing can be said about Christianity. It is a tradition of improvisation. Emergent Christianity, like jazz, is not haphazard, but rather is the result of a careful attention to tradition and our changing cultural situation. Faithful improvisers who have apprenticed themselves to a tradition and are now creating new pathways for ministry are leading emergent Christianity in mainline churches.

In a cultural situation in which authority is suspect at best and institutions find their influence dwindling, it is no wonder that people of faith have desperately sought stability. The rate of change appears to be shifting exponentially, and so it is perhaps understandable that the church finds itself asking, "Is there anything constant? In our identity? In our practices? In our beliefs? In our way of life?" These are the kinds of questions that sober even our best efforts to understand the significance of this time we are living in.

However, Christianity is not primarily a place of constancy. Christianity is a tradition of improvisation. If tradition means the passing on of the faith (literally that which is "handed over"), then perhaps we ought to retell the stories of how that happens.

Improvisation at the Edge of the Promised Land

God's people learned early on about the way that tradition is passed on. After being freed from slavery in Egypt, and after forty years of wilderness wandering, they stood at the edge of the promised land. They were recipients of the promise given to them through Abraham.

As the book of Deuteronomy opens, the people of God remember all that God has done. Moses then offers a sermon on the Ten Commandments that provides one of the most memorable passages in all of scripture, including "the Shema":

> Hear, O Israel: The Lord is our God, the Lord alone. You shall love the Lord your God with all your heart, and with all your soul, and with all your might. Keep these words that I am commanding you today in your heart. Recite them to your children and talk about them when you are at home and when you are away, when you lie down and when you rise. Bind them as a sign on your hand, fix them as an emblem on your forehead, and write them on the doorposts of your house and on your gates. (Deut. 6:4–9)

As Patrick Miller points out, this teaching begins with the command to hear (6:4) and to love (6:5).[6] The pattern of the commandment is quite provoking: First listen and be attentive, then respond in love. Although the object of Israel's love is God, it is clear that there can be no mutually exclusive separation between love of God and love of neighbor (the Ten Commandments are given for the well-being of the community). The Shema provides the central identifying reality for Israel's existence: a relationship with Yahweh who is not only the God of their ancestors but also their God on this day. Deuteronomy 6 is not only significant for the Shema but also the next generation. After all, the generations of old will not enter the promised land. Moses will not lead them in because a new kind of leadership is needed for this new day and this new situation. The retelling of the Ten Commandments and the narrative history that goes with them is a way of framing the future for Israel. And so Deut. 6 offers important guidance for those who are also concerned with the future passing on of the faith:

> When your children ask you in time to come, "What is the meaning of the decrees and the statutes and the ordinances that the Lord our God has commanded you?" then you shall say to your children, "We were Pharaoh's slaves in Egypt, but the Lord brought us out of Egypt with a mighty hand. The Lord displayed before our eyes great and awesome signs and wonders against Egypt, against Pharaoh and all his household. He brought us out from there in order to bring us in, to give us the land that he promised on oath to our ancestors. Then the Lord commanded us to observe all these statutes, to fear the Lord our God, for our lasting good, so as to keep us alive, as is now the case. If we diligently observe this entire commandment before the Lord our God, as he has commanded us, we will be in the right." (Deut. 6:20–25)

Patrick Miller is again helpful when he says, "It takes the present (next) generation back to the past and brings the past afresh into the present. Can they learn afresh what it means to love the Lord wholeheartedly?"[7] In a similar way as before, the very structure of the commandment is important. The children appear to know what the statutes and ordinances are; the question is, What is the meaning of all this?

The answer that follows is not merely static, dogmatic law as such, but narrative. The story of Israel is retold in a way that creates a basis for its current life together. The story is retold so that a creative memory is fostered in the imaginations of the next generation. The effect of this creative memory provides a new vision. The passing on of the faith is not the perpetuation of a static constant, but the improvisation of its significance for a new day.

Improvisation in the Gospel of Mark

Given the experience Israel had of passing on the faith in Deuteronomy, one might expect that by the time Jesus arrived on the scene there must have been a healthy understanding of tradition in the community of faith. But of course that is not the case. In Mark's gospel (as well as in Matthew and Luke), a man who has followed the ordinances and statutes of the commandments quite well but is just beginning to ask questions of significance confronts Jesus:

> As [Jesus] was setting out on a journey, a man ran up and knelt before him, and asked him, "Good Teacher, what must I do to inherit eternal life?" Jesus said to him, "Why do you call me good? No one is good but God alone. You know the commandments: 'You shall not murder; You shall not commit adultery; You shall not steal; You shall not bear false witness; You shall not defraud; Honor your father and mother.'" He said to him, "Teacher, I have kept all these since my youth." Jesus, looking at him, loved him and said, "You lack one thing; go, sell what you own, and give the money to the poor, and you will have treasure in heaven; then come, follow me." When he heard this, he was shocked and went away grieving, for he had many possessions. (Mk. 10:17–22)

Apparently, the man seems to be under the impression that the point was to uphold the law without learning afresh what it means to love God. Yet the tradition always demands that we do something with it–that we appropriate it for the present time–for it does not stand still. As is usually the case, it is the impact of the answer that Jesus gives that the man cannot imagine. It is a future for his life that he cannot see. It is costly grace. Jesus invites him to "follow me" and be apprenticed into a new way of understanding the tradition–a way that embraces the story of God's people, as told in the scriptures, as the source for a new imagination about the future, not a conservation of a mythic past. This new way invites us to let go of all the things we hold too tightly and it always entails "metanoia," which is to say, in biblical terms, a change of heart.

In retrospect, I am amazed that this story made it into the canon. It is a story that tells of the risk of love and the very real possibility of profound disappointment. In the biblical narrative "tradition" is not equated with the status quo. Rather, it highlights the past in a way that speaks truth to the present and hope for the future.

Improvising and Apprenticeship

So far I hope to have shown two things. First, how in the story of the Netzer Co-Op we sought to improvise with what it meant to be church in that time and place. Second, that even though I have only used snapshots here and there, the scriptures speak of an improvisational arc in which God is constantly seeking to redeem and reconcile all of creation back to right relationship again. In both cases, creativity is found at the intersection of the given and the unpredictable.

Jeremy Begbie, speaking about theology through the arts, says, "If you don't apprentice yourself to a tradition, you'll never innovate."[8] Those of us from mainline church traditions engaged in the emergent conversation are deeply convinced that the way forward is not to dismiss wholesale everything our traditions bring to the table, but rather to dive even deeper into our faith communities as we seek to innovate in response to our traditions. Across mainline denominations today there is a growing movement of faithful apprentices who are tapping into their family trees in an effort to do a new thing. We are doing this because we are lovers of improvisation. It seems to me that this is precisely how the Holy Spirit moves. The Spirit is moving forward the kingdom of God in new and surprising ways, perhaps seen most clearly in the deliberate reappropriation of centuries-old traditions assumed by the culture to be obsolete. The Spirit is moving forward the kingdom of God through mainline denominations because creativity is found at the intersection of the given and the unpredictable. The Spirit is moving forward the kingdom of God because the Triune God is a jazz musician whose improvisational arc is bent this way and that way until all of creation is reconciled again.

Postscript

Considering that so much of this chapter has been an exercise in narrative theology, it seems a bit disingenuous to leave you with the impression that this is primarily my story or that my telling of it has been anything of a solo performance. Quite the contrary is true and so it is necessary to mention those who have shaped this story the most—those who have been my improvisational ensemble. To Brianna Morris-Brock, who cofounded the Netzer Co-Op, and to Jeff Bergeron, who cofounded Intermission on the campus of Texas Lutheran University: You both have been the best of friends and conspirators. To Paul Soupiset, Greg Ronning, Terry and Jill Frisbie, and Dan and Maria Harrington, who so graciously mentored us and served as our elders. To the others who shaped our community significantly: Ryan Sladek, Michael Gomez, Chip Russell, Ashley Delaciacoma, Kasey Weikel, Jerry and Donna Greiner, Bill Russell, Aaron Strumpel, and so many more. To Mary Sue Dreier, Christian Scharen, Patricia Lull, Russell Rathbun, and Debbie Blue, who so encouraged me to actually put this story in writing and to make meaning out of it and claim it as God's work in the world. Even more than the need to thank you and acknowledge you here is the need to celebrate the community that it takes to do faithful improvisation. That is exactly what this book you are holding does: It celebrates the communities and conversations that are shaping the mainline church in the twenty-first century.

Notes

[1] Paul Berliner, *Thinking in Jazz: The Indefinite Art of Improvisation* (Chicago: University of Chicago, 1994), 63.

[2] For an introduction to emerging approaches to worship from an evangelical perspective, see Dan Kimball's *Emerging Worship: Creating Worship Gatherings for New Generations* (Grand Rapids, Mich.: Zondervan, 2004). For an introduction from a mainline perspective, see Phil Snider and Emily Bowen's *Toward a Hopeful Future: Why the Emergent Church Is Good News for Mainline Congregations* (Cleveland: Pilgrim, 2010).

[3] "Give Me Your Hand," written by Aaron Strumpel. Recorded on *Enter the Worship Circle, Fourth Circle.* Used with permission. Visit Aaron's websites at http://www.aaronstrumpel.com and http://www.entertheworshipcircle.com to learn more about his music.

[4] At the time we did not reflect on the use of "curator" very much. But since then I've been greatly impacted by Jonny Baker of Grace (London), who has written extensively about curating worship. Many of his thoughts about curating have made their way into this reflection.

[5] Shane Claiborne, *The Irresistible Revolution: Living as an Ordinary Radical* (Grand Rapids, Mich.: Zondervan, 2006).

[6] Patrick Miller, *Deuteronomy: Interpretation: A Biblical Commentary for Preaching and Teaching* (Louisville: Westminster John Knox, 1990), 97.

[7] Ibid., 107.

[8] See "Jeremy Begbie: Theology Through the Arts," YouTube video, posted by Faith & Leadership (Duke School of Divinity), http://www.youtube.com/watch?v=UlR3bOsoAdA.

13

Emerging from the Jersey Shore

Secular, Generational, and Theological Frontiers

Mike Baughman

*I learned in confirmation classes about the fiery beginnings of the Method-
ist Church and its signature symbol of the cross wrapped in the flame of the
Spirit. Where had the fire gone? I learned about John Wesley, who said that
if they didn't kick him out of town after he spoke, he wondered if he had really preached the gospel.*

—SHANE CLAIBORNE, METHODIST DROPOUT[1]

The United Methodist Church is what it is today because once upon a
time, we were a frontier church. We Methodists are the new kids on the mainline block and "illegitimate" ones at that. As the offspring of an unplanned
pregnancy from the Anglican Communion, we are not really Protestant,
not really Catholic, and not really Anglican. We were born on the fringes of
ecclesiastical society, and we roared into the new United States of America as
a frontier church on the fringes of society. When the American frontier was
conquered, our ecclesiology focused upon the frontiers of society—for a time.

We lived at the edges where one world met another: Proper eighteenth-
century Oxford students spent time in prisons, ordained priests preached

in the fields, and upstanding British citizens organized efforts in the new America. Once upon a time, we lived on the frontier. Bishops sent pastors to tiny settlements like St. Louis and Fort Worth when no one else was there. We brought "Sunday school" to the streets and brought literacy to one of the world's eighteenth-century inventions—the urban poor. We built hospitals, community centers, vacation spots, and universities. Once upon a time, we were a frontier church with a frontier ecclesiology.

But things have changed. American Methodism is no longer a frontier church movement. Our institutions are established. Just about anyone in America can easily get to a United Methodist church, and most Americans can get to several. Our geographical frontier has closed. Our health care and educational institutions are self-sufficient. Our former identity as a church on the cultural frontier has faded—perhaps for some surprising reasons.

The *National Study of Youth and Religion* performed two longitudinal studies of the religious lives of teens and young adults in America. After thousands of interviews and surveys, their comprehensive research reveals some useful insights into how this shift took place. They affirm N. Jay Demereath's 1996 argument: Denominations are on the decline because—surprisingly enough—they were successful.

> Liberal Protestantism's organizational decline has been accompanied by and is in part arguably the consequence of the fact that liberal Protestantism has won a decisive, larger cultural victory . . . Protestantism's core values—individualism, pluralism, emancipation, tolerance, free critical inquiry, and the authority of human experience—have come to so permeate broader American culture that its own churches as organizations have difficulty surviving . . . these liberal values have a tendency to undermine organizational vitality . . . evidence supporting [these claims] was abundant in the *NSYR* interviews with emerging adults.[2]

In a stroke of irony, the old agenda of the mainline movement is no longer relevant because its accomplished agenda is old hat. Our postmodern society simply has "no idea about the genealogy of their taken-for-granted ideas, that is, from where historically they came."[3] We lost our place on the cultural frontier for the same reason that we lost our place on the geographical frontier—we conquered it and lost an ecclesiology that called us to the edges of society.

How the Jersey Shore Changed My Ecclesiology

There is power on the fringes. I grew up just off the Jersey Shore. I say "just off" because the Jersey Shore is a beautiful place where the line between ocean and land is obvious. You know what to expect—beautiful views, great water, and good sun. But our house was on a lagoon in the middle of a marsh—where the lines between land and ocean were far less defined. The marsh was muddy, difficult to navigate, and smelled like rotten eggs at low tide, but it was also a place that contained incredible biological diversity: crabs, clams, birds, raccoons, muskrats, snakes, and the strangest fish you'll ever encounter. I remember my dad telling me that, without the marshes, the bay and much of the ocean would lose its life. As I got older, I also learned that the "clean beaches" were unpredictable too. Powerful waves could knock you over, pull you out to sea, lead you to get pinched by a crab, yet also give you the best ride of your life. I often think people are drawn to places where the water meets the land because we innately know there is power there.

The early church, like the places where the water meets the land, was a frontier movement that thrived on the fringes. I sometimes wonder if Jesus viewed the disciples like a kid views a chemistry set: "If I put a zealot, a tax-collector, and an uneducated fisherman together, I wonder what will happen?" The very incarnation itself shows just how committed God is to frontier ministry as the divine expression blurs all lines and breaks through the barriers of heavens and temple curtains to once again have access to us. People are drawn to the frontiers of geography and culture, as well as God, because there is power on the fringes. This is part of what draws me to a hyphenated identity in the postmodern church: I know there is power on the fringes because that's where God likes to hang out. I desperately want the Methodist church that I love to recapture the fire and Spirit that lives on the fringes.

To assume that the frontier is closed is to see the world with blinders. There are vast frontiers before us. In this chapter, I wish to explore three frontiers that the United Methodist Church and other denominations are well equipped to engage: secular, generational, and theological. There are far more frontiers than these three, but an exploration of these frontiers serves as a good place to begin. While I could fill this chapter with critiques of what the United Methodist Church is doing wrong, I'd rather offer possibilities and share stories of those who have already begun to engage the postmodern frontier around us. Indeed, the work has already started.

The Secular Frontier

Where can I go from your spirit?
Or where can I flee from your presence?

−Psalm 139:7

Although John Wesley may not have believed that God determines all things, early in his ministry he expressed confidence in God's presence in all things.[4] Later in life, Wesley preached a sermon, "On the Omnipresence of God," further supporting the importance he placed on this doctrine. The presence of God in all things, Wesley argued, is integrally tied to the sustenance of all things. If something exists, God must be sustaining it and must be able to impact change upon it. Therefore, God is present.[5] Wesley's final emphasis on omnipresence came at his deathbed when he uttered his last words–"the best of all is that God is with us."

As I think about the frontier church movements of the eighteenth and nineteenth centuries, it's easy to see how confidence in God's omnipresence dominated approaches to ministry. With the conviction that God's presence could not be contained in physical sanctuaries, George Whitfield, John Wesley, and Jonathan Edwards spoke in the streets and fields. Even in persecution, they believed that God was present.

As I recall their ministries, I cannot help but think of connections to the emerging churches, which now meet in homes, coffee shops, bars, and even old car dealerships. Eddie Gibbs and Ryan Bolger have described an engagement with the secular to be one of the most significant traits of the emerging church movement. By identifying with the life of Jesus, emerging churches "tear down the church practices that foster a secular mind-set, namely, that there are secular spaces, times, or activities . . . Sacralization in emerging churches is about one thing: the destruction of the sacred/secular split of modernity."[6]

Few aspects of the emerging church movement are more critical for our denominations to adopt than a respectful engagement of the "secular." Rather than engaging the secular in order to bring Jesus into it–as many have done in mainline history–the emerging churches engage the secular assuming that Jesus is already there. In so doing, they implicitly train their congregations and communities to believe that God is more than a sectioned-off part of someone's life.

In many ways, the emerging church movement has been successful at recapturing the frontier church mentality that Wesley encouraged with his statements on the omnipresence of God. Wesley asked, "What are we to make of this awful consideration [that God is present in all places]? . . . Should we not labour continually to acknowledge his presence?"[7]

Imagine what it would be like if we actually believed that God was everywhere. The United Methodist Church has set an ambitious goal: 650 new church starts in four years.[8] Instead of chasing after God into the streets and alleys of society–the fringes–we've decided to make more places for God to hang out as if the divine dance needs another place to wait for us on Sunday. We have constructed walls for God, compartmentalizing the divine into Sunday-morning church buildings–not realizing that God has already snuck out the back door to throw birthday parties for prostitutes, hold funerals for drug users in comedy clubs, and inspire the barista who tends his own flock each day of the week. Starting new, traditional churches will not make us a frontier church. It will just make us the Starbucks of the church world, with Methodist churches across the street from Methodist churches.

The problem is not a lack of church buildings. Our bigger challenge is that we've limited our understanding of church to a building with a steeple, reduced mission to a trip, and lost our ability to wed church living with mission. If we want to communicate the presence of God in the world and sustain congregations that draw people for reasons other than geography, then we should be starting alternative congregations. We should stop building so many churches and start opening coffee houses whose profits dig wells for villages in Africa. We should organize congregations around thrift shops, soup kitchens, day care co-ops, clinics, employment offices, and community centers. Organizing worship communities around a shared mission will yield far better results for the kingdom in a postmodern society than organizing for the sake of being an organized body that worships God. What if we engaged God by worshiping in missional outposts on Sunday mornings instead of retreating into a sanctuary in order to engage God?[9] Far from abandoning worship of God, what I propose is that we push thrift shop clothes racks against the wall, circle up the coffee house chairs, and worship God surrounded by the work of our calling. This could alter our self-perception, ecclesiology, and theology. In so doing, clergy might literally place the communion cup in the middle of the mission field. Then we might know that the blood in the streets and the blood in the cup are one and the same.

These frontier congregation starts do not have to be big. As Shane Claiborne has written,

> This thing Jesus called the kingdom of God is emerging across the globe in the most unexpected places, a gentle whisper amid the chaos. Little people with big dreams are reimagining the world. Little movements of communities of ordinary radicals are committed to doing small things with great love.[10]

These efforts may start and remain small. They may rise and fade as people come and go. Yet we should acknowledge that small and strong are not mutually exclusive terms.

The rising generation is not interested in talk, but action. After years of study, one pollster describes the rising generation as one "looking for meaning, not more doctrines and isms to live by."[11] Young adults believe that "the best thing about religion is that it helps people to be good, to make good choices, to behave well."[12] We have the opportunity to build upon our strongest positive perceptions, adopt a frontier-church ecclesiology, and find ways to offer meaning in the omnipresence of God. This can take place in a wide variety of contexts that extend well beyond the walls of the sanctuary. Simply stating that "God is everywhere" is not enough for our postmodern world. We must live into such a conviction by boldly dismantling the sacred/secular divide.

The Generational Frontier

I can change the world
And I refuse to believe that
I am a part of a lost generation[13]

In order to bring about any significant ecclesiastical shift, we have to address youth and young adult ministry. I do not primarily suggest this because they are the constituents who have the potential to be involved in our churches the longest. Instead, ecclesiastical shifts must begin with efforts at youth and young adult ministries because adolescence, by nature, is a hyperexpression of dominant cultural trends. When one sets aside the particularities of life situation and physical ability, ministry that connects with teenagers will generally reach the rest of the congregation. More important, when God wanted to change the world in the deepest way imaginable, the divine Trinity hired a youth minister–Gabriel–who visited with a teenager and challenged her to change the world.

Yet as many within mainline congregations already know all too well, vital youth and young adult ministries elude much of the church. In order to reach out to the generational frontier, there are a few myths that need to be dispelled.

Myth #1: Churches That Have Hired a Youth Minister Are Already on the Generational Frontier

Despite the emphasis on youth and young adult ministry, we do precious little to support it. We hire youth ministers who have either little theological training or little intent to stay very long. We typically train and hire youth ministers for the wrong reasons (e.g., because they are cool, rather than because they know how to train a team of lay volunteers) and, when it comes to funding, we put youth ministry very low on the priority list. We ought to heed the warnings of Christian Smith in *Soul Searching*:

> When religious communities do not invest in their youth, unsurprisingly, their youth are less likely to invest in their religious faith. Supplies of resources, personnel, organizations and programs are not the whole story, but they are a significant part of it . . . when it comes to youth, religious congregations, denominations and other religious organizations generally "will get back what they invest" and normally not a lot more.[14]

A resurgence of energy into youth ministry is a critical step to engaging the generational frontier. Revitalization of youth ministry is seen by Robert Weems and Ann Michel as a critical tool in developing younger clergy[15] and is a necessary step if we hope to retain students like Shane Claiborne, who could not find vitality in the Methodist church that formed him. As the *National Study for Youth and Religion* affirms, young adults who were involved in religious organizations in high school are more likely to be involved in college and beyond.[16]

Myth #2: Teens Are Too Busy to Be a Part of Church

Research consistently reveals that the mission field for teens is ripe. "Millennials think and talk more about faith, and do more with it, than older people realize . . . in polls, teens cite religion as the second-strongest influence in their lives, just behind parents, but ahead of teachers, boy/girlfriends, peers and the media."[17] Smith highlights this interest: "The problem is not that youth won't come to church (most will), or that they hate church (few do), or that they don't want to listen to religious ministers or mature mentoring adults (they will and do). But this does not mean that youth are currently being well engaged by their religious congregation. They generally are not."[18]

We have failed teenagers in the church by not asking anything of them, and in the process we haven't helped them build a set of core commitments and values. Apart from asking them not to have sex until they get married, we rarely challenge their decisions to prioritize soccer games over worship, to spend money on going to the movies instead of on the poor, or to sit with their friends instead of outcasts in the school cafeteria. It's not that teenagers don't have any time to invest; it's just that the investment of their time is based on a prioritization of what they value. When youth ministers intentionally target the "cool kids" in a school in an effort to make youth group "cool," or when youth ministry is reduced to entertaining kids who are already hyperentertained, then what does this say about the core commitments and values that our churches embody?

Jesus embodied a set of core convictions that were literally worth dying for. When we fail to challenge our youth, young adults, and congregations to invest in such commitments, we deny them the opportunity to find something worth living for. If church is just one of many places where teenagers might go to be entertained, then how are we offering any kind of alternative witness or community?

Myth #3: Youth and Young Adult Ministries Are Programs to Benefit the Congregation

In our increasingly mobile society, it is less and less likely that the teens we raise in a congregation will be the adults who later lead that congregation. Although they may be active in church down the road, they are more likely to move away than remain home, and they may very well end up in another denomination. Student ministries are not primarily for the benefit of one congregation, but for the kingdom. What if we inspired our congregations to be proud of the way we equip disciples, much like Jesus did, and send them into the world to "go and do likewise"? Not in order to further our own particular congregations, but for the well-being of the church at large?

The Theological Frontier

From the cowardice that dares not face new truth,
From the laziness that is contented with half-truth,
From the arrogance that thinks it knows all truth,
Good Lord, deliver me.[19]

When I was a little kid, I made ashtrays for my mom in art class and gave them to her, full of pride, even though she didn't smoke. While dating the woman who became my wife, I kissed her good-bye whenever we parted. When my son was very young, I comforted him whenever he was upset. I did my best to make him feel better, even if he inadvertently caused his own hurt.

I don't make ashtrays for my mother anymore. Instead, I talk to her, cook for her, thank her for all she means in my life. I still kiss my wife good-bye every time we part, but we also pray together every night before we go to sleep. I still comfort my son, but sometimes I don't do that until after we've talked about what he did wrong.

Ten years from now, I'll love my son, wife, and mother differently than I do now. I will know and believe different things about them than I do now. What I have for them is true love, which always responds to the needs of the other and always seeks to know more about the other. True love is bidirectional and dynamic. It's a dance.

If we believe that God left us the agency to decide whether or not to love God in return, then it makes sense to believe that God intends for us to share in *true love* with the divine. We love God, according to who God is, and express it in ways the Spirit makes available to us. I believe that God loves us back in similar ways–according to who we are and what we need, and sometimes this changes in response to where we are on life's journey.

While the generational frontier discussed previously is important, we need to push to an even more uncomfortable frontier. Eddie Gibbs and Ryan Bolger claim that generational studies have "done more harm than good for those churches that believe the church's main problem is a generational one. Generational issues are imbedded in a much deeper cultural and philosophical shift from modernity to postmodernity."[20] The best generational ministries will only take us so far. The mainline churches were formed on the motto *semper reformandi* (always reform), yet our theologies have become relatively stagnant. Why are so many in mainline churches afraid of the spirit of the reformers? The likely answer is that we are the new establishment, although that seems far too obvious, arrogant, and disappointing.

While many assume that the unchanging nature of God accompanied by a stable theology provides comfort to many in our congregations, I wonder if just as many in our culture are disquieted by how established our theology has become—especially when presented in a dogmatic fashion that leaves little room for diverse theological opinions. Many with a "modern" philosophical-theological perspective are disturbed by the very notion of a theological frontier that is willing to examine and potentially discard parts of our theological heritage. Herein lies a fundamental difference that mainline churches must understand (even if they do not agree) in order to thrive in the postmodern world: "Moderns" see contradiction, confusion, irreverence, danger, discrepancy, and discord; "Postmoderns" see layers, nuance, ambiguity, mystery, and major sevenths.

This shift from modern to postmodern could not be more important, nor could it be more ignored by the Methodist Church—even though we should be the ones jumping on the postmodern bandwagon. After all, emergents are thriving on "generative friendships," and the conversations they yield, which is just an updated expression of what John Wesley identified to be a means of grace: holy conferencing![21] Consider the fact that, historically speaking, Methodists are not a confessional church. The closest we have to dogma are the Articles of Religion and a bunch of sermons, which were written to inspire discussion, thought, and consideration! John Wesley's sermon "On Catholic Spirit" established a desire among the Methodist movement for theological diversity, and our theology is determined by a combination of scripture, tradition, reason, and experience. The nature of our theological system and core beliefs should lead us to the frontiers of theology, but despite guaranteed employment, our pastors are tame—so worried to offend that we rarely say anything (or so worried that someone might believe the wrong thing that we rarely give people room to explore).

Embracing the theological frontier will help the church embark upon the generational frontier. Sermons should explore the difficulties of faith and belief and not just tout the benefits of them. For emerging adults, "Bullshit detectors are set on high all the time . . . Like guild merchants of old, [they] bite every metaphorical coin they are handed to see if the metal is real or false."[22]

We shouldn't engage theological frontiers for the sake of being interesting or "relevant" to a rising generation or postmodern mentality, but because of our desire to be faithful. We know that we have not figured everything out and that we still want to "go onto perfection," continuing the reformation cry, *semper reformandi.*

Like many postmoderns, my willingness to question and challenge items at the core of my faith is not an expression of distrust or disobedience to God or the scriptures. On the contrary, it is an act of faith and trust in the belief that God is big enough to handle my questions and doubts. Questions affirm our belief that the scriptures, when searched diligently in community and with all the tools available to us, will stand whatever tests are laid before them. I know that nothing short of the faith that has defined my life is at stake when I ask hard questions of God or the Bible. But because I trust, I ask the questions nonetheless. And so do postmoderns.[23]

Ready for the Frontier

My hope is not to make the United Methodist Church an emergent denomination. The notion that the United Methodist Church or any other denomination could, as a whole, become "emergent" is absurd (especially if one accepts Gibbs and Bolger's strict criteria for what constitutes an emerging church).[24] But that is not to say that the emerging church could not exist within a denominational body in a similar way that the Methodist movement existed within the Anglican Church. Is there a risk that such an emergent body may eventually split from the main body as the Methodist Church twice did from the Anglican Communion? Of course! But it is by no means predetermined.

How can United Methodists engage emergent expressions of postmodern Christianity? Here are a few suggestions.

Resources

Despite the overall decline in attendance, giving in United Methodist churches continues to grow. In 2005, United Methodists donated $4.7 billion to church-affiliated organizations and projects. To put that in perspective, Starbucks's gross income in 2009 was $4.9 billion. And there is good reason to suggest that giving to church programs and projects will continue with the rising generation. Younger generations want to participate in symbolic actions that free them from the unbridled consumerism that defines their lives: "To one in three [young adults] success is the freedom to make a large charitable contribution."[25]

Furthermore, United Methodists have enormous untapped resources at their disposal that could be used to start new congregations on the secular frontier:

> Doug Ruffle of the [Greater] New Jersey Annual Conference did a study of the property assets of local churches in his annual conference. He discovered that the 197 churches in his annual conference that did not receive a profession of faith had combined assets of $170 million. Many of these churches are close to being discontinued. If even five percent of these congregations turned their assets over to their annual conference, that would provide $8.5 million to invest.[26]

We have enough wealth and donations to be able to risk creative, outside-the-box church starts because, if we fail, we do not risk folding as a denomination. Many congregations could support new church starts and not risk very much themselves. Our financial security could promote the experimentation and exploration necessary for creative expressions of frontier ministry.

Structure

Currently, bishops have significant power in the United Methodist Church. They ordain, enforce expectations of local churches, and, most significantly, determine which pastors serve in which congregations. A system like this allows churches to be held accountable and pastors to be challenged to meet a bishop or cabinet member's expectation. Yet the vast majority of emergent expressions in the Methodist Church have developed in grassroots ways. Far from being a bad thing, all movements, it seems, must start in this way. Imagine, however, the potential for emerging expressions of church in a denominational structure that could take place with top-down support and motivation as well. To accomplish this, we could risk putting young clergy in conference leadership positions–not as token members (which is the usual gesture), but with a critical mass that has the ability to influence change on boards and agencies. We could continue the positive trend of inviting people like Phyllis Tickle, Elaine Heath, and Nadia Bolz-Weber to speak to our Diocese, Annual Conferences, and Synod events and to take this one step further by asking successful practitioners to train our bishops, superintendents, moderators, and leaders.

Our Theology

I spent a year serving as a United Methodist minister appointed to an Episcopal church. One time, one of the priests chided our Methodist theology. "Episcopal theology," he said, "is far more stable than your Methodist approach. We believe in an equal balance of scripture, tradition, and reason–a three-legged stool. You add in experience and make the scripture leg bigger than the rest. With four legs–one of them too long–your theology is imbalanced." I agreed and told him that's precisely why I love the Methodist Church. I want a church that is humble enough and open enough to know that our theology should wobble so that there's space for diversity on our theological stool, which might lean a bit to the right and then to the left. I also want a church that has tradition, history, and wisdom to share. This is another gift that United Methodists bring to the emergent table.

Engaging the Frontier

Those of us who desperately love our denominations but who have also swallowed the red pill of postmodern culture cannot go back. The culture from which we came is no longer the culture to which we are called, but we do not feel like we need to leave the church that gave us the best gift of all–the Triune God who is with us! I began this essay with *once upon a time.* I want to end it with *happening right now:*

About 215 years ago, in the rural hills of New Jersey, one of the first Methodist bishops started a congregation, now called Asbury United Methodist Church. Today, the pastor is a second-career woman. The average

age of the congregation is in the eighties. In the surrounding area, there is a significant population of at-risk young adults who have few venues for community. Asbury's pastor, Rev. Gina Yeske, saw a need and offered a vision.

Members from Asbury United Methodist Church donated significant amounts of money and labor to partner with another small congregation (175-year-old Bloomsbury United Methodist Church) to remodel Asbury's church basement into *The Wine Cellar*–a young adult ministry venue with coffee, Wi-Fi, comfortable gathering space, and an altar space between two very old stained-glass windows. In less than a year, a community of roughly twenty-five young adults has grown up around worship, fellowship, and theological reflection. In addition to the pastors, members of the young adult community preach, and they discuss "emerging" theologians ranging from Rob Bell to Mark Driscoll. Yeske muses, "We offer a place of love to those that church and society have lost–and we're building a community for some of the most hurting people in our community." I asked the Rev. Drew Dyson, a doctoral student who lives in the area and helps with *The Wine Cellar* if the congregation members are involved.

> Some are–they do a great job loving these young adults and asking them about their lives. Others cannot stand to be in the room because of the colors on the walls, but they aren't upset about the place. They knew that they were dying as a congregation and really didn't want to change, but they *did* want something to continue in this place that has been holy to them. So they gave their money and their space to make it happen. And it's beautiful.

Rev. Yeske calls *The Wine Cellar* Asbury United Methodist Church's "dying gift."

One year ago, Asbury United Methodist Church was a stagnant, declining church. Yet they captured the energy and frontier spirit that, 215 years ago, led to its foundation. May we find ways to "go and do likewise," living on the fringes of society where the Holy Spirit lives and dwells.

Notes

[1] Shane Claiborne, *The Irresistible Revolution: Living as an Ordinary Radical* (Grand Rapids, Mich.: Zondervan, 2006), 43.

[2] Christian Smith and Patricia Snell, *Souls in Transition* (New York: Oxford University, 2009), 287–88.

[3] Ibid., 288.

[4] John Wesley, "The Imperfection of Human Knowledge," in *The Works of John Wesley*, vol. 6 (Grand Rapids, Mich.: Baker, 2007), 337.

[5] John Wesley, "On the Omnipresence of God," available online at http://new.gbgm-umc.org/umhistory/wesley/sermons/111.

[6] Eddie Gibbs and Ryan Bolger, *Emerging Churches: Creating Christian Community in Postmodern Cultures* (Grand Rapids, Mich.: Baker Academic, 2005), 66.

[7] Wesley, "On the Omnipresence of God."

[8] To see the strategic plan of new church starts by the UMC see Path1 website, http://www.path1.org.

[9] Several denominations have struggled with the role of deacons in their congregations. What if churches were started by deacons with clergy assisting them?

[10] Claiborne, *The Irresistible Revolution*, 25.

[11] John Zogby, *The Way We'll Be* (New York: Random House, 2008), 147.

[12] Smith and Snell, *Souls in Transition*, 286.

[13] "Lost Generation." YouTube video, posted by Jonathan Reed, http://www.youtube.com/watch?v=42E2fAWM6rA&feature=related.

[14] Christian Smith and Melina Lundquist Denton, *Soul Searching: The Religious and Spiritual Lives of American Teenagers* (New York: Oxford University, 2009), 262.

[15] Robert Weems and Ann Michel, *The Crisis of Younger Clergy* (Nashville: Abingdon, 2008), 115.

[16] Smith and Snell, *Souls in Transition*, 282.

[17] Neil Howe and William Strauss, *Millennials Rising* (New York: Vintage Books, 2000), 234.

[18] Smith and Snell, *Souls in Transition*, 266.

[19] Anonymous-Kenyan, "For the Spirit of Truth," in *United Methodist Hymnal* (Nashville: United Methodist Publishing House, 1989), #597.

[20] Gibbs and Bolger, *Emerging Churches*, 22.

[21] See Emergent Village, "Values and Practices," http://www.emergentvillage.com/about-information/values-and-practices.

[22] Zogby, *The Way We'll Be*, 197.

[23] See Mark Feldmeir's *Stirred, Not Shaken: Themes for an Emerging Generation* (St. Louis: Chalice, 2005).

[24] Gibbs and Bolger outline nine characteristics of an emerging church: "Emerging churches (1) identify with the life of Jesus, (2) transform the secular realm, and (3) live highly communal lives. Because of these three activities, they (4) welcome the stranger, (5) serve with generosity, (6) participate as producers, (7) create as created beings, (8) lead as a body, and (9) take part in spiritual activities" (44–45).

[25] Zogby, *The Way We'll Be*, 37.

[26] Craig Miller, *7 Myths of the United Methodist Church* (Nashville: Discipleship Resources, 2008), 173.

Afterword

All in the Family

Doug Pagitt

I tend to use the metaphor of family in conversations about church and church structures far too often. My friend Toby once said, "I don't mind the use of the family as a metaphor for church, but I do mind when it is the only metaphor used." I think Toby is right; family is not the only way to think about the church and I was committed to not use it in my contribution to *The Hyphenateds*. But I have broken that commitment. I think for good cause, however. If there was ever a time to use the notion of family to help us see clearly, it is in the conversation that has taken place in this book.

I live in a blended family, but we only go by one surname–Pagitt. My wife was raised a Rasmussen (she was also a Keiner, but the only name given to her and the only name she used was Rasmussen). Now she, like the other five of us, goes by Pagitt. No hyphens in her name or mine.

In our family we have four children, two that Shelley and I share genes with and two that came into our family through adoption. When Ruben and Chico became Pagitts we did not want them to lose their sense of origin and family. They were five and six years old at the time of adoption and were keenly aware of being Vijaro Meranos. My sons come from a culture where your father's surname does not suffice on legal documents; you must also include your mother's maiden name. They were legally Vijaro Meranos. So when they became Pagitts we had some figuring to do.

We talked long and hard about how to keep the connection to the life they came from while making our life as a new family. We considered adding their familial name to each of ours as middle names. I would become Douglas Arnold *Vijaro* Pagitt. But as it turns out a name change is a rather complex endeavor at any time other than marriage. So we left our names as they were but kept Ruben and Chico's familial names as their "middle names."

One of the options we have in North American culture is to use family names as middle names. And many do so sometimes for important and even fun reasons.

My friend Rachel Held Evans kept her maiden name as a middle name and responded to a Facebook question I posted about the use of hyphenated names with this: "I didn't hyphenate, but I kept my maiden name as my middle name and use it on my blog, books, etc. I guess all those years of being an incomplete sentence (Rachel Held . . .) made me long for completion. :-)"

I know many couples who upon marriage add the other person's family name to theirs as a middle name. In fact, many people's middle names were their mother's or grandmother's maiden name. It is a clever work-around to keep the family connection.

Some go a step further when they marry and make a new name for them both. My friend Lisa Ellis married Eric Woods; they are now the Ellwoods.

The other option is the hyphenated last name. A number of good friends are "hyphenateds," and so we hear of the awkwardness that can come with having a name with punctuation in it. It makes it difficult when making a dinner reservation or filling out a form that doesn't have room for all the letters. People having to put together alphabetical lists are often puzzled by not knowing which name to list.

And hyphenating can create some good teasing opportunities. My friend Paul responded to my Facebook question by writing: "My sister, Sarah Carlson, married Brian Carlson. I encouraged them to hyphenate their last names, but they didn't go for it." And someone else asked: "What does a person do who marries someone with a hyphenated name, double hyphenate?"

With some of this in mind we decided to forgo the hyphen in our family name. But others have not, and for good reason.

They know there is an awkwardness and inconvenience that comes with a longer than normal name. They are willing to take on the burden of having to explain whose name is whose. They are willing to put up with the social judgments that come with a husband taking his wife's name or being a woman who "won't submit to a patriarchal system."

For many people their families of origin are often seen as too important, too formational, too persistent to lay one aside for the other. Nadia Bolz-Weber says, "Matthew and I are both Bolz-Weber . . . because it's a merger and not a hostile takeover."

This is, in my opinion, where the hyphenateds of the emerging church world find themselves. They recognize that they are in a new relationship, but they also know where they come from. The want to be fully in the emerging family, but as a product of another family.

They can no more leave their Lutheran family, Methodist heritage, or Presbyterian spiritual community than we could tell Ruben and Chico that they were no longer Vijaros. It simply would not have been honest. The ecclesial hyphenateds are doing what they can to live in a complex blended family.

And there are those for whom the family they came from was equally important but not a primary means of identity. They were free to think of themselves first by their given name, not their last name. When they introduce themselves they rarely would give it the "Bond, James Bond" approach. They were not rejecting their family heritage, simply seeing themselves as more than their familial name. They are the ones who will, without malice, make a new name as they make a new family.

I see both of these as valid in the ecclesial world. Those who are making a new life in faith as a community and tend to lean into their first name and those who want to honor and stay connected to their forbearers. In fact, our thoughts on whether to hyphenate our church identity or not are quite often a product of our personalities and our experiences of our own families. There is no getting away from the influence of our past, whether we call it by name or not.

So what is this hyphenated thing about? Well, in part, it is all of us trying to figure out the best way to move forward in our world from the particular pasts from which we are emerging. And being a part of a blended family (in my home and faith) is a beautiful thing whether we use the punctuation or not.

Bibliography

Abeysekara, Ananda. *The Colors of the Robe.* Columbia: University of South Carolina, 2002.

Adams, Hazard, and Leroy Searle, eds. *Critical Theory Since 1965.* Tallahassee: University Presses of Florida, 1986.

Alexander, Jeffrey C., and Steven Seidman. *Culture and Society: Contemporary Debates.* Cambridge: Cambridge University, 1990.

Allen, O. Wesley. *The Homiletic of All Believers: A Conversational Approach to Proclamation and Preaching.* Louisville: Westminster John Knox, 2005.

Archbishop's Council on Mission and Fore. *Mission-Shaped Church: Church Planting and Fresh Expressions of Church in a Changing Context.* New York: Seabury Books, 2010.

Bartlett, David L. *Between the Bible and the Church: New Methods for Biblical Preaching.* Nashville: Abingdon, 1999.

Bass, Diana Butler. *Christianity for the Rest of Us: How the Neighborhood Church Is Transforming the Faith.* New York: HarperOne, 2006.

———. *A People's History of Christianity: The Other Side of the Story.* New York: HarperOne, 2009.

Bell, Rob. *Velvet Elvis: Repainting the Christian Faith.* Grand Rapids, Mich.: Zondervan, 2005.

Berliner, Paul. *Thinking in Jazz: The Indefinite Art of Improvisation.* Chicago: University of Chicago, 1994.

Bibby, Reginald. *Restless Churches: How Canada's Churches Can Contribute to the Emerging Religious Renaissance.* Toronto: Novalis, 2004.

The Book of Common Prayer. Oxford, England: Oxford University, 1662.

The Book of Common Prayer. New York: Church Publishing, 1979.

Bosch, David. *Transforming Mission: Paradigm Shifts in Theology of Mission.* Maryknoll, N.Y.: Orbis, 1991.

Campolo, Tony, and Brian McLaren. *Adventures in Missing the Point.* Grand Rapids, Mich.: Zondervan, 2003.

Caputo, John D. *On Religion.* London: Routledge, 2001.

———. *What Would Jesus Deconstruct? The Good News of Postmodernism for the Church.* Grand Rapids, Mich.: Baker Academic, 2007.

Childers, Jana. *Performing the Word: Preaching as Theatre.* Nashville: Abingdon, 1998.

Claiborne, Shane. *The Irresistible Revolution: Living as an Ordinary Radical.* Grand Rapids, Mich.: Zondervan, 2006.

Clayton, Philip. *Transforming Christian Theology: For Church and Society*. Minneapolis: Fortress, 2010.

Cosgrove, Charles, and Dow Edgerton. *In Other Words: Incarnational Translation for Preaching*. Grand Rapids, Mich.: Eerdmans, 2007.

Coupland, Douglas. *Life After God*. New York: Pocket Books, 1994.

Croft, Steven, Ian Mosby, and Stephanie Spellers, eds. *Ancient Faith, Future Mission: Fresh Expressions in the Sacramental Tradition*. New York: Church Publishing, 2010.

Daly, Mary. *Outercourse*. New York: Harper, 1992.

———. *Pure Lust*. New York: Harper, 1984.

Daly, Mary, and Jane Caputi. *Webster's First Intergalactic Wickedary of the English Language*. Boston: Beacon, 1987.

Dennis, Marie, Cynthia Moe-Lobeda, Joseph Nangle, and Stuart Taylor. *St. Francis and the Foolishness of God*. Maryknoll, N.Y.: Orbis, 2002.

DeYoung, Kevin, and Ted Kluck. *Why We're Not Emergent: By Two Guys Who Should Be*. Chicago: Moody, 2008.

Dixon, A. C., and Reuben Torrey, eds. *The Fundamentals*. Vol. 6. Chicago: Testimony, c. 1915.

Douglas, Ian, and Kwok Pui Lan, eds. *Beyond Colonial Anglicanism: The Anglican Communion in the Twenty-First Century*. New York: Church Publishing, 2001.

Engel, Randy. *The Rite of Sodomy*. Export, Pa.: New Engel, 2006.

Feldmeir, Mark. *Stirred, Not Shaken: Themes for an Emerging Generation*. St. Louis: Chalice, 2005.

Foss, Michael. *Power Surge: Six Marks of Discipleship for a Changing Church*. Minneapolis: Fortress, 2000.

Foster, Durwood, ed. *The Irrelevance and Relevance of the Christian Message*. Cleveland: Pilgrim, 1996.

Friedman, Edwin. *A Failure of Nerve: Leadership in the Age of the Quick Fix*. New York: Seabury Books, 2007.

Frost, Michael. *Exiles: Living Missionally in a Post-Christian Culture*. Peabody, Mass.: Hendrickson, 2006.

Gibbs, Eddie, and Ryan Bolger. *Emerging Churches: Creating Christian Community in Postmodern Cultures*. Grand Rapids, Mich.: Baker Academic, 2005.

Green, Laurie. *Let's Do Theology: Resources for Contextual Theology*. New York: Continuum, 2010.

Hadaway, C. Kirk. "Facts on Episcopal Church Growth." Pamphlet. New York: Episcopal Church Center, 2008.

Hall, Douglas John. *Bound and Free: A Theologian's Journey*. Minneapolis: Fortress, 2005.

Hamilton, William. *On Taking God out of the Dictionary*. New York: McGraw-Hill, 1974.

Harrison, Lesley, ed. *Living the Welcome: The Journal*. Toronto: The United Church of Canada Publishing House, 2007.

Heath, Elaine A., and Scott T. Kisker. *Longing for Spring: A New Vision for Wesleyan Community*. Eugene, Oreg.: Cascade, 2010.

Hegel, Georg Wilhelm Friedrich. *Phenomenology of the Spirit*. Oxford University, 1979.

Heifetz, Ronald. *Leadership without Easy Answers*. Cambridge, Mass.: Harvard University, 1994.

Jones, Tony. *The New Christians: Dispatches from the Emergent Frontier.* San Francisco: Jossey Bass, 2008.

Hillerbrand, Hans. *The Division of Christendom.* Louisville: Westminster John Knox, 2007.

Howe, Neil, and William Strauss. *Millennials Rising.* New York: Vintage Books, 2000.

Keller, Catherine. *God and Power.* Minneapolis: Fortress, 2005.

Kierkegaard, Søren. *Attack Upon Christendom.* Princeton, N.J.: Princeton University, 1968.

———. *Concluding Unscientific Postscript to the Philosophical Crumbs.* Cambridge: Cambridge University, 2009.

Kimball, Dan. *Emerging Worship: Creating Worship Gatherings for New Generations.* Grand Rapids, Mich.: Zondervan, 2004.

Leahy, D. G. *Foundation.* Albany, N.Y.: SUNY, 1996.

Loehe, Wilhelm. *Three Books about the Church.* Translated and edited by James L. Schaaf. Philadelphia: Fortress, 1969.

Lose, David. *Confessing Jesus Christ: Preaching in a Postmodern World.* Grand Rapids, Mich.: Eerdmans, 2003.

Luther, Martin. *First Principles of the Reformation or the Ninety-Five Theses and Three Primary Works of Dr. Martin Luther.* Translated by Henry Wace and C. Buccheim. London: John Murray, 1883.

McClendon, James Jr. *Doctrine: Systematic Theology.* Vol. 2. Nashville: Abingdon, 1994.

McClure, John. *The Roundtable Pulpit: Where Leadership and Preaching Meet.* Nashville: Abingdon, 1995.

McLaren, Brian. *A Generous Orthodoxy.* Grand Rapids, Mich.: Zondervan, 2004.

———. *A New Kind of Christianity: Ten Questions That Are Transforming the Faith.* New York: HarperOne, 2010.

Miller, Craig. *7 Myths of the United Methodist Church.* Nashville: Discipleship Resources, 2008.

Miller, Patrick. *Deuteronomy: Interpretation: A Biblical Commentary for Preaching and Teaching.* Louisville: Westminster John Knox, 1990.

Naas, Michael. *Taking on the Tradition: Jacques Derrida and the Legacies of Deconstruction.* Stanford, Calif.: Stanford University, 2002.

Pagitt, Doug. *Church in the Inventive Age.* Minneapolis: Fortress, 2010.

———. *Preaching Re-Imagined.* Grand Rapids, Mich.: Zondervan, 2005.

Pagitt, Doug, and Tony Jones, eds. *An Emergent Manifesto of Hope.* Grand Rapids, Mich.: Baker, 2007.

Pelikan, Jaroslav. *The Vindication of Tradition: The 1983 Jefferson Lecture in the Humanities.* New Haven, Conn.: Yale University, 1986.

Phillips, J. B. *Your God Is Too Small.* New York: Macmillan, 1953.

Pink, Daniel H. *A Whole New Mind: Why Right-Brainers Will Rule the Future.* New York: Riverhead Books, 2006.

Presler, Titus. *Going Global with God: Reconciling Mission in a World of Difference.* New York: Church Publishing, 2010.

Rah, Soong-Chan. *The Next Evangelicalism: Freeing the Church from Western Cultural Captivity.* Downers Grove, Ill: Intervarsity, 2009.

Raschke, Carl. *GloboChrist.* Grand Rapids, Mich.: Baker Academic, 2008.

——. *The Next Reformation: Why Evangelicals Must Embrace Postmodernity.* Grand Rapids, Mich.: Baker Academic, 2004.

——. *Painted Black.* New York: Harper, 1990.

Reese, Martha Grace. *Unbinding Your Heart.* St. Louis: Chalice, 2008.

Rieger, Joerg. *Christ and Empire: From Paul to Postcolonial Times.* Minneapolis: Fortress, 2007.

Rollins, Peter. *The Fidelity of Betrayal: Towards a Church Beyond Belief.* Brewster, Mass.: Paraclete, 2008.

——. *How (Not) to Speak of God.* Brewster, Mass.: Paraclete, 2006.

——. *Insurrection: To Believe Is Human; to Doubt Divine.* New York: Howard, 2011.

Rose, Lucy Atkinson. *Sharing the Word: Preaching in the Roundtable Church.* Louisville: Westminster John Knox, 1997.

Satlow, Michael L. *Creating Judaism: History, Tradition, Practice.* New York: Columbia University, 2006.

Sherwood, Yvonne. *Derrida's Bible: Reading a Page of Scripture with a Little Help from Derrida.* New York: Palgrave Macmillan, 2004.

Sittler, Josepp. *Gravity and Grace.* Minneapolis: Augsburg Publishing House, 1986.

Smith, Christian, and Melina Lundquist Denton. *Soul Searching.* New York: Oxford University, 2005.

Smith, Christian, and Patricia Snell. *Souls in Transition.* New York: Oxford University, 2009.

Snider, Phil, and Emily Bowen. *Toward a Hopeful Future: Why the Emergent Church Is Good News for Mainline Congregations.* Cleveland: Pilgrim, 2010.

Spellers, Stephanie. *Radical Welcome: Embracing God, The Other and the Spirit of Transformation.* New York: Church Publishing, 2006.

Stevens, Jarrett. *The Deity Formerly Known as God.* Grand Rapids, Mich.: Zondervan, 2006.

Stone, Bryan P. *Evangelism after Christendom: The Theology and Practice of Christian Witness.* Grand Rapids, Mich.: Brazos, 2007.

Sweet, Leonard. *FaithQuakes.* Nashville: Abingdon, 1994.

——. *The Gospel According to Starbucks: Living with a Grande Passion.* Colorado Springs: WaterBrook, 2007.

Tappert, Theodore G. *The Book of Concord.* Minneapolis: Fortress, 1959.

Taylor, Mark C. *After God.* Chicago: University of Chicago, 2007.

Tickle, Phyllis. *The Great Emergence: How Christianity Is Changing and Why.* Grand Rapids, Mich.: Baker, 2008.

Tomlinson, Dave. *The Post-Evangelical.* Grand Rapids, Mich.: Zondervan, 2003.

Weems, Robert, and Ann Michel. *The Crisis of Younger Clergy.* Nashville: Abingdon, 2008.

Wesley, John. *The Works of John Wesley.* Grand Rapids, Mich.: Baker, 2007.

Wilson-Hartgrove, Jonathan. *New Monasticism: What It Has to Say to Today's Church.* Grand Rapids, Mich.: Brazos, 2008.

Žižek, Slavoj. *In Defense of Lost Causes.* London: Verso, 2008.

Zogby, John. *The Way We'll Be.* New York: Random House, 2008.